SEX AND TRANSCENDENCE

About the Author

Keith Sherwood is an internationally known teacher and healer. He founded the American Psychic Association and served as its director and editor of its magazine, Psychic. He has appeared on many radio and television programs throughout the United States and Europe, and currently teaches chakra therapy, a synthesis of Western therapeutic techniques, Taoist Yoga, and Tantra. He resides in Portland, Oregon.

KEITH SHERWOOD

SEX AND TRANSCENDENCE

Enhance Your Relationships Through
Meditations, Chakra & Energy Work

Llewellyn Publications
Woodbury, Minnesota

FIRST EDITION
First Printing, 2011

Cover design by Kevin R. Brown
Cover images: background © iStockphoto.com/s.m.Art designs, Shiva image
    © iStockphoto.com/Paul Pantazescu
Editing by Tom Bilstad
Interior illustrations © Wen Hsu

Llewellyn is a registered trademark of Llewellyn Worldwide Ltd.

Library of Congress Cataloging-in-Publication Data (Pending)
ISBN: 978-0-7387-1340-3

Llewellyn Publications
A Division of Llewellyn Worldwide Ltd.
2143 Wooddale Drive
Woodbury, MN 55125-2989
www.llewellyn.com

Printed in the United States of America

Other Books by Keith Sherwood

The Art of Spiritual Healing

Chakra Healing and Karmic Awareness

Chakra Therapy: For Personal Growth & Healing

Contents

List of Figures xvii

Introduction 1

Chapter 1 3

The Universe Is in Orgasmic Bliss — So Are You

The Tantric View of Relationship 3

Shakti and Sexual Energy 5

Importance of Sexual Energy 6

Importance of Trust 7

Attitude Is Everything 8

You Are in Orgasmic Bliss ... 10

... Even if You Don't Realize It 11

If It Ain't Broke, Don't Fix It 12

Taking Personal Responsibility and Becoming Present 13

    EXERCISE: Becoming Present (Standard Method Exercise) 15

    EXERCISE: Orgasmic Bliss Mudra 17

A Final Note 19

Chapter 2 21

Get What You Want Most from Your Sexual Relationship

Not All Desires Are the Same 26

Inauthentic Desires 28

External Projections 29

Karmic Baggage and External Projections 33

The Importance of Saying Yes and No 36

    EXERCISE: The No Mudra 36

    EXERCISE: Overcoming Inauthentic Desires 36

    EXERCISE: The Pleasure Meditation 38

Chapter 3 43

The Importance of Self-Love

Where Love Does Not Exist: The Individual Mind and Ego 45

Where Love Truly Exists: Universal Consciousness 46

The Authentic Mind 48

The Human Energy System 51

The Truth About Self-Love 54

EXERCISE: Building a Foundation for the Bridge 1:
Becoming Present in Paramatman 56

EXERCISE: Building a Foundation for the Bridge 2:
Becoming Present in Jivamatman 57

EXERCISE: Self-Love Meditation 58

EXERCISE: Loving Your Sexual Expression 59

EXERCISE: Loving Your Body Parts 60

EXERCISE: Loving Your Neglected Body Parts 61

Putting It All Together 62

Chapter 4 65

Say Yes to Transcendent Sex

Karmic Baggage and Sexual Energy 66

Karmic Baggage and Non-Physical Beings 68

Recognizing Non-Physical Beings 72

Leave Your Karmic Baggage at the Door 72

EXERCISE: Determining What Resonates 74

Activating and Centering Yourself in Your Heart Chakra 76

EXERCISE: Activating and Centering in the Heart Chakra 77

EXERCISE: Five-Day Regimen to Enhance Sexual Energy 78

Naomi's Experience 83

Chapter 5 87

Fantasy and Karmic Baggage

Your Restrictive Belief System 88

EXERCISE: The Self-Acceptance Mudra 89

Fear and the Internal Dialogue 91

The Power of Positive Intention 94

Personas 95

Dominant and Subordinate Personas 96

EXERCISE: *Experiencing Your Dominant Persona 98*

EXERCISE: *Experiencing a Subordinate Persona 99*

EXERCISE: *Releasing Personas 101*

The Seven-Step Process 105

Chapter 6 107
Get Real — Expressing What You Really Feel

Being a Surrogate 109

Authentic and Inauthentic Emotions 111

Authentic Emotions 112

Inauthentic Emotions 114

Why Do Inauthentic Emotions Rule? 115

Polarity and Authentic Emotions 118

EXERCISE: *Expressing and Resolving Authentic Emotions 120*

EXERCISE: *The Authentic Anger Meditation 121*

EXERCISE: *The Authentic Fear Meditation 122*

EXERCISE: *The Authentic Pain Meditation 123*

EXERCISE: *The Authentic Joy Meditation 123*

Authentic Emotions and Sexual Ecstasy 124

EXERCISE: *Activating the Seven Traditional Chakras 125*

EXERCISE: *Activating the First Through Thirteen Chakras 125*

Chapter 7 129
Sex Is an Inter-Dimensional Sport

Structure of the Human Energy System 134

The Seven Traditional Chakras 136

Etheric and Physical Chakras 140

The Chakras' Sexual Potential 142

EXERCISE: *Enhancing Your Chakras' Sexual Potential* 145

EXERCISE: *Chakra Clensing* 146

Companion Chakras 147

EXERCISE: *First-Pair Meditation* 151

EXERCISE: *Second-Pair Meditation* 152

EXERCISE: *Third-Pair Meditation* 152

EXERCISE: *Fourth-Pair Meditation* 152

Chapter 8 155

Your Energy Field Is a Love Machine

Structure of Your Subtle Bodies and Sheaths 157

Function of Your Subtle Bodies 158

Fragmentation 159

EXERCISE: *The Body Integration Mudra* 161

The Truth About Feelings and Sensations 163

Your Etheric and Physical Chakras 164

EXERCISE: *Activating Your Etheric Chakras* 164

EXERCISE: *Activating Your Physical Chakras* 165

Prepare to Get Grounded 165

EXERCISE: *Reintegrating a Subtle Vehicle* 167

EXERCISE: *Getting Grounded the Right Way* 168

The Importance of Touch, Taste, and Smell 169

Chakras Above and Below Body Space 170

EXERCISE: *Awakening Your Sense of Touch* 172

EXERCISE: *Awakening Your Senses of Smell and Taste* 173

EXERCISE: *Awakening Your Senses of Sight and Hearing* 173

Chapter 9 175

The Problem of Past-Life Lovers

The Principle of Field Dominance 177

Energetic Interactions with Dead People 178

Cords, Controlling Waves, and Attachment Fields 180

Past-Life Lovers 181

Overcoming Past-Life Attachments 182

    EXERCISE: *Severing a Past-Life Connection 184*

    EXERCISE: *Ending Relationships the Right Way 185*

    EXERCISE: *Strengthening Your Boundaries 188*

Chapter 10 191

Gender Is in Everything

Yin and Yang 193

Enhancing the Flow 194

The Quest for More Desire (Sexual Energy) 195

Sweet Surrender 196

    EXERCISE: *Creating Flexibility 197*

    EXERCISE: *The Pelvic Thrust 199*

    EXERCISE: *The Running Cat 199*

    EXERCISE: *The Snake Push 200*

    EXERCISE: *Becoming Honest 201*

    EXERCISE: *Activating the Energy Centers in Your Hands and Feet 204*

    EXERCISE: *Expressing Sexual Energy Through Your Hands 205*

    EXERCISE: *Expressing Sexual Energy Through Your Feet 205*

Chapter 11 207

Spiritual Foreplay

Setting the External Conditions 208

How Flexible Are You? 210

Traditional Sexual Foreplay 210

Spiritual Foreplay 212

Transcending Duality 214

The Kundalini-Shakti 215

The Problem of Qualified Energy 216

    EXERCISE: *The Five-Step Method—Arousing the Serpent Energy 216*

    EXERCISE: *Step One—Scanning Your Energy Field 218*

EXERCISE: *Step Two—Releasing Blockages from the Serpent Energy 219*

EXERCISE: *Step Three—An Appropriate Apology 220*

EXERCISE: *Step Four—Activating the Front and Back of the Seven Traditional Chakras 221*

EXERCISE: *Step Five—The Root Lock 222*

After the Kundalini-Shakti Has Been Aroused 224

EXERCISE: *Enhancing Your Gazing 224*

EXERCISE: *Mutual Gazing 225*

EXERCISE: *Gazing from Your Chakras 226*

Chapter 12...229

Celebrating the Goddess

EXERCISE: *The Yoni Mudra 231*

EXERCISE: *The Ohm Technique 233*

EXERCISE: *Celebrating the Yoni 234*

EXERCISE: *Empowering the Goddess 235*

EXERCISE: *The Maithuna Rite 238*

Chapter 13...241

Your Three Hearts

The Human Heart 243

The Second Heart 245

The Third Heart 245

The Yearning of the Third Heart 246

The Yearning for Truth 248

The Yearning for Freedom 248

The Yearning for Unconditional Love 248

EXERCISE: *Finding the Yearning of the Third Heart 249*

EXERCISE: *Enhancing the Yearning of the Third Heart 251*

Chapter 14 253

Full-Body, Multiple, and Endless Orgasms

Orgasm and Relationship 255

What We Know About Orgasm 256

Physical Changes During Orgasm 257

Genital Orgasm 258

    EXERCISE: The Love Mudra 259

Full-Body Orgasm 260

    EXERCISE: Full-Body Orgasm 262

    EXERCISE: Full-Body Multiple Orgasm 264

Endless Orgasm 265

    EXERCISE: The Endless Orgasm 266

Beyond Spiritual Foreplay 267

    EXERCISE: Putting on the Sock 267

    EXERCISE: The Blacksmith's Posture 267

    EXERCISE: The Ostrich's Tail 267

    EXERCISE: The Yawning Position 268

    EXERCISE: The Afterglow 269

    EXERCISE: The Cradle 270

Chapter 15 273

Say Yes to Transcendent Relationships

Traditional Relationship 273

Transcendent Relationship 275

Transcendent Relationship and Polarity 276

    EXERCISE: Transcending Up-Down Polarity 284

Chapter 16.. 287
Make the Commitment to Transcendence Now

The Truth About Individuality 289

Transcendence Is for Everyone 291

From Friendship to Union 292

Footnotes 295

Glossary 297

Index 311

List of Figures

Figure 1: The Orgasmic Bliss Mudra   18

Figure 2: The No Mudra   37

Figure 3: A Chakra   39

Figure 4: Karmic Baggage   47

Figure 5: The Human Energy System   52

Figure 6: The Yogic Breath   79

Figure 7: The Empowerment Mudra   82

Figure 8: The Fearless Mudra   90

Figure 9: The Self-Acceptance Mudra   92

Figure 10: Authentic Emotion: Anger (Second Chakra)   113

Figure 11: Structure of the Human Energy System   127

Figure 12: Organs of the Human Energy System   135

Figure 13: The Etheric and Physical Chakras   141

Figure 14: The Minor Energy Centers in Hands and Feet   144

Figure 15: Stroking and Polarization   148

Figure 16: Hand in Circular Motion   148

Figure 17: The Body Integration Mudra   162

Figure 18: Chakras Above and Below Body Space   171

Figure 19: The Yes Mudra   202

Figure 20: The Governor, Ida, and Pingala Meridians   223

Figure 21: The Yoni Mudra   232

Figure 22: Energy Centers along the Governor, Ida, and Pingala   238

Figure 23: The Love Mudra   261

Figure 24: The Acupressure Points to Enhance the Afterglow   270

Figure 25a: Female Up-Down Polarity   280

Figure 25b: Male Up-Down Polarity   281

Introduction

The yearning for transcendent sex is a compelling motivator in our relationships. Who among us doesn't desire a relationship that goes beyond ordinary limits? Who wouldn't want to bond more fully, and more fulfillingly, with one's partner? This book will show you how to do just that.

It all begins with the tantric masters, who recognized more than a thousand years ago that human sexuality and the energy at its foundation are powerful forces that can lead us to ecstasy. These forces can also work as extremely effective tools to achieve transcendent states of consciousness and new levels of intimacy with a partner—in other words, a transcendent relationship.

So what exactly is a transcendent relationship? Is it simply a partnership defined by great sex, or is there more to it? First of all, let me assure you that you will indeed experience phenomenal sex that allows you to feel complete oneness with your partner and with Universal Consciousness. But beyond that, you will learn to share pleasure, love, intimacy, and joy freely with a partner, without blockages, karma, or anything else getting in the way. You may wonder at this point if you need the "perfect" partner to achieve such things. The answer to that is a resounding no. If you love your partner and you share sexual chemistry, then the two of you have everything you need to create a transcendent relationship.

What You Will Learn

Sex and Transcendence focuses on how the human energy field affects sex and relationships. It will help you identify and remove the blockages in your energy field that restrict your potential to experience transcendent sex, and also offers energetic solutions to the sexual and relationship problems caused by those blockages.

Each chapter contains practical exercises that you can use, on your own or with your partner, to overcome the limitations imposed on your sexuality by karma, our culture, and any individual personality issues. You will learn how karmic baggage, the foundation of blockages and personality issues, is created, how it disrupts intimate relationships, and how it can be safely and permanently released. You will also learn how polarity (the interaction of Yin and Yang) affects sexual energy, and how fears and fantasies can be used to enhance sexual ecstasy. And finally, you will discover how to tap into the universal qualities of god or goddess energy (personified here as Shiva and Shakti).

Sex and Transcendence is a practical book for both individuals and couples who desire to bring enlightenment to their everyday life. This book includes a wealth of information on how to use your body, mind, and energy field to enhance sexual intimacy. In the last six chapters, special attention has been given to spiritual foreplay and techniques to help you achieve and enhance your enjoyment of a full-body, multiple, and endless orgasm.

Throughout my years of work in this field, I've learned to experience energy fields directly, by seeing and feeling them, and have studied energetic interactions between people engaged in all forms of intimate activity. This has allowed me to develop techniques that can release energy blockages and restore the human energy field to the healthiest condition possible. It is my privilege to share these techniques with you here.

Chapter 1

The Universe Is in Orgasmic Bliss — So Are You

The Taoists tell us that, at the moment the universe was created, the energy that is the foundation of human sexuality split into two halves, which became known by the Chinese as Yin and Yang. Yin represents femininity, body, soul, earth, moon, water, night, cold, darkness, and contraction. Yang, on the other hand, represents masculinity, mind, spirit, heaven, sun, day, fire, heat, sunlight, and expansion. Everything in the universe can be defined by its particular balance of Yin and Yang; however, nothing is completely one or the other. Everything that exists has elements of both, because Yin and Yang are never static—they are always interacting with one another. An excess of Yin becomes Yang, and an excess of Yang becomes Yin. In a perfect example of this, water, which is Yin, when frozen becomes ice, which is Yang.

The Tantric View of Relationship

Human sexuality cannot be understood outside the concept of Yin and Yang. In the tantric view, a human being and his or her relationships are a mirror of the universe—or even better, the whole universe in microcosm. The universe itself is seen as a union of the male and female principles, as represented by the divine couple Shiva and Shakti.

In tantra, the male Shiva and the female Shakti are revered as both the divine couple and as the archetypes for consciousness (Shiva) and energy (Shakti). The ancient Vedic texts, which are sacred to yoga and tantra, describe through metaphor and myth a person's relationship to his or her energy field and the energy field's relationship to other people and the cosmos. The most well-known Vedic texts, the Upanishads and the Bhagavad Gita, tell us that after the universe was created, Shiva and Shakti emerged from the singularity called Universal Consciousness via the *tattvas*, which are steps in the evolution of the physical and non-physical universe.

Thirty-six tattvas are responsible for the incredible diversity of our universe. The first tattva was the original world as it emerged from Universal Consciousness, a world without form. From this, Purusha and Prakriti emerged. Purusha, the predecessor of Shiva, was the primordial consciousness and Prakriti, the predecessor of Shakti, the primordial source of power (sexual energy). The next tattva, which resulted from their joining, was called Mahatattva. It was at this stage that perfect balance in the primordial, nonphysical universe was disrupted and evolution—as human beings can conceive it—began. In the next tattva, Shiva and Shakti emerged, and it was at this point that sexual ecstasy first made its appearance.

In tantra, evolution is considered to be an ongoing process through which Shakti (Yin) is continuously impregnated by Shiva (Yang). This constant act of creation and its associated sexual delight are central to tantric experience and to the tantric view of transcendence (enlightenment). The universe is continuously being created through the union of opposites: Yin/Yang, Shiva/Shakti.

The divine couple serves as the archetype for sexual love (*Eros*) and a transcendent relationship. The sexual ecstasy that two individuals experience together is seen as being fundamentally the same as that experienced by the divine couple. This is why, in tantra, human sexuality is elevated beyond the mere act of procreation, it becomes a vehicle for achieving transcendence. Sex is used to break down the barriers that make people feel separate, and transports them into a state of union with each other and with Universal Consciousness.

Like the ancient tantric masters, you can experience similar states of sexual ecstasy. Then, with the help of this book, you can take the next step. You can use the previously dormant powers of your energy field to achieve transcendence or enlightenment, where pleasure, love, intimacy, and joy emanate spontaneously from within you, and you can share those uplifting qualities with your partner.

The first step in that process will be to learn as much as possible about Shakti, the female principle and the source of orgasmic bliss.

Shakti and Sexual Energy

After emerging from Universal Consciousness, the goddess Shakti, in the form of creative, sexual energy, began to function as the driving force of evolution. This sexual energy is responsible for creating the diversity of life that exists in both the physical and nonphysical universe. Without Shakti, there would be no awe-inspiring universe, no sentient beings to be aware of it, and no pleasure, love, intimacy, and joy. Shakti's creative sexual energy connects everything that exists, in both physical and nonphysical dimensions, and this energy provides the medium through which all things manifest.

Unlike energy on the physical-material plane, which in its different forms can produce physical qualities such as force, electrical charge, or heat, sexual energy is actually nonphysical and has only universal qualities. I'll be talking more about universal qualities later on, but right now, you need to know these are life-affirming elements that bring people together in the most direct and joyful way possible—for example, pleasure, love, intimacy, joy, truth, freedom, and unconditional love (bliss). Universal qualities don't cause attachment and bind people to each other in unhealthy ways; rather, universal qualities, and the energy that supports them, enhance freedom, self-awareness, and self-confidence. Universal qualities never change. They can't be influenced by any of the forces that exist in the physical universe, and they are what make transcendent sex possible.

Usually we're more aware of energy with physical qualities because we can perceive it in the physical-material world. You can sense it when you feel anxious, or depressed, or when you feel your energy contract in reaction to stress, shock, illness, or trauma. But underlying the universe of physical energy is a universe of sexual energy with only universal qualities. This energy—Shakti's energy—forms the foundation of our universe and each human being within it.

Importance of Sexual Energy

Unfortunately, even though sexual energy permeates the entire universe in both the physical and nonphysical dimensions, most people are unaware of it and its importance except during intimate physical contact. There are times, however, when it's impossible to ignore the presence of sexual energy and the universal qualities that emerge from it. You experience sexual energy whenever you're excited by another human being, and whenever you share pleasure, love, intimacy, and joy with your partner. You also experience it when you feel a surge of vitality or creativity, and whenever you feel a profound sense of well being, contentment, or satisfaction.

Some of you may already recognize the extraordinary power of sexual energy. You may realize this force is so powerful that, when it's unleashed during sexual ecstasy, it can catapult you into a state of transcendence where problems and worries disappear and you can, at least temporarily, participate in the bliss that is continuously experienced by the living universe. We all have vast reserves of sexual energy within us—an infinite supply.

The tantric masters acknowledged the transcendent nature of sexual energy and used the act of lovemaking as a tool to achieve an internal state of oneness that partners could then share with one another. Although many people are aware of the potentially transformative power of sex, few people are aware that their physical-material body, and the energy field that interpenetrates it, have been designed specifically to allow us to experience oneness and to share these universal qualities with other people.

The energy field that exists in and around your physical-material body actually consists of a number of inter-dimensional energetic bodies that allow you to express yourself and interact with other people. The chakras, auras, meridians, and minor energy centers are located throughout your energy field, which fuels them with sexual energy. You will learn more about your energy field later in this book. For now, remember that form follows function—your primary purpose for being alive is to serve as a vehicle through which universal qualities can be shared with other people.

To share universal love and the pleasure, intimacy, and joy that emerge from it, you must first embrace the sexual energy that emerges from deep within you. Only then can your energy field and physical-material body perform the functions for which they were designed.

Importance of Trust

For more than thirty years, I've worked with people who've made self-realization and achieving a transcendent relationship their highest priorities. I've found that the full experience of sexual energy, as promoted by the tantrics, only becomes possible when people have enough trust in themselves and their partner to embrace it. This level of trust can't emerge until a person is able to release fear, judgment, and cultural taboos that restrict the free flow of sexual energy.

Trust is the awareness that it's safe to radiate sexual energy freely. The ability to trust yourself will allow you to express your energy without old fears getting in the way. However, most people have been programmed to abide by certain cultural taboos and to be afraid of one's body and its natural urges. This makes it difficult to trust yourself and your partner, and without trust it will be difficult—if not impossible—to break through the blockages and boundaries that limit you. Any programming or past experiences that inhibit the free radiation of sexual energy through your energy field stand in the way of your achieving a transcendent (transformative) relationship.

In their pioneering study of human sexuality, Masters and Johnson were surprised to discover that "negative or restrictive attitudes toward sex, absorbed from religion or basic cultural attitudes, can have ... an enormous impact ... If you believe that sex is dirty, that orgasms (and sexual pleasure in general) are unnecessary and an indication of a less than good character, then you will take that attitude into the bedroom with you."[1]

That attitude will influence you not only in the bedroom, but also in other aspects of your life. The effects of programming that limits the free flow of sexual energy can be seen everywhere—in the people around us, in cultural institutions, and in religious doctrine and tradition. All this programming is the result of a belief system that seeks to dictate how we interact and how we express sexual energy. In fact, the belief system you carry with you through life can be one of the biggest obstacles in your experience of the transformative power of sexual energy, because it can inhibit you from trusting yourself, your body, and your partner.

This is especially true if you live in a patriarchal culture—and all major Christian and Islamic cultures are patriarchal. The more male-dominant the culture, the more rigid it will be, and the more challenging it will be for you to trust yourself and other people. As previously stated, without trust it will be difficult, if not impossible, to radiate sexual energy freely and to share pleasure, love, intimacy, and joy at the appropriate time with an appropriate partner. In patriarchal cultures, the pressure to conform to the dominant belief system can be so strong that only those with a deep trust in themselves (and their partner) will risk the censure of family and friends—and in some cases the threat of violence—to pursue self-realization and a relationship that goes beyond the accepted norm.

Attitude Is Everything

Although each patriarchal culture has its own belief system, some attitudes that have been widely accepted particularly affect one's ability to trust oneself and one's partner:

Blaming the victim: Those who seek a transformative relationship don't blame other people. They see others as having the potential for transcendence, like themselves, and as being limited only by the choices they make. It's important to recognize that blaming another person for the blockages in his or her energy field serves no useful purpose and is always inappropriate.

Romanticizing the culture of ego: Violence, control, and manipulation, as well as gratifying one's individual desires at the expense of others, are all encouraged by patriarchal cultures. People who yearn to experience transcendence, within themselves or with a partner, can't indulge in these behaviors since they create mistrust and disrupt the flow of sexual energy.

Oppressing women: The oppression of women and the suppression of sexual energy go hand in hand. These practices create negativity and prevent people from experiencing the universal qualities of joy, truth, freedom, and unconditional love (bliss).

Giving away personal responsibility: People who consciously or unconsciously give away responsibility lose control over their energy field, disrupting the flow of sexual energy and making it difficult to experience a transformative relationship. It is essential, therefore, to take back authority if it has been lost. Make a conscious decision to trust yourself and say yes to what enhances the flow of sexual energy and no to what does not.

Victimizing the innocent and the vulnerable: The innocent and the vulnerable include children, animals, and those who are unable to sustain themselves without outside support. In societies where the values of patriarchy have penetrated deeply, people will be victimized through overt and/or covert abuse, neglect, and repression, often based on their class, gender, race, or national origin. Those who seek self-realization and a transcendent relationship must recognize that all living beings emerge from Universal Consciousness and must be accorded the dignity they deserve. Thus, all activities that victimize other beings should be avoided.

It's only when these types of attitudes have been abandoned in favor of personal integrity that the trust necessary to achieve a transcendent, transformative relationship will emerge. By personal integrity, I mean much more than personal honesty. You live with integrity by embracing what is authentic within yourself and by having the courage to express it, even when there is opposition from cultural institutions, other people, and your own restrictive belief system.

In fact, it's only when you can accept what is deepest and most authentic within yourself—and when you sense that your partner has the integrity and ability to do the same—that barriers to transcendence will begin to dissolve. Trusting yourself and allowing the sexual energy that radiates through your energy field and physical-material body to flow freely is absolutely essential to the experience of transcendent sex and relationships.

You Are in Orgasmic Bliss ...

Human sexuality is not grounded exclusively in the chemical reactions that take place within the physical-material body. Sexuality in the physical world is actually the outer manifestation of a deeper sexuality, which emerges through your energy field and is dependent on your ability to radiate sexual energy freely. This deeper sexuality is known in tantra as *orgasmic bliss*, and even if you've had difficulty radiating sexual energy freely, in reality you're already in this transcendent state.

Orgasmic bliss is an enduring condition, deep within your energy field, created through the union of consciousness (Shiva) and sexual energy (Shakti). The merging of consciousness and sexual energy provides you with a safe haven, deep within you, where you already experience oneness and where nothing can interfere with your experience of transcendent sex and relationships.

Although orgasmic bliss cannot easily be described in words, you can imagine a state that combines the anticipation and increased sexual excitement experienced during the moments before a full-body orgasm with the satisfaction and release that takes place during and after it. This timeless state goes far beyond the pleasures associated with a purely genital orgasm. When orgasmic bliss emerges into your conscious awareness, it will feel like an electric buzz that envelops you with vitality, creativity, and a love of life that radiates through your entire energy field and fills your physical-material body.

It's this enduring state of orgasmic bliss that makes transcendent, transformative sex possible. But orgasmic bliss is not something you have to develop or something that can be achieved through self-improvement or learned through a course of study. It's not reserved for a special, select group or for people who believe in some special doctrine. This state exists as a birthright within every man and woman alive today.

... Even if You Don't Realize It

Despite the fact that you're already in orgasmic bliss, you're probably not conscious of it or experiencing its benefits. That's because all the little things that intrude on one's conscious mind—goals, desires, personality issues—also impede one's energy field. These myriad distractions can include the desire to change your partner in some way; the need to feel secure, or loved, or appreciated; the unconscious desire to control your environment; or even some goal you're trying to achieve. All such matters will prevent you from consciously experiencing orgasmic bliss and sharing it with your partner.

I call this complex of attitudes, beliefs, and feelings *personality issues*, and all such issues can block your ability to experience the transformative power of sexual energy. This can happen when circumstances cause your energy to contract, or when you become attached to someone or something.

When you become attached to a personality issue, you can become overwhelmed by an idea, attitude, or emotion that alienates you from your body and the people with whom you share relationships. Once you become alienated from your body and from other people, you can be duped into believing that the best way to overcome the issue is to improve yourself in some way.

There are as many types of personality issues as there are people, but one of the most common is "the blame game." People who are trapped in the blame game experience a loss of sexual energy, motivation, and power, blaming others for their condition and then using forgiveness to shift responsibility.

If It Ain't Broke, Don't Fix It

Techniques to improve oneself come in many forms. Throughout human history, people have tried to become more loving, more sensitive, or just better in some way—often with little lasting success. The concept of self-improvement rests on the false assumption that there is something inherently wrong, damaged, or flawed in a person that, through effort or hard work, can be changed or improved. If it's not a physical or biological flaw, then it must be something in one's "software program" that is defective or which, with a little tinkering, could be improved.

It's important here to debunk the myth of self-improvement because it is in itself a personality issue. As with other personality issues, trying to "improve" yourself will create internal conflict, disrupt the flow of sexual energy through your energy field, and prevent you from achieving transcendent sex.

The truth is that you emerged from Universal Consciousness and that you participate in relationship—that is, experience oneness—on all dimensions of the multi-dimensional universe. This makes you, regardless of your present condition, a vehicle for universal love with the capacity to manifest all the universal qualities that arise from Universal Consciousness through your energy field and physical-material body. You also have vast resources of consciousness and sexual energy available to you. Consciousness is awareness, and the more aware you become, the more you will understand about yourself and your environment. As you become aware, you'll begin to recognize that you are far more than you hitherto believed. There is nothing to "improve," only personality issues that must be released or transcended, and dormant powers that must be actualized.

You can serve as this perfect vehicle because of your relationship to Universal Consciousness and Shakti—because, on every dimension of the physical and nonphysical universe, you have an energy system through which you can share universal love, as well as any other universal quality you choose, through transcendent sex.

On the physical-material plane, you have a body that is made of flesh and blood. On the nonphysical planes, you have nonphysical bodies, composed of energy with universal qualities, which interpenetrates your physical body. These nonphysical bodies, and the energy system that supports them, make up what is known as your *energy field*. Your energy bodies and energy system can never change, nor can they be damaged in any way. And no amount of "tinkering" can change how they process energy or radiate the universal qualities that are essential for the experience of transcendent sex.

The bottom line is that you and the people you love are perfect in purpose, design, and function. There is no need to "improve" yourself in any way. As a multi-dimensional being with vast resources of consciousness and sexual energy, you are ideal the way you are. However, in order to experience and share transcendent sex, you must learn what your energy bodies and energy system can do. Then you must remove blockages and restore your energy field and energy system to a healthy working condition so that you can use them efficiently, in all situations, no matter how challenging.

Taking Personal Responsibility and Becoming Present

Unfortunately, we don't receive an energy field instruction manual when we're born, nor when we come of age, so it's unlikely that yours is in perfect working condition. Like everyone else, you were left on your own without the skills necessary to maintain your energy system in a healthy state or guide you toward transcendence. It's time for you to take personal responsibility for the condition of your energy field, and the first step toward doing so is to center yourself in the present, the now—the only time-space in which you can experience transcendence.

Through becoming and remaining present in the ever-present now, every living organism experiences the benefits of its relationship with Universal Consciousness and Shakti. Only humans have fallen out of the ever-present now. This is because of our attachment to personality issues that trap us in the past and the future, and which prevent us from radiating sexual energy freely.

Those of us on the planet today, perhaps more than at any other time in human history, suffer greatly from this fall and its consequences. Modern men and women tend to position their consciousness in either the front or the back of their body. Their posture, voice, and breathing reflect this. They walk tilted backward or forward. Their breath is shallow and incomplete, and their voices don't resonate from deep within them.

In the East, adepts saw the folly of living in the past and the future. The tantrics, in particular, sought a way to overcome the limitations imposed by time. They succeeded, first by recognizing that past and future are part of the landscape that enriches an eternal present, and then by observing that if a human positions one's awareness in the front of his or her energy field and ahead of his or her physical body, relative to time, one positions him- or herself in the future. And if one positions his or her awareness in the back of one's energy field and behind one's physical body, relative to time, one positions him- or herself in the past. These insights made it possible for tantrics to position their awareness in the center of their energy field and squarely inside themselves, where there is no past or future—only the ever-present now exists.

Indeed, the tantric view puts human beings directly at the center of things. Past and future become the scenery that spills out of their consciousness and colors their world, but they are not trapped by them any longer. Humans remains centered inside themselves, where they can know and be themselves. And they are centered in their energy field, the vehicle through which orgasmic bliss emerges and through which they can share pleasure, love, intimacy, and joy through transcendent sex.

Like a tantric adept, you can experience the ever-present now by becoming present in your physical-material body and the energy field that interpenetrates it. By reorienting yourself in that way, you will be taking an important step in the process of transcendence.

THE UNIVERSE IS IN ORGASMIC BLISS—SO ARE YOU   15

Exercise: Becoming Present
(Standard Method Exercise)

This exercise is designed to reposition you in the ever-present now, re-gardless of your physical and energetic condition. It takes about twenty minutes, and you should try to do it every day. You'll find it easiest to perform in the lotus position, sitting with your back straight and your legs crossed, or sitting upright in a straight-back chair.

Central to the exercise is learning to relax the major muscle groups of your physical-material body, which you will do by contracting and releasing them. This helps to quiet your mind by releasing residual stress. The technique you will use is called the Standard Method Exer-cise, which I've used successfully for more than twenty-five years. It's easy to learn and it can be used by anyone, regardless of his or her prior experience in energy work.

It's important to note that in this exercise your *intent* serves the same function as a computer software program. Just as a software pro-gram instructs a computer to perform a particular task, your intent in-structs your authentic (higher) mind to turn your perception inward. Your perception consists of your senses, which gather physical-material input, as well as your other, nonphysical means of knowing, such as intuition. If you use your intent properly, without watching yourself, trying too hard, or mixing your intent with sentiment and self-doubt, your perception will automatically turn inward.

Your initial goal is to perceive your energy field, which may look and/or feel like a large cavity that interpenetrates your physical-ma-terial body. This field can extend up to twenty-six feet (eight meters) beyond the surface of your body. Your ultimate goal is to become pres-ent through centering yourself within your energy field. Many people who've practiced this exercise report that, once they become present, distracting thoughts decrease or stop. They also report that their body seems lighter and they feel more authentic, and more aware of both their internal and external environment.

Once you are comfortably seated, close your eyes and breathe deeply through your nose without separation between inhalation and exhalation. Slowly count backward from five to one. As you count back-ward, mentally repeat and visualize each number three times to your-self. Take your time and let your mind be as creative as it likes. After you reach the number one, repeat this affirmation to yourself: *"I'm now deeply relaxed, feeling better than I did before."*

Continue by counting backward from ten to one, letting yourself sink deeper on each descending number. When you reach the number one, affirm: *"Every time I come to this level of mind, I'm able to use more of my mind in more creative ways."*

Next, inhale and bring your attention to your feet. Contract the muscles of your feet as much as possible. Hold your breath for five sec-onds. Then release your breath and allow the muscles of your feet to relax. Inhale deeply again and repeat the process with your ankles and calves. Continue in the same way with your knees, thighs, buttocks and pelvis, middle and upper abdomen, chest, shoulders, neck, arms, and hands. After you've tightened and relaxed all those body parts, squeeze the muscles of your face and hold for five seconds. Then release and say as you exhale, "Ahh." Next, open your mouth, stick out your tongue, and stretch the muscles of your face as much as possible. Hold for five seconds. Then release the muscles of your face and as you exhale say, "Ahh."

Finally, contract your entire body and squeeze the muscles of your face while you hold your breath for five seconds. Expel the breath through your nose and relax. Now affirm, *"It's my intent to turn my per-ception inward."* You'll become aware of your energy field by seeing, feeling, or sensing it.

Once you're aware of your energy field, assert, *"It's my intent to be present in my energy field."* Immediately your orientation will shift. From your new vantage point—within your energy field—you will become aware that you are centered in the ever-present now.

Take fifteen minutes to enjoy this experience. Then count from one to five and open your eyes. When you do so, you will feel perfectly re-laxed and better than you did before. The more often you practice the exercise, the greater the benefits will be, and the easier it will be to re-main present in the ever-present now.

Exercise: Orgasmic Bliss Mudra

As soon as you're able to stay present for fifteen minutes, you can take the next step in the process of transcendence: you can bring orgasmic bliss into your conscious awareness.

To do so, you will use a *mudra* specifically designed for that purpose. A mudra is a symbolic gesture that can be made with the hands and fingers or in combination with the tongue and feet. Each mudra has a specific effect on the human energy field and the energy flowing through it. The Orgasmic Bliss Mudra, which follows, is designed to bring orgasmic bliss into your conscious awareness, once you've become present in your energy field.

At first, practice the mudra by yourself. Once you feel more confident, you can practice it with your partner while you're sitting one yard (one meter) apart, facing each other. Most people report a dramatic shift in their inner state while practicing the mudra. Worldly concerns recede into the background and a timeless state of peace quickly fills the vacuum. But the peace people experience is not the same as stillness. The peace that emerges from this mudra will be full of energy and will provide the space for orgasmic bliss to emerge and radiate through your energy field.

To begin, use the Standard Method Exercise to relax your physical-material body and become present. Then place the tip of your tongue on your upper palette, and bring it straight back until it comes to rest at the point where the hard palate rolls up and becomes soft. Once the tip of your tongue is in that position, put the bottom of your feet together so that the soles are touching. Then bring your hands in front of your solar plexus and place the inside tips of your thumbs together. Continue by bringing the outside of your index fingers together from the tips to the first joint. Next, bring the outside of your middle fingers together from the first to the second joint. The fourth and fifth fingers should be curled into your palm (see Figure 1). Once your tongue, fingers, and feet are in position, close your eyes and breathe through your nose.

Remain present and perform the mudra for ten minutes. When you are finished, release your fingers first. Then separate the soles of your feet and finally bring your tongue back to its normal position. Next, count from one to five, and when you reach the number five, open your eyes. You will be wide awake, perfectly relaxed, and you'll feel better than you did before.

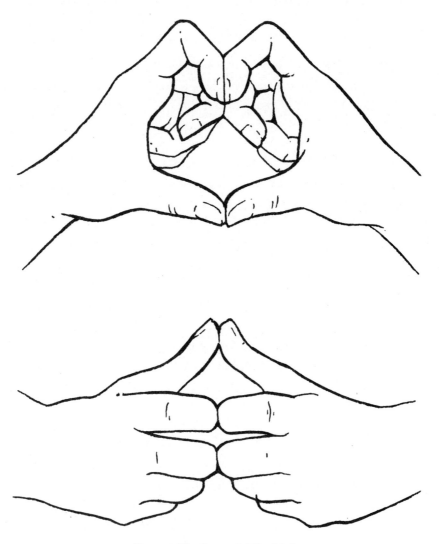

Figure 1: The Orgasmic Bliss Mudra

A Final Note

Before we move on, it's important to note that your ability to experience transcendent sex and relationships is not dependent on factors such as looks, personality, and compatibility, or values, beliefs, and how much you're able to give to and take from your partner on the physical-material level. These are indeed factors in our relationships, but they only set the conditions. The factors that most influence your experience of transcendent sex and relationships will be the condition of your energy field and your ability to experience orgasmic bliss.

The more access you have to orgasmic bliss, the more "at home" you'll feel in your body and the more personal chemistry you'll have with your partner. In fact, people have chemistry with each other precisely because they're able to find space within themselves through which orgasmic bliss can emerge. The key that unlocks the mystery surrounding human relationships is simply this: it's not individual qualities people seek most from a partner, it's the universal qualities that emerge from orgasmic bliss as pleasure, love, intimacy, and joy.

Chapter 2

Get What You Want Most From Your Sexual Relationship

Traditionally, when merchants in rural India want to haggle over the price of cows or crops; or when village elders, stroking their white beards, want to mull over decisions; or when priests, huddled around a sacrificial fire, wish to intone mantras; or when women wish to gather to catch up on the news; or when farmers wish to herd their animals to escape the withering summer sun; or when teachers wish to meet with their students for instruction, these people gather beneath the overarching canopy of the village banyan tree, which provides a vast, cool, outdoor assembly space.

When one tree fulfils the wishes of so many, is it any wonder that one of the most popular Indian parables—and one retold for countless centuries under countless banyan trees—is that of the Wish-Fulfilling Tree. The Wish-Fulfilling Tree, as the allegory has it, grows high in the Himalayas, and anyone who discovers this tree there and stands beneath it will find that all of his or her wishes become fulfilled. Thus, children standing under the tree will wish for candies until their stomachs ache and the sweets become tasteless. Young men and women will wish for wealth, fame, and sexual pleasures, until they find themselves slaves to lust and fortune. The secret of the tree, of course, is that it does not grow atop the Himalayas, but within every human heart. Consider, for instance, Jason's heart, in the following story.

It had been a long week. When Jason arrived home, his wife Sharon met him at the door. She'd spent the whole day preparing for his arrival. Two glasses of wine stood on the dinner table beautifully set with candles, a linen tablecloth, and napkins. Romantic lighting sparkled and the scent of roses filled the room.

Sharon looked lovely. Her dark eyes were soft and inviting, and she'd donned a revealing dress that would create a sensation if she were to wear it in public. Everything was perfect, except Jason's shoulders were tight, his neck was stiff, and thoughts of his secret affair with his domineering female boss cascaded through his mind like a waterfall. He found himself unable to enjoy a single moment, and after dinner, when they began kissing, he was not able to become sexually aroused.

So, what was Jason's problem? The Wish-Fulfilling Tree in Jason's heart was deeply conflicted. The desire for Sharon that he usually felt, as well as the authentic feelings that supported his desire, were being blocked by the conflicting desires and inauthentic feelings for his boss. After all, he did not want to lose his job, so he had succumbed to the advances of his buxom blonde boss in the same way that he had always submitted to the will of his dominating mother. In other words, the old karmic baggage of his mother-son relationship had mixed with the lust and power his boss was projecting at him. These old patterns were sabotaging his natural desire for Sharon.

Similar to Jason, you may find that these two "demons," karmic baggage and external projections, complicate your authentic desires. In fact, you may have experienced this many times. Karmic baggage and projections coming from another person are composed of dense energy that can create feelings of being pressured, with accompanying aching muscles, stress, anxiety, self-doubt, and confusion. Often we are not even aware of the source of our discomfort. This is one reason why the two demons of karmic baggage and external projections are the principle sources of human suffering, including physical disease.

Just as Jason's karmic baggage and external projections limited his awareness and disrupted his authentic relationship, so may have yours, too. These demons can obstruct the flow of sexual energy through your energy field and create attitudes, beliefs, feelings, and inauthentic desires that thwart your experience of pleasure, love, intimacy, and joy.

The karmic baggage in your energy field is composed of energy with individual qualities. Jason's karmic baggage, for instance, involves the quality of being the victim of domination, an emotion that had become habitual because of the overbearing presence of his mother during his formative years. If you have lived with dominance during the stage of life when your emotional patterns form, as had Jason, you can see why you may have become attached to this baggage, thus allowing it to become integrated into your individual mind and ego.

The external projections in your energy field are energetic projections. These also have individual qualities—such as anxiety, self-doubt, or submission—and are caused by energy that some other person may have projected at you. Once Jason had submitted to the advances of his boss, Jason became attached to this external projection until it became integrated into his individual mind and ego and became part of the similar karmic baggage from his domineering mother, which he had long been carrying in his energy field. Thus his natural desire for his wife was conflicted with his inauthentic desire to carry on with his secret affair.

Conflicting desires that emerge from karmic baggage and external projections can interfere with you at the most inconvenient moments, just as they did with Jason. They can disrupt not only your desire for conventional romance, but also for transcendent sex and relationships. After all, a conflicted mind cannot experience transcendence. The simple truth is that your heart really is a Wish-Fulfilling Tree: you really do get what you wish for most. If your wishes are in conflict, however, the tree may not know which wish to deliver to you. You may remain in limbo, your wishes and your mind forming a tangled mass of confused energy. And this will also affect your body.

Therefore, if you do not want to remain in limbo like Jason, you must determine what you really want. What you want most will be determined by which of your desires are stronger: those inauthentic desires that emerge from your individual mind and ego and are supported by karmic baggage and external projections, or those authentic desires that emerge from and are supported by your soul.

Now, before you object and insist that what you want most is to share transcendent sex and relationships, please take a moment to reflect on the Principle of Desire: *desire is a function of mind*. Desire manifests in all fields of activity. Desires that are stronger and more active will dominate weaker, less-active desires in all energetic interactions that take place in both the physical and non-physical universe.

Because virtually all energetic interactions between humans are manifestations of desire and of the will and/or intent that supports desire, humans get what they want most. This happens whether they're conscious or unconscious of their hidden desires and/or fears (fear is the flip side of desire) that motivated them to interact in the first place.

To illustrate this point, let me introduce Bob, who is an adolescent male. Bob has a desire for a healthy meal of lentil soup made with vegetables straight from the garden and accompanied by whole grain bread. After all, his family has always eaten healthy food. Bob, however, has a problem. He has a conflicting desire to gobble down a huge order of fried onion rings. If his desire for the junk food is stronger than his desire for the healthy meal, then the inauthentic desire will dominate, compelling Bob to go for the onion rings. And the inauthentic desire will do that by bombarding him with attitudes, beliefs, feelings, and sensations that have their basis in the karmic baggage and external projections in his energy field. For instance, Bob may have been eating healthy foods his entire life. However, now he is a teen, a stage in life when young men naturally become a little rebellious (karmic baggage). For instance, Mahatma Gandhi, as a teen, rebelled against his vegetarian upbringing. He decided that what was wrong with India was vegetarianism, and so he began eating meat and vowed to convert all of India to meat eating. It was the only vow he ever broke. So, Bob, like Gandhi, is now vulnerable to peer pressure. His buddies may be putting a lot of pressure on him (external projections) to be cool by rebelling against his habit of eating healthy food.

The same psychic mechanisms come into play in Jason's desire to continue his affair with his boss. It's important to note that by creating desires, attitudes, beliefs, feelings, and sensations that are antagonistic to transcendent sex and relationships, karmic baggage and external projections create a counterfeit mind—called the *individual mind and ego*—which can oppose the desire, will, and intent of your *authentic mind*, your true mind, which is aligned with and enhances the goals of transcendent sex and relationships. Just as a great banyan tree remains basically itself—not breaking when buffeted by storm winds, or dying when a vine climbs up around its trunk, or being bothered when priests or merchants or mothers meet under its vast canopy—your authentic mind is your true vehicle of awareness and self-expression. It is not really reactive to karmic baggage or external projections as long as you take care of it. And your authentic mind remains the same even when its influence and ability to function have been inhibited by the build-up of karmic baggage and external projections in your energy field.

Your authentic mind is composed of your energy bodies and your energy system, which support it. This includes mental functions—your memory, centers of deductive and inductive reasoning, and your organs of perception and self-expression. It's important to note that your authentic mind is formed exclusively of consciousness and energy with universal qualities. And when it motivates you to act, the only influence your authentic mind will have is to vitalize you or whatever it's acting upon. In the same way a great banyan tree does not alter, control, manipulate, or change the qualities of a breeze, or a vine growing up its trunk, or the people who meet under it, your authentic mind does not alter, control, manipulate, or change the qualities of anything with which it interacts. In fact, like Universal Consciousness, all actions motivated by your authentic mind enhance your experience of pleasure, love, intimacy, and joy. All the people meeting under the banyan tree feel nurtured by its presence.

By adding what you just learned about your authentic mind to what you already know about the Principle of Desire, you will not be surprised to learn that getting what you want most also implies that you must exercise your free will just as you must exercise your other muscles. If you exercise your free will, you can change what you want most by enhancing authentic desires (which emerge from your authentic mind) at the expense of inauthentic desires (which emerge from your individual mind and ego).

How are some other ways you can enhance your authentic desires? Both yoga and tantra agree that by enhancing the health of your energy field and the flow of sexual energy through it, you can nourish authentic desires and prevent or discourage inauthentic desires. When you do this, inauthentic desires will no longer dominate your awareness and interfere with your relationships.

Not All Desires Are the Same

According to the Vedic texts at the basis of yoga and tantra, the Tree of Authentic Desire has four main branches—Artha, Kama, Dharma, and Moksha. The four branches of authentic desire enhance the flow of sexual energy, keep you present in your energy field, and support transcendent sex and relationships. These four branches of desire are the normal, natural functions of life on earth. They shouldn't be confused with desires for specific things, which create attachment and which emerge through your individual mind and ego.

The first branch of authentic desire is called Artha. In Sanskrit, *Artha* means "the desire for material comfort or wealth." Artha is not the same as greed, which can emerge only from the individual mind and ego. Unlike greed, Artha provides the energy necessary to create a living environment that supports transcendent sex and relationships.

In the midst of everyday life it's easy to forget that, in order for a relationship to flourish, an environment must be created that takes people's material needs into consideration. By acknowledging and fulfilling Artha you can secure the time, space, and material comfort you need to make your relationship flourish and to share universal qualities with your partner.

Kama is the second branch of authentic desire. Kama denotes both pleasure as well as the desire for pleasure. It's worth noting that yogic texts state that Universal Consciousness created the universe for its own pleasure. Thus, it comes as no surprise that Kama enhances the energy necessary for you (and your partner) to experience pleasure, love, intimacy, and joy.

Just as Artha should be distinguished from greed, the desire for pleasure should not be confused with lust—the superficial and incomplete enjoyment of physical pleasure, for instance, with a prostitute—in the absence of real and relational intimate contact. Kama refers to a human's authentic desire to share pleasure through sexual union and real intimate contact.

Pleasure in all its forms emerges as a function of sexual energy. By giving yourself permission to experience pleasure, you will be freeing yourself from restrictive beliefs that may have blocked the flow of sexual energy through your energy field and prevented you from experiencing transcendent sex and relationships.

Dharma is the third authentic desire. In Sanskrit, *Dharma* means "that which holds together" (in essence, that which prevents worldly relationships from dissolving into chaos). Dharma has two applications. There is universal Dharma, which is the duty that everyone has to seek transcendent relationship. And there is individual Dharma, which is the specific path each person must follow in order to achieve it.

Moksha is the fourth authentic desire. In Sanskrit, *Moksha* means "transcendence," which is spiritual freedom and liberation from karmic attachment and external projections. Of the four authentic desires, Moksha is the most important because without Moksha there would be nothing to motivate people to progress beyond crude physical pleasure and the basics of personal and group survival—which include food-gathering, status, and reproduction.

It's Moksha that motivates people to engage in activities that lead to transcendent sex and relationships. Without Moksha there would be no reason to favor authentic desires over inauthentic desires, no reason to experience orgasmic bliss, and no reason to engage in any activities that lead to union with another person or universal consciousness.

Because everyone seeks transcendence in some way or another, Moksha is the true state of every human being. And although your desire for transcendence may have been dormant until now, you can awaken and augment it by participating in a process that leads to spiritual union with your partner, your self, and with Universal Consciousness. Further-more, the desire for Moksha—or transcendence—is the most important branch of the Tree of Desire, because transcendence is the fulfillment of Artha, Kama, and Dharma. Transcendence provides the ultimate comfort (Artha), it grants the most sublime pleasure (Kama), and it also consti-tutes one's highest duty (Dharma).

Inauthentic Desires

Besides authentic desires, you have inauthentic desires, which emerge through your inauthentic mind and ego. You experience inauthentic de-sires when they bombard you from within, and you experience them when people you know project them at you.

How do you distinguish which desires are authentic and which are inauthentic?

There are legions of inauthentic desires, but they all have several things in common by which you can recognize them. First, they disrupt the flow of sexual energy through your energy field. That, in turn, can prevent you from turning your organs of perception inward and becom-ing present. Second, they attach you to fields of energy with individual qualities—including fields that compel you to think, worry, pass judg-ment, and compare yourself to others. Third, they make it difficult for you to embrace Artha, Kama, Dharma, and Moksha. So, if the desires you experience badger you or create an irrational need to have, own, or consume something or to engage in sexual activities that you find unpleasant or distasteful, you're being disturbed by inauthentic desires.

If you're being plagued by the desire to give away personal power or personal responsibility, you are being disturbed by inauthentic desires. Indeed, once you've become attached to your individual mind and ego, you can desire almost anything—even things that are self-destructive, perverted, or that prevent you from experiencing soulful pleasure, love, intimacy, and joy and sharing them with a partner. In the end, if you're being disturbed by any desire that opposes transcendent sex or relation-ships, that desire must be inauthentic.

External Projections

So, suppose you have recognized that you do have inauthentic desires. Now what? Karmic baggage is the source of most inauthentic desires. Remember that Jason was psychologically predisposed to submit to his domineering female boss due to the karmic baggage from his overbearing mother that he suffered from all through his childhood. However, inauthentic desires can also emerge from external projections, especially when these external projections reinforce the karmic baggage. Remember that Jason's boss was actively lusting after him, and it was Jason's karmic submission to his mother that made him vulnerable to the dominating energy his busty, blonde boss was projecting externally at him. Because Jason's karmic baggage "rhymed" or vibrated in resonance with the energy his boss was projecting, he accepted her energy as authentic and then integrated it into his individual mind and ego.

So, as you can see, to accept an external projection and integrate it into your individual mind and ego all you have to do is grant it legitimacy. And you can do that by accepting that the projected attitude, belief, feeling, sensation, or desire you're experiencing is your own. This was easy for Jason to do, because he had long experienced similar feelings.

Thus, it may be easy to become attached to an external projection. If a projected thought passes through your mind, and you become the thinker of the thought—by believing it's your thought and then by investing your personal will, desire, and/or intent in the thought—you will become attached to it. Once you're attached to the thought, it's just a matter of time before it becomes integrated into your individual mind and ego. The same process can take place if you believe in or invest your personal will in a feeling or desire that has been projected at you.

The intrusion of external projections into your energy field is an invasive process that actually begins in the womb and can continue throughout the successive stages of your life. After all, Jason was subjected to the domineering energy of his mother, even before he was born. Below are ten guidelines that will help you to determine which thoughts, emotions, feelings, and desires are generated by your own mind and which enter your field as an external projection. What they have in common is that they are not the real you. It is as if some Christian emperor were to conquer the Indian village and attempt suddenly to change the banyan tree into a Christmas tree by dressing it up in ornaments and trying to make it feel as if it had not been doing a good job of protecting and nourishing everyone in the village for thousands of years. The banyan tree would feel that it was not really being itself.

1. Thought precedes emotion. If you feel or desire something not related to what you're doing or what you've experienced through your organs of perception, it's source is probably an external projection.

2. Thoughts, feelings, and desires that are new to you or out of the context of what you're doing are generally caused by external projections.

3. Heavy, dense, and oppressive emotions, feelings, and/or desires that press on you from the outside are caused by external projections.

4. Feelings, thoughts, and desires that hammer at you even after you've rejected them are caused by external projections.

5. Sudden and dramatic emotional shifts or dramatic shifts in the quality and intensity of your desires are caused by external projections.

6. Accusations and the perpetual charges "You're wrong" or "You're not good enough" are caused by external projections.

7. Sudden weakness, confusion, or anxiety about what you want are caused by external projections.

8. Dramatic shifts in your level of sexual energy or what sexually stimulates or satisfies you are caused by external projections.

9. Physical experiences, such as heat, pressure, thrills, and so on that are out of context to what you are doing or what you want are caused by external projections.

10. Thoughts, feelings, and sensations that try to manipulate, change, or control what you want or which dwell on your defects—

especially those you cannot change—are caused by external projections.

Attachment to external projections has become so common that by
the time most people reach puberty they're literally surrounded by energy with individual qualities that have been projected at them. That
qualified energy is like an ill-fitting suit. It can disrupt the flow of sexual
energy through your energy field, forcing you to contract, and disrupting your ability to participate in transcendent sex and relationships.

The three most common types of external projections that can interfere with your authentic desires—particularly your desire for transcendent sex and relationships—are controlling waves, cords, and attachment fields.

Controlling Waves

Controlling waves are waves of subtle, non-physical energy with individual qualities. These waves can be projected on the subtle dimensions
of the non-physical universe, but not in the physical-material universe.
They are normally projected by someone who seeks to control and/or
change an aspect of another person's personality.

Controlling waves are normally wedge-shaped when they emerge
from the perpetrator's energy field and are projected at the target.
However, once the controlling wave has entered the targets' energy
field it will quickly expand to fill a large portion of it on the dimension
on which it has been projected.

Whenever someone attached to a personality issue (and therefore to
energy with individual qualities) projects an attitude, thought, emotion,
feeling, or inauthentic desire at another person, he or she can project a
controlling wave. When the controlling wave is projected at the front
of the target's energy field, the perpetrator will have expectations that
have not been fulfilled. When the controlling wave is projected at the
back of the target's energy field, the perpetrator will be trying to regain something that he or she perceives he or she has lost. Those who
are unsure of their position will project a controlling wave at either the
right or left side of the target's energy field.

It's worth mentioning that controlling waves can put pressure on the karmic baggage already present in the target's energy field, just as the controlling energy of Jason's boss put pressure on Jason's karmic baggage. The increased pressure caused by a controlling wave is the most common source of stress and stress-related symptoms.

Even if the perpetrator is only partially conscious that he or she is projecting a controlling wave, the wave can attach the target to the perpetrator for years. In most cases, however, the controlling wave will remain intact as long as it serves the perpetrator's purpose, which can be as simple as holding on to the target, even if the desire or need for relationship isn't reciprocated.

Cords

Cords are another type of external projection that can be projected from one person to another. Structurally and functionally they differ from controlling waves in several important ways. Cords are generally denser than controlling waves. The structure of cords don't change after they've been projected. In fact, cords closely resemble long, thin tubes that have a consistent diameter along their entire length.

Cords are a manifestation of dependency, need, and/or desire that can border on obsession. Unlike a controlling wave—which is primarily an instrument of control—a cord manifests the perpetrator's desire or need to hold on to or have contact with his or her target.

Cords remain active as long as the perpetrator holds on to the false impression that he or she needs or desires something (even if it's just contact) from the target. As long as the cords are active, the perpetrator can continue to project energy with individual qualities through them. Once the perpetrator abandons the false impression that he or she needs or desires something from the target, the cord will become dormant, and energy from the perpetrator will no longer flow through it.

Even if a cord has become functionally dormant, however, it will remain structurally intact, keeping the target connected to the perpetrator, in some cases for years after the initial projection.

It is important to note that in all cases of sexual abuse there will be two penetrations: a physical penetration, and a violent penetration of qualified energy in the form of a cord. It's not the physical penetration but the cord that causes the most extreme symptoms. Indeed, it's the continued presence of a cord that explains the pervasive fear the victim of sexual abuse can have for the perpetrator, even years after the abuse has taken place.

Attachment Fields

An attachment field is another type of external projection that can disrupt the flow of sexual energy through a person's energy field and interfere with his or her authentic desires and relationships. An attachment field normally has a long, rectangular shape and will be extremely dense and sticky. It's because of these qualities, particularly its density, that an attachment field can penetrate the target's energy field.

Attachment fields are often projected between family members, which is why old adages such as "The apple doesn't fall far from the tree" and "Like father, like son" are true—more often than not.

The perpetrator's motive for projecting an attachment field, whether he or she is fully conscious of the projection or not, will be to compel the target to do what he or she wants.

An attachment field acts like a computer virus, disrupting the target's normal decision-making process by introducing powerful feelings, emotions, thoughts, and desires into his or her energy field. In the process, an attachment field can disrupt the target's ability to radiate sexual energy. It can prevent the target from remaining present in his or her energy field. And, it can disrupt the target's ability to experience authentic desires and share them with his or her partner.

Karmic Baggage and External Projections

From what you've just learned, it should be clear that, like karmic baggage, external projections can disrupt your ability to radiate sexual energy freely and experience authentic desires. Karmic baggage is the core problem, but external projections add an additional punch to karmic baggage. For some people, it's the knockout punch that disrupts their motivation and makes it impossible for them to enjoy transcendent sex and relationships. If you're like most people, you're being affected by the karmic baggage you've collected in your energy field, and you've become attached to external projections from other people—family, friends, lovers, former lovers, and so on.

In one of her first sessions with me, Sandra was surprised to learn that her ability to experience sustained intimacy with her partner was dependent on how much influence karmic baggage and external projections had on her energy field and her ability to radiate sexual energy freely. Sandra began the session by declaring:

> *"So, I have past-life karma and friends and family members who are projecting at me and screwing up my relationships. And if that's not bad enough, now you're telling me if I get attached to all those projections, I'll get trapped by inauthentic desires, which will compel me to do things that will disrupt my experience of transcendent sex and relationships?"*

I replied, *"Do you do everything you want, or do you sometimes do things and wonder why you did them afterwards?"*

"I wonder why I do a lot of things …"

"And do you feel ambivalent?"

"Yes … and confused and sometimes I become obsessive because I feel so conflicted."

"Ok, then you tell me what is going on," I asked.

"What's going on is … I'm being trapped by desires that don't quite seem like the real me, that seem to come from somewhere else, but yet seem strangely familiar." Sandra leaned forward and muttered, *"I think I could live with the idea of karmic baggage."*

Sandra then continued. *"However, what I'm having trouble with is the idea that people I know are manipulating me with their projections."*

"Listen, Sandra, I know it's hard to accept. But people believe they have good reasons to project. Otherwise they wouldn't do it."

"Really, even if projections disrupt my relationships?"

"You're giving the average person too much credit. Most people don't connect cause and effect, particularly in the non-physical universe. So they don't know that their projections can disrupt another person's relationship."

"But that doesn't explain what motivates people to project at people they know."

"Sandra, people project for a host of reasons. But in the end people project because they want to influence other people. They may be motivated by a need to control or they may want to change, manipulate, connect to, or harm the person they're projecting at. In most cases the perpetrator isn't even aware that the projection of a thought, emotion, or feeling motivated by karmic baggage or their own inauthentic desires can disrupt another person's energy field or their ability to enjoy the benefits of transcendent sex and relationships. Sometimes it's simply a question of mechanics. A person will become attached to a thought, emotion, or feeling that has emerged from his or her karmic baggage or an external projection that's trapped in his or her energy field. Then an inauthentic desire will emerge, and he or she will project the qualified energy that supports it at another person, because he or she blames them for something or perceives he or she needs or wants something from the targeted person."

"Are you saying that the projection will be directed at whomever the perpetrator is thinking about?" asked Sandra.

"Exactly. And when a person with strong desires, feelings of dependency, anger, or jealousy intentionally projects at another person, its impact will be stronger and will last longer. That's why, even if someone wants to go beyond the limits of a traditional relationship, if the inauthentic desires emerging from his or her karmic baggage and/or from external projections are strong enough, he or she is out of luck. It also explains why it's so important to say yes to authentic desires and say no to inauthentic desires if you want to engage in transcendent sex and relationships."

The Importance of Saying Yes and No

You already say yes to authentic desires when your personal will supports them and they're not opposed by stronger desires that emerge from your individual mind and ego. In fact, authentic desires are hardwired into your energy field and your authentic mind.

The metaphor of a growing seed and the soil that nourishes it illustrates what I mean. The seed—which represents your relationship—must be nourished by the soil—represented by authentic desires—if it's to grow and bear fruit. The fruit, of course, includes pleasure, love, intimacy, and joy. But to consistently experience these universal qualities and share them with a partner you must recognize that it's just as important to say no to inauthentic desires as it is to say yes to authentic desires.

In order for you to say no to inauthentic desires I've included the No Mudra in two parts. At first, you should perform the No Mudra on its own. Then you can perform the mudra after you've become present in your energy field and filled it with sexual energy. By performing the No Mudra, becoming present, and filling your energy field with sexual energy, you will be able to resist (say no to) inauthentic desires as well as to karmic baggage and the external projections that support them.

Exercise: The No Mudra

The No Mudra is designed to deny inauthentic desire receptors in your authentic mind and energy field. To perform the mudra, use your thumbs and index fingers of both hands to form two loops that are connected to one another like two links of a chain. Then bring the tips of your middle fingers, ring fingers, and pinkies together so that they resemble the sides of a triangle (see Figure 2). Perform the No Mudra for at least ten minutes a day for three days.

Exercise: Overcoming Inauthentic Desires

After you've performed the No Mudra on its own, you can take the next step by performing it after you've become present in your energy field and filled it with sexual energy. To begin, find a comfortable position by

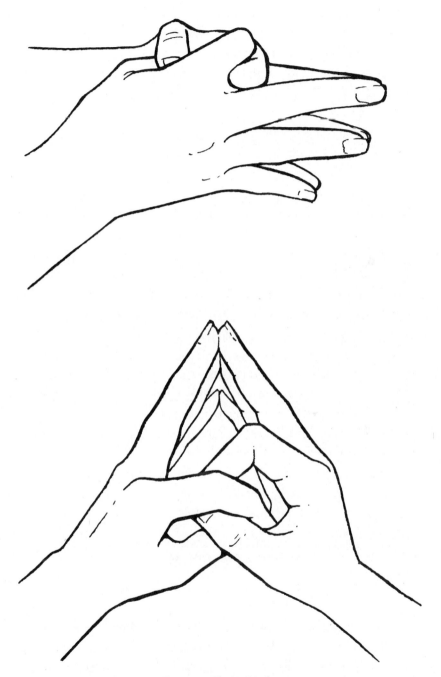

Figure 2: *The No Mudra*

either sitting, lying, or standing with your back straight. Then choose an inauthentic desire that has been disturbing you and your relationships. It could be the desire to control your partner, the desire to punish him or her or to get more sympathy from your partner. Any inauthentic desire that emerges regularly and disrupts your ability to experience and share pleasure, love, and intimacy with your partner will work.

Once you've chosen an inauthentic desire, keep it in mind. Then close your eyes and start breathing deeply through your nose—without separation between inhalation and exhalation. Continue breathing this way for five minutes. Then count backward from five to one, and then from ten to one. Use the Standard Method Exercise to relax the muscles of your physical-material body. Once your muscles are relaxed, assert, *"It's my intent to become present in my energy field on the dimension where I've become attached to the inauthentic desire I have in mind."*

Take a few moments to experience the shift. Then assert, *"It's my intent to fill my energy field with sexual energy on the dimension where I've become present."*

Continue by performing the No Mudra. Hold the mudra for ten more minutes. After ten minutes release the mudra and count from one to five. When you reach the number five, open your eyes. You will feel wide awake, perfectly relaxed, and better than you did before.

You should perform the techniques you just learned as part of your daily regimen or until the inauthentic desire you had in mind no longer disturbs you. By consistently saying no to inauthentic desires you will gradually overcome them. And by overcoming them you will be able to experience more pleasure, love, and intimacy to share with your partner.

Exercise: The Pleasure Meditation

What if you could water and fertilize the Tree of Authentic Desire so that all of its branches are strong and its flowers are fragrant and numerous? In fact, you can learn how to do just that. Once you can say no to inauthentic desires, you can take the next step by saying yes to and nourishing the sexual pleasure that emerges naturally through your energy field, via your chakras.

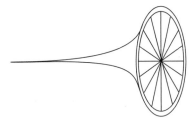

Figure 3: *A Chakra*

Your chakras—along with your meridians, auras, and minor energy centers—compose your energy system (see Figure 12). Your energy system plays an essential role in your ability to participate in transcendent sex and relationships.

Your chakras keep you connected to Universal Consciousness, and it's through your chakras that sexual energy, emerging from Universal Consciousness, can enter your energy field and provide you with pleasure.

Your chakras are composed exclusively of energy with universal qualities. Each chakra looks like a brightly colored disk that spins rapidly at the end of what looks like a long axle or stalk. The wheel portion is about three inches (eight centimeters) in diameter and perpetually moves or spins around a central axis. Emerging from the center of the disk are what appear to be spokes (see Figure 3).

Although you have chakras within your body as well as above and below it, it's the seven traditional chakras inside your body that we will be concerned with in this exercise.

The seven traditional chakras emerge from points that correspond to your spine and head.

Figure 12 illustrates that the first chakra emerges from a point that corresponds to the base of your spine. Your second chakra emerges from a point four finger widths below your navel. Your third chakra emerges from your spine at a point that corresponds to your solar plexus. Your fourth chakra emerges from a point that corresponds to the center of the breastbone. Your fifth chakra emerges from a point one-half inch (one centimeter) below your Adam's apple. Your sixth chakra emerges from a point that corresponds to the center of your brow. Your seventh chakra emerges from a point that corresponds to the crown of your head.

For more on the seven traditional chakras and the chakras above and below your body space, go to chapter 7.

In the Pleasure Meditation, you will use tone to activate your seven traditional chakras so that sexual energy radiates freely and you can experience and express the pleasure you feel, without judgment or fear getting in the way.

To perform the Pleasure Meditation, you will undress and place a large mirror in front of you so that you can see both your face and your genitals. In the first part of the exercise, you will become present in your energy field and perform the No Mudra. Then you will watch yourself in the mirror while you chant the appropriate tone that activates and enhances the flow of sexual energy through your seven traditional chakras, beginning with your first chakra at the base of your spine.

The point of this exercise is to enjoy the pleasure that emerges from each chakra while you watch yourself without fear or judgment. By being present and performing the No Mudra while you activate each chakra, you should be able to enjoy the unique vibration of each chakra and your own reaction to it.

Each chakra vibrates at a particular frequency that corresponds to one of the seven tones you will be chanting during the exercise. The tone for the first chakra, at the base of spine, is G. And you will find G easily if you chant "oo" as in the word "who." The tone for the second chakra is A. And you will find A easily if you chant "oh" as in the word "hoe." The tone for the third chakra, by the solar plexus, is B. And you will find B easily if you chant "aw" as in the word "awe." The tone for the fourth chakra, at the center of your breastbone, is C. And you will find C easily if you chant "ah" as in the word "ha." The tone for the fifth chakra, at the throat, is D. And you will find D easily if you chant "eh" as in the word "hey." The tone for the sixth chakra, at the brow, is E. And you will find E easily if you chant "ee" as in the word "eel." The tone for the seventh chakra, at the crown, is F. And you will find F easily if you chant "om," as in the word "ohm."

Once you're clear which tone corresponds to which chakra, you can continue the exercise by chanting the appropriate tone three times from each chakra. Do this ascending from the first to the seventh chakra. After you have completed chanting, take five more minutes to observe yourself in the mirror. After five minutes you can lie on your back or sit upright with your eyes closed for another ten minutes. After that time, count from one to five and open your eyes. You will feel wide awake, perfectly relaxed, and better than you did before.

In this chapter you have learned to say no to inauthentic desires and yes to the pleasure that emerges naturally from your seven traditional chakras. This is like learning how to water and fertilize the Tree of Authentic Desire. Now you are ready to take the next step in the process of transcendence. You are ready to enhance your self-love.

Chapter 3

The Importance of Self-Love

According to an ancient spiritual text known as the Bhairava Tantra,

One day it began to rain, and the rain continued for days and months on end. Everything was submerged underwater, and there was no land or landmark of any kind in sight. A lone bird was hovering over this vast expanse of water, and, seeing no landmark anywhere, became lost and could not return to its home. Then the water gradually receded a bit, and a log of wood came into sight. The bird at once landed on the wood and, using it as a base, flew back and forth from there in order to find food and whatever else it needed. Each time the bird flew off in any direction, it kept the piece of wood in sight and, in this way, always returned to the same base without any difficulty.[2]

If you want to enjoy the beauty of transcendent sex and relationships, you must learn where love truly exists in infinite supply and where love does not exist. Then—like the lone bird in the story—you must learn to cultivate a kind of dual awareness, engaging in all our worldly activities but always keeping your base in mind, keeping in your awareness the field of life where love truly exists. Then you can really live in love. And this is your birthright.

After all, you emerged from Universal Consciousness and you participate in relationship on all physical and non-physical dimensions of the multi-dimensional universe. This makes you a multi-dimensional being with the capacity to experience and share pleasure, love, intimacy, and joy with your partner through transcendent sex and relationships.

You have already learned to enhance your enjoyment of pleasure in chapter 2. But before you can consistently enjoy pleasure, love, intimacy, and joy, and share these universal qualities with your partner, there are two questions that must be answered. The first question is whether you must love yourself first in order to experience love, intimacy, and joy and share these with a partner. And if the answer to that question is yes—and you lack sufficient self-love—the second question is what can you do to increase self-love?

I will answer both questions in this chapter. But before I do that I must clear up the confusion about self-love, because people rarely differentiate between Universal Consciousness, the source of love, the authentic mind, the vehicle through which love emerges, and the individual mind and ego, which are composed of karmic baggage and external projections.

To overcome the confusion, it would be instructive to take a closer look at love and how it's related to Universal Consciousness, your authentic mind, and your individual mind and ego. With that knowledge, you'll have a clearer picture of what self-love is and how you can increase it—if necessary—so that you can experience more of it and share more of it with your partner.

We'll begin by looking at your individual mind and ego, which are both composed of energy with individual qualities. After that we'll look at Universal Consciousness—the foundation of your authentic mind. Then we'll look at your authentic mind, which is composed of three parts—Paramatman, Jivamatman, and your subtle energy system—which supports and nourishes them both.

Where Love Does Not Exist:
The Individual Mind and Ego

The individual mind and ego—which so many people regard as their primary vehicles of awareness and self-expression—are neither structural parts of the human energy field nor functional parts of the authentic mind. They are not really a very safe place. In fact they are like the limitless expanse of water where the lone bird could find no place to rest. Neither the individual mind nor the ego has definite structures that define it. In fact, each is composed of an evolving community of energy fields that have only individual qualities.

All humans have come into this life with layers of energy with individual qualities in their energy field (see Figure 4). And virtually all humans have added additional layers, by integrating external projections into their energy field throughout the successive stages of their life.

Although there is a dizzying number of such fields in both the individual mind and ego, all these fields have several things in common. They all have the ability to assert will and (inauthentic) desire as well as to express awareness, emotion, feeling, and sensation. And they all have a personal agenda, which motivates them to act on their own behalf, either alone or in concert with other qualified energy fields.

Although they can function individually, it's by functioning together that the individual mind and ego can filter or even distort a person's perception of people, places, and things. And by distorting a person's perception, the individual mind and ego can weaken a person's commitment to himself or herself and to the people with whom he or she shares relationship.

Although the fields of qualified energy that compose your individual mind and ego are capable of asserting energy with individual qualities (in the form of thoughts, attitudes, emotions, feelings, and inauthentic desires), they can't express or share love. Nonetheless, it's possible for your individual mind and ego to usurp the functions of your authentic mind and to function as a surrogate mind, which can disrupt your ability to experience and share pleasure, love, intimacy, and joy.

Activities that emerge from your individual mind and ego (which disrupt your ability to experience pleasure, love, intimacy, and joy) are worrying, judging, and comparing yourself to others, as well as activities that emerge from inauthentic desires and activities that block the flow of sexual energy through your energy field and prevent you from remaining present.

It's worth knowing that fields of energy contained in the individual mind and ego are part of a larger field of qualified energy known as Maya. In Sanskrit, *Maya* can be defined as "the appearance of reality." Although disagreement exists among the world's religions and spiritual traditions, it's generally agreed that the field of Maya (which exists alongside authentic fields of energy on all physical and non-physical dimensions) has existed and will continue to exist as long as there is a phenomenal, day-to-day universe.

The field of Maya and the individual fields of energy within your individual mind and ego have a tremendous impact on you and your relationships. And if the density, polarity, and level of activity of your individual mind and ego become great enough (and you become attached to the energy emerging from them), the flow of sexual energy through your energy field will be blocked and you will have difficulty experiencing and sharing pleasure, love, intimacy, and joy. Without the ability to experience and share pleasure, love, intimacy, and joy, your life can become dry and lifeless, and you can fall prey to a worldview that stresses ownership, control, and manipulation.

Where Love Truly Exists: Universal Consciousness

The ancient texts of yoga and tantra all agree that Universal Consciousness is the foundation of your authentic mind, as well as of everything else in the physical and non-physical universe, including time, space, energy, and consciousness. Although Universal Consciousness is the foundation of the phenomenal universe, it has no individual qualities. So, a precise definition of Universal Consciousness is impossible. Furthermore, because your spirit, intellect, soul, and physical-material body

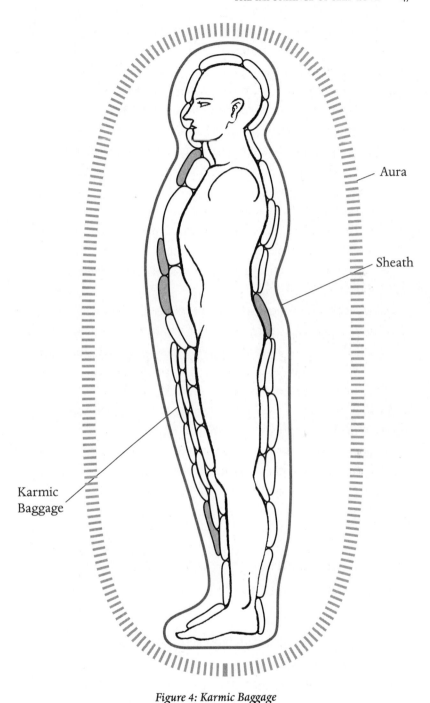

Figure 4: Karmic Baggage

emerged from Universal Consciousness, none of them has the capacity to conceive of or understand what Universal Consciousness is, even though it is their root cause or creator. The paradox this represents can be likened to the problem faced by beings in a dream who vainly try to conceive of their creator, the dreamer, to whom these beings owe their existence and in whose consciousness they exist and function.

What we do know is that love emerges from Universal Consciousness and that it's through Universal Consciousness that you have the consciousness to recognize love.

Although modern psychologists and health practitioners rarely make a distinction between the different types of love, the ancients took great pains to differentiate between them. The classical Greeks described three types of love: *Agape*—universal love; *Filio*—brotherly love, and *Eros*—sexual love.

The love that emerges directly from Universal Consciousness is universal love, which the Greeks called Agape and the yogis called *Ananda*. Universal love is unconditional. It sets no conditions, and shines like the sun on saint and sinner alike. Because universal love sets no conditions, universal love can't blow hot or cold. It can't be controlled or limited by inauthentic desires, judgment, or fear. And universal love can't be reserved for any selected group or individual.

Because universal love emerges directly from Universal Consciousness, we can say that both are essentially the same (God is love). And like Universal Consciousness, universal love must exist outside normal time-space, in the ever-present now. This means that universal love can't be the love we're talking about when we address the question of self-love. Nor can Universal Consciousness be someone who needs (more) self-love to engage in relationship, because everything necessary for self-love—including pleasure, love, intimacy, and joy—emerges directly from it.

The Authentic Mind

Like the universe, your authentic mind emerged from Universal Consciousness through the tattvas. The word "tattva" comes from the Sanskrit root *tat,* which means "that," and *tvam,* which means "thou"

or "you." Thus "tattva" means "thou are that." "Thou are that" signifies the ancient truth that you are always in union with Universal Consciousness and that you can experience the benefits of union (which
include pleasure, love, intimacy, and joy) by remaining present in your
authentic mind.

As evolution proceeded—via the tattvas—a hierarchy of physical
and non-physical dimensions was created in both the physical and non-
physical universe. You exist on all of these dimensions. And on all of
these dimensions your authentic mind has the capacity to experience
and share pleasure, love, intimacy, and joy through transcendent sex
and relationships. In fact, your authentic mind can be considered as a
vast interdimensional organism, composed of energy bodies with different functions and an energy system that nourishes them and that
provides them with sexual energy. These energy bodies and the organs
of your energy system allow you to share all forms of love, including
universal love. Though it's designed to function as a unified whole,
your authentic mind is divided into three essential parts: Paramatman,
Jivamatman, and the human energy system.

Paramatman

Para, in Sanskrit, refers to the supreme or universal. In conjunction with
the word *Atman*, it refers to that which is transcendent. Paramatman
can be considered transcendent, as in universal mind. It is mind without
differentiation. This means that Paramatman is not composed of different energy bodies with different structures and functions. On each dimension, Paramatman emerges as one unified field or body, composed
of consciousness and energy with universal qualities. As a unified field
or body, Paramatman contains everything necessary for you to be present and to be aware of your internal and external environment. However, its structure prevents it from participating directly in the individual
activities of transcendent sex and relationships.

Paramatman does have a direct connection to Atman. Atman is a
thumb-sized spot on the right side of your chest where universal love
emerges into your conscious awareness. Once you become aware of
Atman you will begin to experience the yearning for freedom, truth,

and/or universal love. And it's by following inward the yearning for one of these three that you will become aware of your a priori union with Universal Consciousness.

Jivamatman

In Sanskrit, *Jiva* means "embodied soul." Jivamatman refers to the part of your authentic mind that is differentiated into spirit, intellect, soul, and body. Jivamatman is composed exclusively of energy with universal qualities. And it's through Jivamatman that Universal Consciousness can express universal love, which has been differentiated into pleasure, (human) love, intimacy, and joy.

Like Paramatman, Jivamatman evolved from Universal Consciousness by way of the tattvas. But unlike Paramatman, Jivamatman is not composed of one undifferentiated body. On each dimension Jivamatman is composed of energy bodies, sheaths, and auras whose structures vary according to their functions.

You may not be aware of it, but it's through the energy bodies, sheaths, and auras in Jivamatman that you develop an authentic identity; acquire knowledge; express authentic emotions, feelings, and desires; and experience pleasure, love, intimacy, and joy.

Energy Bodies

Within the field of Jivamatman you have non-physical energy bodies that interpenetrate your physical-material body. These energy bodies are the same size and shape as your physical-material body. And they're composed entirely of energy with universal qualities. Energy bodies allow you to be present in your energy field and experience the activities of the physical and non-physical universe via your awareness and your organs of perception.

Sheaths

Like energy bodies, sheaths interpenetrate your physical-material body. However, sheaths are larger than energy bodies and extend several inches (centimeters) beyond the space normally occupied by them (see Figure 5). Like your energy bodies, sheaths are composed entirely of energy with universal qualities. However, unlike your energy bodies, which only allow you to be present, sheaths allow you to interact directly with your external environment and other sentient beings. In fact, it's your sheaths that give you the flexibility to express yourself and to communicate with other people, empathize with them, and accumulate knowledge about your external environment.

Auras

Auras are egg-shaped fields of energy with universal qualities that surround your energy bodies and sheaths on all physical and non-physical dimensions. They are composed of two parts: a large cavity (which surrounds your energy bodies and sheaths), and a surface boundary (which surrounds the cavity and separates it from the external environment).

Under normal conditions your auras provide you with boundaries that protect you from the intrusion of external projections that could disrupt the flow of sexual energy through your energy field and prevent you from experiencing and sharing pleasure, love, intimacy, and joy (see Figure 5 on the next page).

It's important to note, however, that if the surface of an aura has been weakened by shock or trauma (caused by the violent intrusion of qualified energy into your energy field), the aura can be contaminated by energy with individual qualities. If this energy gets stuck in your energy field, it's only a matter of time before it becomes integrated into the karmic baggage you carry in your individual mind and ego.

The Human Energy System

To support Paramatman and Jivamatman, you have a subtle energy system composed of chakras, meridians, and minor energy centers.

There are one hundred and forty-four chakras within your energy system. Eleven chakras are located within personal body space (the space on the subtle dimensions that interpenetrates your physical-material body): the traditional seven chakras as well as two etheric chakras and two physical chakras.

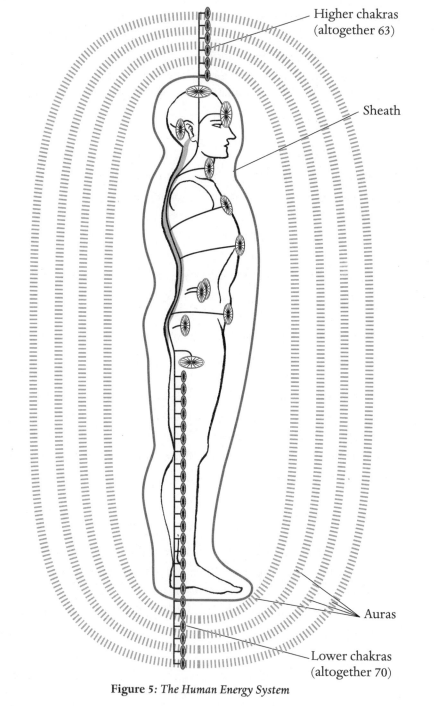

Higher chakras
(altogether 63)

Sheath

Auras

Lower chakras
(altogether 70)

Figure 5: *The Human Energy System*

The seven traditional chakras are located along the spine and in your head. The upper etheric chakra is located on the left side of your pelvis, between your second and third chakras. Your lower etheric chakra is located on the right side of your pelvis, between your second and third chakras. Your upper physical chakra is located in the back of your head directly behind and below your sixth chakra. And your lower physical chakra is located in the back of your pelvis, just below your second chakra. Sixty-three chakras are stacked above your personal body space, directly above the seventh chakra, and seventy chakras are stacked below your personal body space, directly below the first chakra (see Figure 5).

Sexual energy radiates through all one hundred and forty-four chakras and is continuously being transmuted into the precise frequencies needed to maintain the health of your energy system and the communities of energy bodies, sheaths, and auras that your energy system supports.

Additionally, minor energy centers are located throughout your body. Four principle centers are located in your extremities—one in each hand and one in each foot. Others are scattered throughout your energy field. The minor energy centers have two principle functions: they facilitate the movement of sexual energy through your energy field, and they balance the pressure within it.

Your meridians transfer sexual energy from your chakras to your energetic vehicles in Paramatman and your energy bodies, sheaths, and auras in Jivamatman. This enables you to remain present in your authentic mind, form an authentic identity, and participate in all the activities of a transcendent sex and relationships.

Your auras also cooperate with your energy system by serving as reservoirs of sexual energy, which your energetic vehicles in Paramatman and your energy bodies and sheaths in Jivamatman can draw on in times of need. However, to perform its functions properly, the surface of an aura must be strong, firm, and free from the influence of external projections and the inordinate accumulation of karmic baggage.

Before we move on, it's worth noting that there has been a convolution between your energy system and your physical-material body. In

fact, your ability to experience the physical-material world and participate in it fully is made possible by the synchronistic function of your
energy system and the organs of your physical-material body.

The Truth About Self-Love

From what we've learned so far it should be clear that sexual energy
in the form of love radiates from Universal Consciousness into your
energy field first, and it's only after you've experienced it as self-love
that you can share it with another person. So, the answer to our first
question—whether you must love yourself first in order to share love,
intimacy, and joy with your partner—must be a resounding yes.

In order to answer the second question—what you can do to increase your self-love if it's lacking—you must first recognize that it's impossible to love yourself or share love with your partner without having
enough sexual energy in your energy field. This means that to enhance
your self-love you must enhance the total amount of sexual energy you
have available. And that energy must be able to radiate freely into the
part of your energy field that can share it with yourself as self-love.

Because your individual mind and ego are composed entirely of
energy with individual qualities, it would be foolish to try to increase
your self-love by trying to enhance the amount of qualified energy you
have or by transferring energy with individual qualities from one part
of your energy field to another.

When it comes to self-love, there is an additional problem with the
individual mind and ego, because what motivates them both is not love
but survival and the compulsion to satisfy the inauthentic desires that
emerge from the karmic baggage that supports them. Indeed, to ask
the individual mind and ego to enhance your self-love—if it is lacking—
would be comparable to asking another person who is antagonistic to
you to enhance your self-love by sharing more of his or her antagonistic
energy with you. The individual mind and ego is like the vast sea in the
Bhairava Tantra, as the sea could provide no protection or comfort to
the lone bird.

When we review what we know about Universal Consciousness, it quickly becomes clear that Universal Consciousness couldn't enhance your self-love either, because it would have to descend into the dualistic universe to do so. Because Universal Consciousness couldn't do that and remain a singularity, it would be absurd to believe that it's Universal Consciousness that must do something to enhance your self-love so that you could share more love with another person.

Now that we've eliminated your individual mind and ego and Universal Consciousness, we must turn to your authentic mind to find out how you can enhance your self-love when it's lacking. When we review what we've learned about your authentic mind, we quickly recognize that to enhance your self-love, it's Jivamatman that must receive more love, because it's only through Jivamatman that you can form an authentic identity and share pleasure, love, intimacy, and joy with another person.

If it's Jivamatman that must receive more love to enhance your self-love, then it must be Paramatman that must provide love, because it's through Paramatman that universal love, in the form of sexual energy, enters your energy field from Universal Consciousness.

Indeed, research has confirmed that if you center yourself in your authentic mind you can enhance the amount of sexual energy Paramatman receives from Universal Consciousness. Then you can enhance your self-love by transferring the excess of sexual energy from Paramatman to Jivamatman.

The ability to transfer sexual energy from Paramatman to Jivamatman while maintaining your awareness of the external environment, is called *dual awareness.*

Let us now review the story with which we opened this chapter, for it illustrates how useful dual awareness can be:

One day it began to rain, and the rain continued for days and months on end. Everything was submerged underwater, and there was no land or landmark of any kind in sight. A lone bird was hovering over this vast expanse of water, and, seeing no landmark anywhere, became lost and could not return to its home. Then the water gradually receded a bit, and a log of wood came into sight. The bird at once landed on the wood and, using it as a base, flew back and forth from there in order to find food and whatever else it needed. Each time the bird flew off in any direction, it kept the piece of wood in sight and, in this way, always returned to the same base without any difficulty.[3]

Exercise: Building a Foundation for the Bridge 1: Becoming Present in Paramatman

To enhance your self-love the first thing you must do is center yourself in Paramatman. After that you will center yourself in Jivamatman. Once you can do both, you will enhance your self-love by performing the Self-Love Meditation.

In the exercise that follows you will become present in Paramatman. Begin by finding a comfortable position, with your back straight. Then close your eyes and breathe deeply through your nose without separation between inhalation and exhalation. After two or three minutes, count backward from five to one, then from ten to one. To relax the muscles of your physical-material body, you will use the Standard Method Exercise of alternatively tensing and releasing your muscles. After completing the Standard Method Exercise, assert: *"It's my intent to become present in Paramatman."* Then assert: *"It's my intent to turn my organs of perception inward in Paramatman."* After a few moments your orientation will shift and you'll become aware of a large cavity that interpenetrates your physical-material body. This cavity is the field of Paramatman, and it will extend up to twenty-six feet (eight meters) beyond your physical-material body in all directions.

From your new vantage point—within Paramatman—you will become aware of the love that emerges from Universal Consciousness and radiates through you. Take fifteen minutes to enjoy the experience. Then count from one to five. When you reach the number five, open your eyes and bring yourself out of the exercise. You can practice this exercise every day for fifteen minutes. The more often you practice, the greater the benefits will be and the easier it will be to experience universal love radiating into Paramatman from Universal Consciousness.

When you are confident that you can remain present in Paramatman for at least fifteen minutes, you can take the next step. You can become present in Jivamatman, and experience dual awareness, by turning your organs of perception inward in the field of Jivamatman.

Exercise: Building a Foundation for the Bridge 2: Becoming Present in Jivamatman

To become present in Jivamatman, find a comfortable position with your back straight. Then close your eyes and breathe deeply through your nose without separation between inhalation and exhalation. After two or three minutes count backward from five to one, and then from ten to one. To relax the muscles of your physical-material body you will use the Standard Method Exercise of alternatively tensing and releasing your muscles.

After completing the Standard Method Exercise, assert: *"It's my intent to become present in Jivamatman."* Then assert: *"It's my intent to turn my organs of perception inward in the field of Jivamatman."* After a few moments, your orientation will shift and you'll become aware of a large cavity that interpenetrates your physical-material body. This cavity is the field of Jivamatman, and it will extend up to twenty-six feet (eight meters) beyond your physical-material body. Once you've become aware of Jivamatman, allow your organs of perception to extend their awareness beyond the cavity into the external environment. By extending your awareness, you will experience dual awareness in the field of Jivamatman.

Many people report that as soon as they experience dual awareness, thoughts stop or at least stop disturbing them, their body becomes lighter, and they experience more self-control.

Take fifteen minutes to enjoy the experience. Then count from one to five, open your eyes, and bring yourself out of the exercise.

Exercise: Self-Love Meditation

Once you can remain present in both Paramatman and Jivamatman for at least fifteen minutes, you can begin to enhance your self-love by practicing the Self-Love Meditation. In the Self-Love Meditation you will become present in Paramatman first. Then you will fill Paramatman with sexual energy. Once you've filled Paramatman with sexual energy, you will become present in Jivamatman and fill Jivamatman with sexual energy. Once both fields are filled with sexual energy, you will turn your organs of perception inward on Jivamatman. Then you will extend your awareness from Jivamatman into the external environment. By turning your organs of perception inward and extending your awareness into the external environment, while remaining present in Jivamatman, you will experience dual awareness. And as soon as sexual energy pours into Jivamatman from Paramatman you will experience the benefits of more self-love.

To begin the Self-Love Meditation, find a comfortable position, with your back straight. Then close your eyes and breathe deeply through your nose, without separation between inhalation and exhalation. After two or three minutes, count backward from five to one, then from ten to one. To relax the muscles of your physical-material body you will use the Standard Method Exercise of alternatively tensing and releasing your muscles.

After completing the Standard Method Exercise, assert: *"It's my intent to become present in Paramatman."* Take a minute or two to enjoy the shift. Then assert: *"It's my intent to fill my field of Paramatman with sexual energy."* Once you're satisfied that Paramatman has been filled with sexual energy, assert: *"It's my intent to become present in Jivamatman."* Then assert: *"It's my intent to turn my organs of perception inward on Jivamatman."* Once you've turned your organs of perception inward on Jivamatman, take a few moments to enjoy the shift. Then assert: *"It's my intent to fill my field of Jivamatman with sexual energy."* Continue by asserting: *"It's my intent to extend my awareness from Jivamatman into the external environment and experience dual awareness."* Almost immediately you'll experience your self-love grow stronger.

Take fifteen minutes to perform the Self-Love Meditation. Then count from one to five, open your eyes, and bring yourself out of the meditation. If you practice the exercise regularly it's only a matter of time before you develop dual awareness and experience the benefits that come from enhanced self-love.

Exercise: Loving Your Sexual Expression

Once you've enhanced your self-love you can enhance your experience of sexual love, Eros, and the unique way you express it. The exercise that follows is called the Eros Meditation. It's designed to enhance your experience of Eros by having you activate your chakras while you stimulate yourself sexually. You will need a large mirror, which you will place in front of you. It must be large enough for you to see both your face and genitals clearly.

To prepare yourself for the Eros Meditation, perform the No Mudra, which you learned in chapter 2, for five minutes. Then use the techniques you learned earlier in this chapter to become present in Paramatman and Jivamatman. Once you are present in both fields and have achieved dual awareness, you will spread your legs and look at yourself in the mirror while you stimulate your genitals with your positive (right) hand. After a minute or two, you will begin to chant in succession the tones that corresponds to each of your seven traditional chakras, beginning with the first chakra at the base of your spine and ending with the seventh chakra at the top of your head.

You will chant from each chakra for two minutes. Try to keep eye contact with your mirror image at least part of the time.

Chant the tone for each chakra like it has been described in chapter 2. The tone for the first chakra is pronounced "*oo,*" as in the word "who." The tone for the second chakra is pronounced "*oh,*" as in the word "hoe." The tone for the third chakra is pronounced "*aw,*" as in the word "awe." The tone for the fourth chakra is pronounced "*ah,*" as in the word "ha." The tone for the fifth chakra is pronounced "*eh,*" as in the word "hey." The tone for the sixth chakra is pronounced "*ee,*" as in the word "eel."

The tone for the seventh chakra is pronounced *"om,"* as in the word "ohm."

Once you've chanted from your seventh chakra, close your eyes, lie back and for the next ten minutes enjoy Eros and the unique way you express sexual love. After ten minutes count from one to five and open your eyes. You will feel wide awake and better than you did before.

There is a variation to this exercise, which is even more intimate. In the variation you will substitute your partner for the mirror. During the exercise your partner will be a passive observer. While he or she watches you, you will stimulate your genitals and chant the appropriate tone from each of your seven traditional chakras.

During the exercise it's important to keep as much eye contact with your partner as possible. If you have enough trust and you keep eye contact, you will be able to see and even feel the effect your sexual love has on your partner. This will be a deeply personal experience, and the more authentic you can be, the more powerful and intimate it will be for you and your partner.

When it comes to stimulating yourself, it might interest you to know that Alfred Kinsey, while interviewing men and woman for his landmark works, *Sexual Behavior in the Human Male* and *Sexual Behavior in the Human Female*, discovered that 90 percent of males and 62 percent of females masturbated regularly. Kinsey came to the conclusion that masturbation is a normal part of human sexuality for people who are in relationship with another person and for those who are not.

Exercise: Loving Your Body Parts

Once you've enhanced your self-love and your enjoyment of sexual love, Eros, you can begin to love your unloved body parts. You may not realize it, but you continually love the body parts that give you pleasure by allowing sexual energy to radiate through them. The sexual energy that radiates through those body parts provides them with the nourishment they need to function healthfully and integrate their functions with the rest of your body.

When sexual energy radiates freely through a body part, you will enjoy how it feels, how it looks, and you will be able to share the energy emerging from it with your partner.

William Shakespeare wrote, "Self-love is not so vile a sin as self-neglecting." By neglecting a body part, disapproving of it, or withholding love from it—either consciously or unconsciously—you will force the body part to contract. This in turn will disrupt your ability to enjoy the body part and share your enjoyment with your partner.

There are a number of reasons why you might disapprove, neglect, or deny love to a body part. You could find a body part unattractive or feel you might be rejected because of it. You could have been taught that a body part must be kept hidden or that you must control the energy radiating from it. If it's too beautiful (particularly your primary or secondary sexual organs), the body part might attract unwanted attention or people might become jealous of it.

Regardless of the reasons why you disapprove, neglect, or deny love to a body part, by doing so you will restrict the flow of sexual energy through it, and this will force the body part to contract. Once it has contracted, the body part will respond either by becoming overly sensitive or by losing sensation and becoming numb.

In any case, the lack of sexual energy radiating from the body part will inhibit you from sharing pleasure, love, intimacy, and joy with your partner.

By mastering the following exercise, you will be able to fill any unloved body part with sexual energy. This will enhance your self-love and your ability to share sexual energy and sexual love freely with your partner.

Exercise: Loving Your Neglected Body Parts

In the exercise that follows you will combine your intent and mental attention (the awareness of your authentic mind) with sexual energy. By combining your intent and mental attention with sexual energy you will be able to fill a neglected body part with sexual energy and share your love with it. Once you've filled a body part with sexual energy it will radiate freely on it's own. And the neglected body part will automatically integrate itself with your other body parts, so that you can share more love with your partner.

Before you proceed, you need to know that you won't focus your mental attention on an unloved body part while you close yourself off to everything else (which is the technique you use in concentration). Instead, you will center yourself in your authentic mind and enjoy the body part you are focused on with your mental attention. Only by enjoying the body part while you let everything else move through your field of awareness, without becoming distracted or attached to it, you will be able to love an unloved body part.

Putting It All Together

The first step in loving an unloved body part is to choose one to work on. You could choose your thighs, feet, lips, or any other part of your body that has been denied the nourishment it needs to radiate freely.

Once you've chosen a body part, find a comfortable position with your back straight and close your eyes. Then count backward from five to one, then from ten to one. Use the Standard Method Exercise to relax the muscles of your physical-material body. Then assert: *"It's my intent to become present in my authentic mind."* Take two or three minutes to enjoy the shift. If your intent is to fill, for example, your thighs with sexual energy, your intent will be: *"It's my intent to focus my mental attention on my thighs and fill them with sexual energy."* Once you've asserted your intent, relax. Sexual energy will fill the body part you have in mind without any further effort on your part.

Allow the process to continue for ten minutes while you stay present in your authentic mind and your mental attention remains focused on the unloved body part. After ten minutes assert: *"It's my intent to release my mental attention."* Then count from one to five. When you reach the number five open your eyes. You will feel wide awake, perfectly relaxed, and better than you did before.

You may have to repeat the exercise several times for the body part to radiate sexual energy normally. However, it's not unusual to experience an enhanced flow of sexual energy through the body part the first time you practice the exercise. Your experience may vary, but if you practice the exercise regularly it won't be long before you can share sexual energy radiating from a previously unloved body part with somebody you love.

Now, like the lone bird who discovered the wooden log, you have discovered where love is not and where love truly exists. Also, you have learned how to build a bridge between where love is and where it is not, and to bring that love into your life.

Chapter 4
Say Yes to Transcendent Sex

For more than ten years Mona had worked as an interior designer, and her charm and creativity had opened the way for her professional success. When Mona met Allen, she felt the chemistry immediately. Although they worked for the same firm and attended several business conventions together, Mona and Allen were not directly involved in the same projects, so there was little chance for them to get to know each other. Mona was in her mid-thirties when she met Allen. Allen was several years older. Both were single and eager to participate in an intimate relationship.

Mona had been working with me for over a year when she explained the following.

The attraction was immediate, but it was six months before we were alone for the first time. It was during a business convention, and we took a long walk in the gardens surrounding the conference center. We spoke about our mutual interests, and before we parted we exchanged addresses and telephone numbers. For the next several weeks we exchanged e-mails and occasionally spoke by phone. Although none of the topics were intimate, I could still feel the attraction growing. And—although I tried to hide it—I knew I was growing more attached to Allen.

It wasn't long before we began to see each other socially, but he moved so slowly that I quickly became impatient. I wanted him so badly, I began to do things to make him jealous. I flirted with other men and made myself less available to him. I took days to return his phone calls. Even after we slept together, I continued to play games with him.

I had this obsessive feeling that I wouldn't be happy until I knew Allen was mine. This feeling drove me crazy. Anyway, just before Allen dumped me, I began seeing my former boyfriend, Hubert, to make Allen jealous and get him to commit. I see now, however, that it was the worst thing I could have done. Allen stopped calling me, and a short time later he sent me a short e-mail bluntly announcing our relationship was over.

I know now that I had been playing a stupid game. However, I didn't really think about the consequences. I had just wanted Allen, and I had wanted him on my terms. I felt that if I could have made him jealous and have pushed him into making a commitment I would have gotten him and that having him would have made me happy. It was only after Allen ended the relationship that I recognized that I'd confused intimacy with dependence. However, the need I had felt was so compelling that love had taken a back seat. Of course, in hindsight I can now see that because of my personality issues, what I had wanted most was not love, but to have a relationship that made me feel safe and in control.

Karmic Baggage and Sexual Energy

In Mona's case personality issues sabotaged her relationship. What Mona couldn't see at the time was that to experience a truly satisfying relationship she had to overcome the karmic baggage that supported her personality issues and disrupted her ability to share pleasure, love, intimacy, and joy with her partner.

When karmic baggage compels a person to manipulate or control his or her partner it's only a matter of time before sexual energy becomes blocked, body parts contract, and intimate relationship collapses.

You've most likely experienced karmic baggage many times. It's the dense energy in your energy field that creates pressure and muscle aches when you're stressed. Karmic baggage produces anxiety, self-doubt, and confusion whether it's consciously or unconsciously activated. Indeed, it's karmic baggage and the personality issues it supports that are the main obstacle to your experience of transcendent sex and relationships.

To understand more deeply what karmic baggage is, you must first understand how the principle of karma influences your life and relationships. The ancient Sanskrit word *karma* comes from the root *Kri*, "to act," and the word signifies an activity or action. In the West "karma" has been defined as the cumulative effect of action, which is commonly expressed as "You reap what you sow." This same principle is echoed in the Bhagavad Gita, the most sacred Vedic text. In the Gita we learn that "He that leadeth into captivity shall go into captivity; he that killeth with the sword must be killed with the sword."

When people in relationship are motivated by personality issues and the karmic baggage that supports them, it's the principle of karma that regulates their interactions. This means that in all situations where you are motivated by a personality issue, nothing happens by chance because the principle of karma connects the effects of all actions to their causes.

It may seem unfair or at the least inconvenient, but in the end you're responsible for what happens to you and your relationships because of your attachment to your personality issues and the karmic baggage that supports them. As a result you will eventually pay the price because all actions that emerge from karmic baggage will disrupt your ability to participate in transcendent sex and relationships.

If you're dependent, your attachment to the karmic baggage that created the pattern will compel you to be dependent or at least reactive to anything that smacks of dependency. If you're dominant, your attachment to karmic baggage can compel you to dominate people even if it interferes with your relationships.

The truth is that karma does more than explain how forces in the physical and non-physical universe interact. Karma manifests will and intent. Much like gravity, karma will attract you to objects, fields of qualified energy, and living beings, and then bind you via inauthentic desire to the object, energy field, or living being to whom you're attracted.

It's important to note that even though the personality issues that emerge through your individual mind and ego (and the karmic baggage that supports them) appear to be the exclusive vehicles of human consciousness, they function like a ventriloquist's puppet: The puppet appears to exhibit all the features of awareness and cognition. It speaks, displays emotion, and reacts to the ventriloquist and audience it's entertaining. However, no matter how clever it is or how realistic it may appear to be, your awareness, your authentic identity, and the sexual energy that supports them come through the ventriloquist (the authentic mind), which is the only vehicle through which you can experience the benefits of inspiring sex, intimacy, and joy with your partner.

From what we know about the principle of karma and fields of energy with individual qualities, we can define karmic baggage as any field of qualified energy that has been integrated into your individual mind and ego and that can cause attachment.

To the untrained observer it may appear that external circumstances have the most profound effect on the quality of your relationships, but appearances are deceiving. It's not your partner, career, family, physical environment, or the condition of your physical body that will have the most influence on how much pleasure, love, and intimacy you experience in your relationship. Rather, the quality of your relationships—especially your intimate relationships—will depend almost entirely on how much karmic baggage you carry in your energy field and its effect on your ability to share sexual energy as pleasure, love, intimacy, and joy.

Karmic Baggage
and Non-Physical Beings

When you center yourself in your energy field and turn your organs of perception inward, the karmic baggage you carry will look like individual bricks piled one on top of another (see Figure 4). The bricks you've carried in your field the longest will be at the bottom of the pile. Each brick is exclusively composed of energy with individual qualities. The individual qualities I'm referring to include mass, density, polarity, surface texture, personal will, desire, (or fear), as well as awareness and a limited degree of emotion, feeling, and sensation.

The longer a brick (individual field of karmic baggage) has been in your energy field, the more dense it will become because of the pressure exerted on it by bricks piled on top of it. Because the oldest fields of karmic baggage are under so much pressure, their individual qualities will rarely emerge into your conscious awareness, which means that you may be unaware of some of the desires (fears), attitudes, emotions, feelings, and sensations that motivate you most deeply and that in many cases have had the most disruptive effect on your relationships. Such bricks are like the foundation stones of a building, which are often out of sight.

It's worth noting that to a human being without sufficient understanding, karmic baggage can appear to have both positive and negative effects. However, even karmic baggage that appears to be positive can nevertheless attach you to inauthentic desires, restrict the flow of sexual energy through your energy field, and disrupt your relationships.

Non-physical beings make the situation even more complicated. They can be found in all fields of karmic baggage. Like physical beings, non-physical beings are composed of the same common elements necessary for life: consciousness, energy, and matter (in the case of non-physical beings, subtle matter), as well as awareness and a limited degree of feeling and sensation. All they lack is a physical-material body. But it's never been a prerequisite for life to be clothed in a physical-material body.

The fact is that non-physical beings emerged into the phenomenal universe eons ago by way of the tattvas, along with you and me. And today they can be found in every dimension in numbers far exceeding the number of living creatures that exist in the physical-material universe.

There exists a great diversity of life forms on the non-physical dimensions. However, the one thing they have in common is their propensity to disrupt the functions of your energy system once they've been introduced into your energy field and you've become attached to them.

The primary activities that can introduce non-physical beings into your energy field are channeling and/or the invocation of non-physical beings such as gods and angels, elementals, spirit guides, deceased human beings, ascended masters, nature spirits, and/or power animals (for guidance, comfort, and/or sustenance).

Many of the activities that introduce non-physical beings into the human energy field have been with humanity for millennia and have been embraced by the world's religions, by alternative healers, and by New Age practitioners. Many of them, in fact, have a long tradition and were even embraced by our ancestors, who adhered to the ancient and nearly universal practice of shamanism.

Shamans and priests in traditional cultures were aware that the universe was animate and were trained to be more discerning than people living in advanced technological cultures. They called non-physical beings spirits, elementals, nymphs, sprites, fairies, entities, spirit guides, angels, demons—classifying them based on their disposition towards human beings.

For shamans and priests in traditional cultures there was a spirit in the mountain, a spirit in the stream, a spirit of love, a spirit of hate, as well as spirits that could badger human beings, create cravings, cause depression and an assortment of other conditions that could disrupt the quality of a person's sexual life and relationships. In one way or another, traditional people incorporated these spirits into their religion and strove to accommodate them through sacrifice, ritual, and petitionary prayer.

In Christian cultures, particularly in the patriarchal cultures of Europe, non-physical beings were viewed quite differently. In the manner of traditional tribal peoples, early Christians recognized that non-physical beings could penetrate the human energy field and interfere with a human's well-being and relationships. In response, Christians held firmly to a dualistic cosmology, with two hierarchies of non-physical beings that competed with one another for dominance. The first hierarchy was under a personal god called Jehovah. The second was under the control of an oppressive male deity, called Satan, who opposed Jehovah and strove to dominate mankind. Though they acknowledged that non-physical beings could trap a human being in the phenomenal universe, Christian clerics failed to realize that good and evil were two sides of the same coin and that non-physical beings in both hierarchies could prevent a human being from sharing pleasure, love, intimacy, and joy through transcendent sex and relationships.

In contrast, yoga and tantra recognized that non-physical beings were an essential part of the ecology of the non-physical universe and that they were subject to the ancient Hermetic Principle of Correspondence, which states "As above, so below; as below, so above." These ancient traditions acknowledge that non-physical beings have the will to fulfill their individual needs—even at your expense—and that these non-physical beings also have an individual mind and ego as well as a personal agenda that is self-serving and orientated towards self-preservation.

With this in mind it comes as no surprise that neither yoga nor tantra accepted the widely held belief (common in both East and West) that some non-physical beings have no self-will, ego, and/or personal agenda.

Whether you choose to demonize non-physical beings or sanctify them, the fact remains that at the core of every field of karmic baggage in your energy field is one or more of these non-physical beings. And although the cognitive ability of non-physical beings, as well as their ability to act and express themselves, is severely limited in comparison to the wide spectrum enjoyed by human beings, they do have individual will, a form of finite consciousness, rudimentary emotions and feelings, and the ability to express these qualities through time-space.

It comes as no surprise then, that when a human being becomes attached to karmic baggage, he or she also becomes attached to the individual qualities of non-physical beings. This means that non-physical beings are at the root of many of mankind's most entrenched problems. The long list of crimes charged against non-physical beings includes blocking people from experiencing universal qualities such as pleasure, love, intimacy, and joy, and separating them from Universal Consciousness.

Although non-physical beings can't separate anyone from Universal Consciousness, they can prevent people from remaining present.

Non-physical beings can restrict the flow of sexual energy through the human energy field and they can prevent people from participating in transcendent sex and relationships. For instance, both Jason (the fellow who was dominated by his female boss) and Mona (who tried to manipulate Allen into being her boyfriend) may have been the victims of a domineering non-physical being similar to Yahweh, whose personality has been described as that of a stereotypical Jewish mother.

Recognizing Non-Physical Beings

There are many ways non-physical beings can limit your ability to participate in transcendent sex and relationships. Non-physical beings can rob you of personal power by blocking the flow of sexual energy through your energy field, and they can limit your ability to use intuition and empathy as relationship tools. They can prevent you from experiencing orgasmic bliss. They can trap you in the past and future. And non-physical beings can prevent you from loving yourself and sharing pleasure, love, intimacy, and joy with your partner.

Non-physical beings can also project a flood of inauthentic desires, which can overwhelm the four authentic desires (Artha, Kama, Dharma, and Moksha). If all that were not enough, non-physical beings in the field of the soul can exhibit a wide range of feelings and emotions that routinely counterfeit authentic human sentiments. In the field of intellect, they can exhibit awareness, ideation, belief, judgment, and prejudice, and they have a predisposition to try to understand what can be known only through intuition, insight, and direct experience. In the field of spirit, non-physical beings can exhibit glowing or burning sensations, an intense sense of mission, as well as a litany of spurious revelations, which can make you feel special or unique in some way.

Leave Your Karmic Baggage at the Door

Although it would be great to magically wipe the karmic slate clean so that you could experience all the benefits of transcendence right now, there is no magic pill that can do that. Fortunately, however, there are two things you can do to minimize the effect of karmic baggage and non-physical beings on your relationships. The first is to recognize that attitudes and beliefs that emerge from your karmic baggage (and from non-physical beings) cannot be objectively true and can't resonate with you. The second is to substitute what resonates and is objectively true for what doesn't resonate and isn't objectively true.

Two thousand years ago Jesus declared, "You shall know the truth and the truth shall set you free." This verse—based on the observation that what is objectively true will create a sympathetic resonance in your energy field—offers you a tool, resonating, to overcome the karmic baggage and the non-physical beings you're attached to and that are hostile to transcendent sex and relationships.

But before you can use resonating as a relationship tool it's important to note that when something is objectively true and you affirm it, the resonance it creates will enhance the flow of sexual energy through your energy field. That, in turn, will make it easier for you to remain present and engage in transcendent sex and relationships.

On the other hand, when something isn't objectively true, it won't resonate, even if you believe it or it has been part of your belief system for years. In fact, when you affirm something that isn't objectively true, the flow of sexual energy through your energy field will be blocked slightly, making it difficult for you to remain present and to engage in transcendent sex and relationships.

Because it's necessary to embrace the objective truth and to express it freely in order to transcend the limits of a traditional relationship, substituting what is objectively true is essential.

To substitute the objective truth for the beliefs that aren't objectively true, you must first determine if what you believe resonates or not. To do that, you will state something you believe (but which might have emerged from karmic baggage) in a normal voice and observe its affect on your energy field.

As an example, you could assert, *"It's appropriate to deceive my partner in order to get what I want."* If this statement is objectively true, it will resonate, your sexual energy will flow more freely and you will find it easier to stay present in your authentic mind. If your belief emerges from karmic baggage (and the non-physical beings within it) and is not objectively true, the flow of sexual energy through your energy field will be blocked slightly and you will find it difficult to stay present in your authentic mind.

If you're centered in your authentic mind when you practice resonating, you can check the effect that your assertion makes on the flow of sexual energy through your energy field and your ability to remain present.

Those of you who use resonance as a relationship tool will find that it can clear up confusion and ambivalence. It can help you to trust your personal insights and intuition, and resonance can help you to gain control of your energy field so that the decisions you make and the activities you engage in enhance your ability to participate in a transforming relationship.

Exercise: Determining What Resonates

To use resonance as a relationship tool, begin by sitting in a comfortable position with your back straight. When you're ready, close your eyes and count backward from five to one, then from ten to one. Use the Standard Method Exercise to relax the muscles of your physical-material body. Then begin breathing deeply through your nose. When you're ready, assert, *"It's my intent to become present in my authentic mind."* Then assert, *"It's my intent to turn my organs of perception inward."* Take five minutes to enjoy the shift. Then assert something you believe is objectively true three times, in a normal voice. For example, Mona could have asserted, *"My need to control has been disrupting my relationship with my partner."*

After making the assertion three times, observe the condition of your energy field. Did more sexual energy radiate through it after you made the assertion, or not? And did you stay present in your authentic mind without effort, or not? If more sexual energy radiated through your energy field and you stayed present without effort, the statement resonated. Then you know that your need to control has been disrupting your relationship. If Mona had used this technique, she might have been able to transcend her karmic baggage and to enjoy real intimacy with Allen.

In order to check your findings, you can assert, *"My need to control has not been disrupting my relationship with my partner."* Make the opposite assertion three times, in a normal voice. After making the opposite assertion, compare the results. Did sexual energy flow more freely, and did you become present more easily when you made the first or the second assertion?

If you're not sure of the results, then practice resonating at another time, when you're more relaxed and more able to be objective. Most problems with resonating can be corrected by practice and by making sure you're present in your authentic mind before you make an assertion.

By knowing what is objectively true and accepting it—rather than blindly accepting what you believe or what emerges from your karmic baggage (and non-physical beings)—you will live with more integrity. By living with more integrity you will weaken your attachment to karmic baggage and non-physical beings. And that will enhance the flow of sexual energy through your energy field.

By using resonance and substituting the objective truth for ideas and beliefs that aren't objectively true and that emerge from your belief system and the karmic baggage that supports it, you will find it easier to trust yourself and to accept what you learn from personal insight and intuition. In addition, you will find it easier to overcome the personality issues that emerge from your karmic baggage and disrupt your ability to participate in all aspects of a transcendent relationship.

You can practice resonating by first checking the resonance of these common beliefs and their opposites.

1. I'm (not) prevented from sharing love because my lover is blocked.

2. My sexual energy is (not) blocked because my lover is selfish.

3. My boyfriend/girlfriend is (not) looking for a mother/father, not a lover.

4. Men/Women (don't) avoid me because I'm a powerful, mature woman/man.

5. My girlfriend/boyfriend is (isn't) more interested in control than love.

Activating and Centering Yourself in Your Heart Chakra

Another way to minimize the effect of karmic baggage (and non-physical beings) on your relationships is to activate and center yourself in your heart chakra. Your heart chakra emerges from a point at your spine that corresponds to the eighth cervical vertebra. From its point of origin the heart chakra extends forward to a point in your physical-material body that corresponds to the center of your breastbone.

As you know, sexual energy radiates through your chakras. That energy is continuously being transmuted into the precise frequencies needed to maintain the health of your energy system and to support the communities of energy bodies and energetic vehicles in it. What you may not know is that the chakras link your energy field to Universal Consciousness. By maintaining that link, your chakras allow consciousness to be transmuted into sexual energy and that sexual energy to radiate through your energy field.

By activating and centering yourself in your heart chakra, you can strengthen your link to Universal Consciousness and enhance the flow of sexual energy into your energy field. That will have a profound effect on your ability to remain authentic and minimize the effects of karmic baggage and non-physical beings.

In addition to minimizing the effect of karmic baggage and non-physical beings, your heart chakra has individual functions that affect your relationships. In the world of spirit, the heart chakra upholds your right to engage in spiritual practice and share your spiritual experiences when appropriate, even when there is internal (from the individual mind and ego) and external (from people, institutions, and culture) opposition.

In the world of intellect, the heart chakra upholds your right to trust your personal intuition and insight and use your intellect freely, no matter how these functions choose to manifest: verbally, through metaphor, the written word, and/or through the arts.

In the world of soul, the heart chakra upholds your right to feel, express, and resolve your authentic emotions and/or desires, and to curtail their outward expression when circumstances demand it. The fact is you have the inalienable right to manifest your authentic desires and to express and resolve all your authentic emotions (including anger, fear, pain, and joy). And no outside authority—including your partner—has the right to make you feel ashamed or guilty for their spontaneous and/or appropriate expression.

Before you activate and center yourself in your heart chakra, it's worth noting that in ancient yogic and tantric texts the chakras have been described as miniature suns—each spinning and radiating a different quality of color in the visual spectrum of light. As each chakra rotates, the disk portion glows with a faint light. The intensity of the light will increase when the chakra becomes more active and more sexual energy radiates through it (see Figure 3).

Exercise: Activating and Centering in the Heart Chakra

In the following exercise you will activate and center yourself in your heart chakra. To begin, find a comfortable position, with your back straight. Then close your eyes and start breathing through your nose, without separation between inhalation and exhalation. Continue for two or three minutes, then count backward from five to one, then from ten to one. Use the Standard Method Exercise to relax the muscles of your physical-material body. Once your muscles are relaxed, assert, *"It's my intent to activate my heart chakra."* Take one or two minutes to enjoy the enhanced activity of your heart chakra. Then assert, *"It's my intent to center myself in my heart chakra."* As soon as you've centered yourself in your heart chakra, you'll feel a glowing sensation emerging from it. Normally this will be accompanied by a feeling of lightness, which will heighten your sense of well-being.

You can enhance these effects first by asserting, *"It's my intent to turn my organs of perception inward on the level of my heart chakra."* Then assert,

"It's my intent to stay centered in my heart chakra while I experience the universe through dual awareness." By turning your organs of perception inward on the level of your heart chakra and then letting your awareness expand into the external environment (while you remain centered), you will experience the world from your heart chakra with dual awareness. The enhanced flow of sexual energy radiating through your heart chakra will make you less reactive to karmic baggage and external projections.

While you remain centered in your heart chakra, resist the tendency to drift or to follow the movement of energetic waves and/or fields. Only energy with individual qualities will move in waves and/or fields. And if you allow yourself to become distracted by their movement, your center of awareness will shift from your heart chakra back into your individual mind and ego.

Take fifteen minutes more to enjoy this exercise. After fifteen minutes, count from one to five. When you reach the number five, open your eyes. You will feel wide awake, perfectly relaxed, and better than you did before.

The amount of sexual energy you have available to share with another person is not entirely dependent on your ability to love yourself, to overcome karma, or to activate your chakras. It is also dependent on how much sexual energy your energy system is capable of handling at any given time. To strengthen your energy system and enhance its ability to handle more sexual energy I've included a five-day regimen. Practice the exercises each day, for five days, to get the most benefit. Then repeat the regimen if necessary.

Exercise: Five-Day Regimen to Enhance Sexual Energy

Day 1

Yogic breath: When your breath is shallow and incomplete, or when you unconsciously hold your breath between inhalation and exhalation, you will inhibit the amount of Prana—a form of sexual energy that enters your energy field with each inhalation. In yoga, there is a technique that will help you to redress this situation. The technique is called the Yogic Breath. By breathing Yogically, you will restore your breathing to its natural state and enhance the level of Prana (sexual energy) that radiates through your energy field.

The Yogic Breath is a synthesis of the three basic breaths, which is why it's sometimes called the complete breath. The three breaths are the abdominal breath, the mid-breath, and the upper-breath. In the abdominal breath, your abdomen is expanded and stretched downward as air and sexual energy fill it. In the mid-breath, air and sexual energy—after filling your abdomen—expand upward to fill your chest cavity. In the process, your rib cage expands and shoulders lift. In the upper-breath, air and sexual energy will continue to rise, filling your nasal passages and your head (see Figure 6).

In complete Yogic Breathing, you will enhance the flow of sexual energy through your energy field and enhance your ability to handle it by drawing sexual energy down through your abdomen to your feet and up to the top of your head.

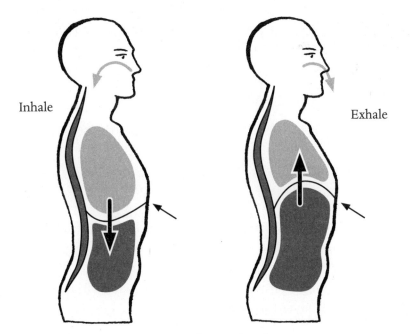

Inhale

Exhale

Figure 6: *The Yogic Breath*

To begin the Yogic Breath, find a comfortable position with your back straight. Once you're comfortable, place your right hand on your abdomen, just below your solar plexus. This will help you to feel the ebb and flow of your breath and will make it more fluid and rhythmic. Then close your eyes and inhale—first filling your lower lungs with air. With your hand on your abdomen, you will feel the muscles of your diaphragm stretch as your stomach becomes slightly extended. Continue to inhale and feel how air fills the middle and upper part of your lungs. Your shoulders will lift and the muscles of your rib cage will stretch as your lungs expand.

During the mid-breath, some people feel discomfort in their upper back, between the shoulder blades. The discomfort is caused by muscles in the back that, over time, have contracted and become stiff. This is largely due to improper breathing. Don't let a little discomfort discourage you. Continue, but gently. In a few days the discomfort will disappear and your muscles will return to their normal state of elasticity.

After air and sexual energy have filled your lungs, let them continue to rise, filling your nasal passages and head. Continue breathing without separation between inhalation and exhalation. When you exhale, reverse the process, by letting your nasal passages empty first—then your upper, your mid, and finally your lower lungs. Your shoulders will naturally drop and your diaphragm will return to its normal position. Continue the exercise for about ten minutes. After ten minutes open your eyes and once again breathe normally.

Once you begin breathing Yogically, you should feel immediate results. Most people report that they experience more sexual energy, greater inner strength, and more vitality.

Day 2

The Empowerment Mudra: The Empowerment Mudra is designed to balance the enhanced flow of sexual energy that you experience during and after Yogic breathing. It does that by distributing sexual energy uniformly through the organs of your energy system (chakras, auras, meridians, and minor energy centers).

To perform the mudra, find a comfortable position, with your back straight. Then place the tip of your tongue directly behind the point where your teeth meet your upper gum. Put the outside tips of your thumbs together to form a triangle. Then put the tips of your index fingers together to form the second triangle. Once the tips of your index fingers are touching, put the outside of your middle and ring fingers together, from the first to the second joint. Then put the inside tips of your pinkies together to form a third triangle.

When you look down at your hands, you will see three triangles. The first triangle has been created by your thumbs. The second triangle has been created by your index fingers, and the third triangle has been created by your pinkies (see Figure 7). Hold the mudra for ten minutes with your eyes closed. Then release the mudra, count from one to five, open your eyes, and bring yourself out of the exercise.

Day 3

On Day 3 you will begin with the Yogic Breath. Once you feel the rhythm of your breath, move your hand from your abdomen and perform the Empowerment Mudra. Continue practicing the Yogic Breath and the Empowerment Mudra together for fifteen minutes with your eyes closed. After fifteen minutes count from one to five, open your eyes, and bring yourself out of the exercise.

Day 4

Begin by counting from five to one, then from ten to one. Then use the Standard Method Exercise to relax your physical-material body. Once your physical-material body is relaxed, assert, *"It's my intent to become present in my authentic mind."* As soon as you're present, begin to breathe yogically. Remain present and continue to breathe yogically for two or three minutes. Then perform the Empowerment Mudra. Continue practicing all three techniques for another ten minutes with your eyes closed. After ten minutes, release the mudra and count from one to five. When you reach the number five, open your eyes. You will feel wide awake, perfectly relaxed, and better than you did before.

Figure 7: *The Empowerment Mudra*

Day 5

Repeat Day 4, but after you've completed the Empowerment Mudra, close your eyes and assert, *"On each inhalation it's my intent to fill my energy field with sexual energy."* This will enhance the flow of sexual energy through your energetic vehicles in Paramatman and your energy bodies, sheaths, and auras in Jivamatman. After fifteen minutes, release the mudra and count from one to five. When you reach the number five, open your eyes. You will feel wide awake, perfectly relaxed, and better than you did before.

By practicing the five-day regimen you will enhance the amount of sexual energy your energy field can handle. That will make it easier for you to overcome the effects of karmic baggage and the demands of the non-physical beings contained within it. And the five-day regimen will also bring you another step closer to experiencing transcendent sex and relationships.

Naomi's Experience

Naomi—a married woman, thirty-seven years of age—experienced a dramatic shift the first time she practiced the five-day regimen and centered herself in her heart chakra. She'd been married to an engineer named Ned for nine years. And until Naomi's shift, Ned had shown no interest in participating in the work of transcendence. She recounted her experience during an individual session.

Naomi sighed, then took a deep breath and declared:

> *"OK, last night I completed the five-day regimen. Then I activated and centered myself in my heart chakra, but I think I may have enhanced the flow of sexual energy too much."*
>
> *"How can you enhance the flow of sexual energy too much?"* I asked in surprise.

Naomi began to laugh self-consciously. Then she explained how her libido had been liberated. After she finished, Naomi waited for my response.

"If your libido became active," I replied, *"then you must have experienced a burst of sexual energy after you activated and centered yourself in your heart chakra. It must have come as quite a shock to Ned."*

"To us both," Naomi added with a sniffle.

"And, Ned, how did he respond?"

"Remarkably well, I think. In fact, after he got over his initial shock, he was very open and receptive."

"And what about you? How did you feel when you made love?"

"I'm not sure I understand?"

"I'm asking you how you felt when you and Ned made love."

"I didn't say we made love." After receiving a knowing look from me, Naomi sighed. *"Okay. If you must know—it wasn't exactly what I expected. It began with a big bang. But then some things happened which surprised me."* Naomi hesitated before she added, *"The truth is—I felt very excited and at the same time a deep inner peace. Usually I have this armor around me, which blocks me from feeling very much."*

"That's karmic baggage."

"You're probably right. But this time it just melted away. And after it did I felt very feminine."

"And your body?"

"That's the strange part. After the initial explosion it felt very light. I didn't seem to have any weight."

"And how did you feel about Ned while all that was going on?"

"It wasn't really about him. That was the interesting part."

"Did you feel like the two of you merged and became one?"

"There didn't seem to be any separation if that's what you mean."

"Good. From what you've said, it sounds as if you made a significant shift when you performed the five-day regimen and centered yourself in your heart chakra. It's that shift that allowed you to become more intimate on more dimensions."

"But it felt so natural," Naomi declared.

"Of course it felt natural. It's what your physical-material body and energy field were designed to do perfectly. Like a toaster that's designed

to toast bread, everything in your physical-material body and energy field was designed to enhance your experience of pleasure, love, intimacy, and joy with Universal Consciousness, your self, and your partner."

Chapter 5

Fantasy and Karmic Baggage

It is difficult for us to realize ultimate reality within our daily lives. After all, we all exist on different levels simultaneously. In fact, we are something like Russian nesting dolls. Perhaps you have seen a set: these are painted, wooden, hollow dolls of decreasing size, one placed within another. If you screw off the head of one of the dolls, you find another one nested neatly inside. In the levels of reality that make up our existence, the innermost levels (or "dolls") are more resonant with ultimate reality, whereas the outermost dolls are just the opposite. As an example, imagine a beautiful young Muslim woman named Medhi, in a village in Afghanistan. Medhi is wearing a burkha that covers her entire body from head to foot, hooded and veiled so that no polluting male gaze can penetrate her coverings, yet she may secretively be listening—through earphones—to a rock concert to save the Brazilian rainforest, a place the conservative elders who keep a close watch over her may never have heard of. She might even have a belly full of Coca-Cola and be having a sexual fantasy of making love with Michael Jackson. Yet, this sexual fantasy and her entire love-the-West persona is only a reaction to the restrictive belief system imposed on her by her elders and her religion. The circumstances that give rise to this persona are just the results of Medhi's karma, forming part of her karmic baggage. If you were Medhi, how could you free yourself of this karmic baggage in order to experience the more authentic levels of existence (the "dolls") within yourself?

Now that you've used resonance to discern what is objectively true, have enhanced the flow of sexual energy through your energy field, and activated and centered yourself in your heart chakra, you'll have developed important skills that will minimize the effect of karmic baggage on your energy field and your relationships. This is because karmic baggage is one of the outer dolls. However, there are other ways to deal with karmic baggage. You can overcome some of its most onerous effects by using personas. Personas are fields of karmic baggage that share the same, or a similar, resonance. They are the building blocks of your personality issues, and you can use them as tools for your transcendence. How to do this will be explained later in this chapter. The other way to deal with karmic baggage is to interact directly with the restrictive parts of your belief system by using positive affirmations and intentions. Positive affirmations and intentions also have a resonant frequency that is in harmony with the inner dolls of your personality.

Your Restrictive Belief System

The restrictive beliefs embraced by all cultures and transmitted through their traditions and institutions make demands on believers that inevitably restrict the flow of sexual energy through their energy systems. In the more general activities of acculturation, we see a similar process at work. Indeed, the acculturation process invariably involves and even encourages people in authority to project energy with individual qualities at people who are subordinate to them. Because of these projections and the restrictions put on them by a restrictive belief system, children will inevitably contract emotionally, intellectually, and even physically. Contraction will disrupt the flow of sexual energy through their energy field. And that will create attachments that will make them feel insecure and fearful. If Medhi, the young Afghani woman, should attend a French college and go to the beach during the holidays, she may find it difficult to don a bikini and undulate in a disco at night to the throb of a reggae beat.

You might believe that adopting a belief system, even if it's restrictive, is a necessary part of the acculturation process. However, it's important to recognize that all fields of karmic baggage that manifest their qualities through a restrictive belief system enhance self-limiting and/or destructive tendencies such as chronic insecurity, fearfulness, hyper-sensitivity, depression, indolence, and aggression. In extreme cases, a restrictive belief system can even create obsessions, which in turn can cause anti-self and anti-social behavior.

It's important to note that whenever you resist the restrictive parts of your belief system and the karmic baggage that supports them, you will be punished by having a wall of fear projected at you that will limit the flow of sexual energy through your energy field and your access to pleasure. Such fear—projected both by individual fields of karmic baggage and frustrated personas—can manifest as nervousness, anxiety, self-doubt, terror, rage, or conflicting emotions and feelings that your individual mind and ego can use to support what is called your *internal dialogue*. This internal dialogue is the relentless cascade of thoughts and feelings that emerges from your individual mind and ego when sexual energy has been blocked and you've been forced to contract. Because fields of karmic baggage and frustrated personas will use fear to bludgeon you into submission, you must first find a reliable way to overcome fear before you can overcome the most restrictive parts of your belief system (see figure 8).

Exercise: The Self-Acceptance Mudra

The Self-Acceptance Mudra will help you to accept yourself even when you've been trapped by restrictive parts of your belief system or when frustrated personas try to coerce you into abandoning your values to meet their demands. Medhi could also use this mudra to great effect. The Self-Acceptance Mudra does this by preventing karmic baggage and personas from using qualified energy to coerce you into making inappropriate choices and decisions.

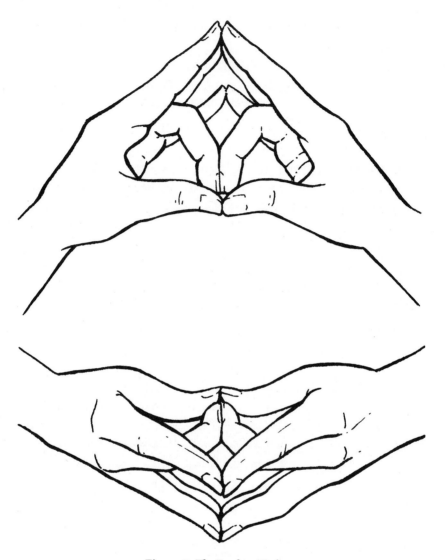

Figure 8: *The Fearless Mudra*

To perform the mudra, find a comfortable position, with your back straight. Then bring your tongue to your top palate and slide it back until the hard palette curls upward and softens. Keep the tip of your tongue in contact with your upper palette, while you place the soles of your feet together. Next, bring the mounds of Venus and the edges of the thumbs together. Then slide your right index finger over your left index finger, so that the tip of the right finger rests atop the second joint of your left finger. The middle fingers are placed together so that the tips are touching. Once they're touching, place the outsides of the ring fingers together, from the first to the second joint. Then bring the inside of the pinkies together from the tips to the first joints (see Figure 9).

Practice the mudra for ten minutes. Then release your fingers and bring your tongue and feet back into their normal position. By practicing the Self-Acceptance Mudra regularly, individual fields of karmic baggage and personas will have less power to bend you to their will and to disrupt your experience of pleasure, love, intimacy, and joy.

Fear and the Internal Dialogue

Mudras can help you to overcome the wall of fear that individual fields of karmic baggage and personas project at you. However, mudras won't help you to overcome the fundamental problems created by the process of acculturation and the influence of restrictive belief systems.

If you were programmed negatively as a child—by family, friends, and institutions that adhere to a restrictive belief system that limits your access to pleasure, love, intimacy, and joy—then you have suffered until now from its effects. And you will continue to suffer, perhaps more heavily in the future, as programming makes it increasingly difficult for you to trust yourself. Furthermore, the confusion a restrictive belief system creates will continue to take its toll on you and your relationships.

The problem you face with a restrictive belief system can be likened to the problem faced by a businessman who discovers that a trusted employee has stolen something valuable from him. No excuse after the fact will convince the businessman to trust his employee again.

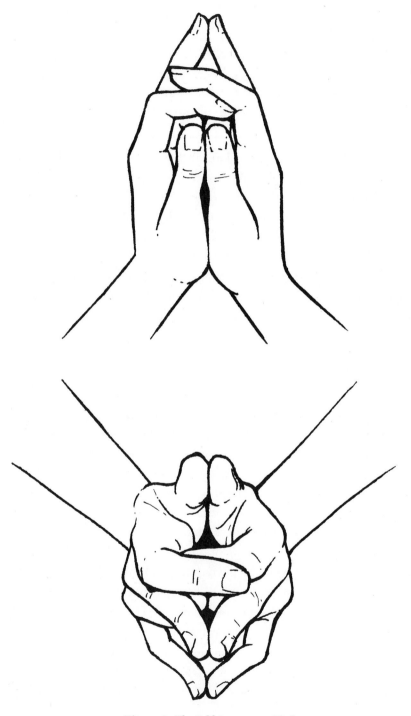

Figure 9: *The Self-Acceptance Mudra*

A restrictive belief system that affectively steals pleasure, love, intimacy, and joy from you and that destroys self-trust can be likened to an employee who has stolen something valuable from you. And like the businessman in the metaphor, you need to ask yourself whether you can trust someone who has betrayed you. The obvious answer is no.

Unfortunately, like most people, you're probably not prepared to say no to something familiar—even if it's something that has prevented you from experiencing pleasure, love, intimacy, and joy—unless you can replace it with something better.

With that in mind, I've included a simple method for you to replace restrictive parts of your belief system with something better—the objective truth.

The objective truth is something that supports pleasure, love, intimacy, and joy. It can be an affirmation that is true everywhere, at all times and in all situations. *"God is love"* is such an affirmation; so is *"This too shall change."* Besides replacing self-limiting beliefs—which emerge from individual fields of karmic baggage—affirmations that are objectively true will enhance the flow of sexual energy through your energy field and keep you present in your authentic mind.

In the following exercise you will substitute affirmations that are objectively true—called *positive affirmations*—for beliefs that aren't objectively true and that restrict the flow of sexual energy through your energy field.

I've compiled a list of positive affirmations you can substitute for restrictive beliefs whenever the karmic baggage and personas that supports them bombard you with thoughts, emotions, feelings, and/or sensations that are antagonistic to transcendent sex and relationships.

To substitute a positive affirmation for a restrictive belief, just repeat the appropriate affirmation to yourself out loud, rather than in thoughts, until it has replaced the restrictive beliefs that are disturbing you. Anyone can use these affirmations fruitfully.

1. I am an eternal being who exists from everlasting to everlasting.

2. I am a God [Goddess] with only universal qualities.

3. I have an unlimited supply of sexual energy within me.

4. I have not been given a spirit of fear, but of power, love, and a sound mind.

5. I am more than the sum of my parts. I am a whole being.

6. I am the master of my mind and my energy field.

7. Pleasure, love, intimacy, and joy are my natural state.

8. I will know the truth, and the truth will set me free.

9. My purpose is to share love through transcendent sex and relationships.

10. I am stronger than my programming; I am a transcendent being.

The Power of Positive Intention

A positive intention is another powerful tool useful in overcoming a restrictive belief system. Because a restrictive belief system can put a brake on your motivation, and a lack of motivation can disrupt your ability to participate in transcendent sex and relationships, the positive intentions that follow can be extremely useful.

A positive intention is positive because it manifests the intent of your authentic mind. Negative intentions emerge from a restrictive belief system and express the intent, attitudes, ideas, emotions, and feelings of your individual mind and ego. Examples of negative intentions are *"I need to control my partner to feel secure"* or *"I'll never be accepted for being myself."*

You can substitute any of the positive intentions that follow for negative intentions, whenever you've been bombarded with intentions antagonistic to transcendent sex and relationships. A list of commonly used positive intentions follows. Repeat the appropriate intention to yourself out loud rather than in thoughts until it has replaced the negative intentions disturbing you.

1. It's my intent to transcend the restrictive elements of my belief system.

2. It's my intent to take full responsibility for my life and well-being.

3. It's my intent to experience my bliss as a God [Goddess].

4. It's my intent to remain present in my authentic mind.

5. It's my intent to activate and center myself in my heart chakra.

6. It's my intent to love what gives me pleasure.

7. It's my intent to experience more pleasure, love, intimacy, and joy.

8. It's my intent to share transcendent sex and a relationship with my partner.

9. It's my intent to know my purpose and to do what is appropriate.

10. It's my intent to love who I am and not what other people want me to be.

Personas

To use personas as tools for transcendence, you must first recognize that personas contain non-physical beings that seek pleasure. And the non-physical beings contained within personas have a personal agenda or path to pleasure, which can emerge into your conscious awareness as a fantasy.

Knowing that there is a cause-and-effect relationship between personas and fantasies, particularly sexual fantasies, will allow you to trace fantasies back to the personas that created them, and from there to the karmic baggage that supports the persona. Once you've traced a fantasy back to the karmic baggage at its root, you will be able to use the karmic baggage as a doorway into your authentic mind. That will allow you to release the karmic baggage (and persona) so that it won't be able to block your access to pleasure, love, intimacy, and joy any longer.

To trace a fantasy back to the karmic baggage at its root and then release it, you will use the Seven-Step Method, which is described later in this chapter. However, before you can use the Seven-Step Method to release karmic baggage and personas, you will need to know more about personas and their effects on your energy field and intimate relationships.

Personas emerge from your individual mind and ego and are composed of two or more fields of karmic baggage having the same or similar resonance. Because all personas are composed of two or more fields of karmic baggage, they all contain non-physical beings.

Personas can be active or inactive. Inactive personas remain buried in your unconscious. However, inactive personas can't stay inactive indefinitely. Under the right conditions, they will become active and then burst into your conscious awareness.

As soon as a persona has become active, it will usurp the functions of your authentic mind, which includes your organs of perception, organs of expression, memory, and deductive and inductive reasoning. Once the functions of your authentic mind are under the control of an active persona, the persona will emerge as a personality issue and will badger you with inauthentic desires, thoughts, feelings, and sensations until you submit to it and fulfill its desire for pleasure. If you refuse to submit to the thoughts, feelings, and sensations the persona has used to badger you, they will intensify until they become a virtual flood of mind stuff called the internal dialogue. The internal dialogue can be compared to a child's tantrum: it's a device a persona will use as a last resort to force you to give the persona the pleasure it demands.

Personas are not part of your authentic mind. However, they do provide a structure for the karmic baggage in your energy field. Individual fields of karmic baggage with the same or similar resonance collectively express their will, inauthentic desire, and the thoughts, feelings, and sensations that emerge from them through personas.

It's worth mentioning that members of the same family tend to have personas that are quite similar or even identical because parents and relatives attached to personas tend to project energy with individual qualities towards people they want to influence, particularly their children.

Dominant and Subordinate Personas

The last thing you need to know about personas is that you have a dominant persona and scores of subordinate personas. Your dominant persona is the oldest and most compelling persona in your energy field. And it contains the largest number of non-physical beings and fields of energy with individual qualities. It's also the persona you identify with most often because it's been with you the longest. In fact, your dominant persona commands your personality and has probably done so all your life.

Subordinate personas have not been with you as long. Because they've been in your energy field for less time, they contain fewer non-physical beings. And the non-physical beings in subordinate personas normally have less power to attach you to inauthentic desires, fears, attitudes, beliefs, emotions, feelings, and sensations that support them.

Some subordinate personas support your dominant persona energetically. Others oppose it. When subordinate personas oppose your dominant persona, they can undermine your well-being and the stability of your relationships. In some cases, especially those that are life-threatening, and/or when you temporarily release your inhibitions—for instance, under the influence of alcohol or stimulants—subordinate personas, including those that lie dormant in your unconscious, can make an unexpected and dramatic appearance.

When the qualities of a persona are particularly distasteful—for example, because the desires, attitudes, thoughts, and emotions associated with it are incompatible with your present belief system—you may push the persona out of your conscious awareness through denial. However, a persona denied can never be completely hidden. Sooner or later it will re-emerge into your conscious awareness and become active again. In fact, the re-emergence of a persona that has been hidden through denial, with all its obsessive and compulsive characteristics, explains many forms of anti-self and anti-social behavior that burst forth suddenly and without any apparent cause. This re-emergence also explains why one person in a relationship may experience an abrupt change in his or her attitude, feelings, and commitment towards his or her partner.

Exercise: Experiencing Your Dominant Persona

To learn more about personas, you must be able to experience them directly. And to experience a persona directly you must experience its qualities: size, shape, density, and surface texture as well as inauthentic desires, fears, attitudes, emotions, feelings, and sensations that emerge from the persona.

The first persona you will experience directly is your dominant persona. When you experience your dominant persona directly for the first time, it will appear like a large field of energy surrounded by a thin skin or surface boundary. Within this surface boundary will be energy fields with individual qualities that look like bricks haphazardly piled one on top of another. Each brick represents a field of karmic baggage. Ordinarily, the stacks of karmic baggage in your dominant persona will be located in your auric field. However, it's not unusual for elements of your dominant persona to extend into the space occupied by your energy bodies and sheaths.

When you're ready to have a direct experience of your dominant persona, find a comfortable position with your back straight. Then close your eyes and breathe Yogically. After two or three minutes, count backward from five to one, and then from ten to one. To relax the muscles of your physical-material body, you will use the Standard Method Exercise. After completing the Standard Method Exercise of alternatively tensing and releasing your muscles, assert, *"It's my intent to activate and center myself in my heart chakra."* Take a few moments to enjoy the shift. Then assert, *"It's my intent to become present in my authentic mind."* Once you've become present, assert, *"It's my intent to experience my dominant persona."* Take two or three minutes to experience it. Then assert, *"It's my intent to turn my organs of perception inward on the levels of my dominant persona."* Take two or three minutes to experience the individual qualities emerging from your dominant persona.

Once you've had a direct experience of your dominant persona, you can go one step further by centering yourself in it while you experience dual awareness. It's important to note that by remaining centered in your authentic mind while you experience dual awareness you will stay detached from the qualities that emerge from your dominant persona.

To continue, assert, *"It's my intent to center myself in my dominant persona while maintaining dual awareness."* By centering yourself in your dominant persona, you will experience its individual qualities as well as what gives it pleasure and how it affects your relationships. Stay centered in your dominant persona for ten more minutes, while you experience dual awareness. Then assert, *"It's my intent to return to normal consciousness."* After you've returned to normal consciousness, count from one to five and open your eyes. You will feel wide awake, perfectly relaxed, and better than you did before.

Exercise: Experiencing a Subordinate Persona

Now that you've had a direct experience of your dominant persona, you're ready to have a direct experience of a subordinate persona. Like your dominant persona, subordinate personas can disrupt your ability to experience pleasure, love, intimacy, and joy, especially when they bombard you with their desires, attitudes, thoughts, and emotions.

To have a direct experience of a subordinate persona, you will use your intent to isolate it from the other subordinate personas in your energy field. In this exercise, the subordinate persona you will isolate will be the persona whose individual qualities most recently emerged into your conscious awareness. To begin the exercise, find a comfortable position, with your back straight. Then close your eyes and breathe yogically. After two or three minutes, count backward from five to one, and then from ten to one. To relax the muscles of your physical-material body, you will use the Standard Method Exercise. After you've completed the Standard Method Exercise of alternatively tensing and releasing your muscles, assert, *"It's my intent to activate and center myself in my heart chakra."*

Take a few moments to enjoy the shift. Then assert, *"It's my intent to become present in my authentic mind."* Once you've become present, assert, *"It's my intent to have a direct experience of the subordinate persona that emerged into my conscious awareness most recently."* Then assert, *"It's my*

*intent to turn my organs of perception inward on the levels of the persona that
I've isolated."*

Continue to experience the persona for ten minutes. Then assert,
"It's my intent to return to normal consciousness." When you've returned to
normal consciousness, count from one to five and open your eyes. You
will feel wide awake, perfectly relaxed, and better than you did before.

Now that you've experienced your dominant persona and a subordinate persona, you can choose a fantasy that has blocked your access
to your authentic mind and let it lead you to a subordinate persona. For
example, you could choose a fantasy where you participate in sexual
activities that you would normally find distasteful or you could choose
a fantasy that has you violently overcome an enemy or competitor.

It's worth noting before you proceed that fantasies always come
from subordinate personas because, unless you are in a state of transcendence, your day-to-day activities are regulated by your dominant
persona.

When you've chosen a fantasy, you will use the Seven-Step Process
to lead you to your authentic mind, and in the process you will release
the persona that blocked your access to pleasure, love, intimacy, and joy
and was responsible for the fantasy. Once you've released the persona,
you will activate the chakra that nourishes your energy bodies, sheaths,
and auras on the dimension where you located the persona. Then you
will fill the space vacated by the persona with sexual energy.

It's important to note that during the Seven-Step Process the persona you've chosen to release will grow larger and appear to extend it's
influence over your energy field. Although this can be a little unnerv-
ing, the good news is that sexual energy will expand along with it, and
sexual energy is infinitely stronger than energy with individual qualities. So, if you stay centered in your authentic mind, your sexual energy
will insulate you from the effects of the persona.

As your sexual energy and the persona expand, the limited space in
your energy field will force them to interact. And it's precisely this interaction that makes it possible for you to release the persona.

It's worth noting that individual fields of karmic baggage within a
persona are composed of an inner cavity filled with qualified energy.

Surrounding the inner cavity is a porous membrane. As the persona expands, the qualified energy in it will become less dense, and the pores in its surface boundary, which resemble the pores in the surface of your auras, will grow larger. When the pores become large enough, sexual energy, which has continued to expand along with the persona, will pour through its surface membrane. Once sexual energy penetrates the persona, the qualified energy and the non-physical beings in the persona will be released permanently from your energy field because sexual energy and energy with individual qualities cannot occupy the same space at the same time. And, with the active elements of the persona released, you will find yourself centered in your authentic mind, on the dimension where the persona was located.

Exercise: Releasing Personas

To release a persona by using the Seven-Step Process, it's important to follow all the steps in the order presented below in summary form, before going into more detail:

Step one is Awareness: In step one, you will pick a fantasy and isolate the subordinate persona that supports it from any other personas that surround it.

Step two is Acceptance: In step two, you will suspend judgment and accept the qualities that emerge from the persona.

Step three is Enjoyment: In step three, you will go beyond acceptance and enjoy the qualities emerging from the persona.

Step four is Identification: In step four, you will suspend your identification with all your other personas—including your dominant persona—and actively embrace the qualities of the persona you have in mind.

Step five is Participation: In step five, you will participate with the persona by letting the qualities of the persona radiate through your energy field, no matter how negative and/or unpleasant they may be.

Step six is Becoming: In step six, you will abandon the restrictive part of your belief system, which normally inhibits you from engaging in the activities the persona finds pleasurable.

Step seven is Permission: In step seven, you will give yourself permission to perform the activities that will give the persona pleasure and are a function of the persona's intent, desire, and/or will.

Now that you have been introduced to the Seven-Step Process, I will go into each level in greater detail:

Awareness

The easiest way to become aware of a persona you want to release is to start with a fantasy and then trace it back to the persona that has exactly these qualities. For example, if you have an escape fantasy, you can start with the fantasy and then use your intent to trace the fantasy back to the persona and the attitudes, emotions, feelings, and sensations that support it. If you do that, the persona will emerge from the background field of personas and karmic baggage. The more specific you make your intent, the better it will be.

If the fantasy leads you to a feeling of heaviness in your abdomen, you could assert, *"It's my intent to become aware of the heaviness in my abdomen and the persona that has caused it."*

After you've located the appropriate persona with your intent, the persona will begin to expand, and its energy will become less dense and easier to accept. As it expands, you will sense, or even see, which activities give the persona pleasure.

Once you become aware of a persona, it's important to remain focused on it to the exclusion of everything else. Only then can you proceed to the next step in the Seven-Step Process—Acceptance.

Acceptance

Once you've become aware of a persona, you must accept it by accepting its qualities and what gives it pleasure. This means you must abandon any attempt to change the persona, to deny it, or to bury it in your unconscious. By accepting the persona, it will expand even further. And by accepting the persona's individual qualities, without attempting to change them, you will prepare yourself for the next step in the process—Enjoyment.

Enjoyment

To enjoy a persona, you must abandon your aversion to its qualities, at least temporarily, no matter how negative and disturbing they may be.

Like a lion in the wild that kills to eat, the persona you've chosen to release is simply acting in accord with its nature. Judging a persona for having qualities you find distasteful is absurd and only makes it more difficult for you to use it as a tool for transcendence.

Indeed, using a persona as a tool for transcendence and then releasing it is not part of a war of good against evil. It's a technique designed to restore your energy field to its natural state of well-being. Recognizing this will make it far easier for you to enjoy the persona.

By enjoying the persona and its qualities, you will allow it to expand even further. In most cases, the persona will expand downward. As the persona expands and becomes less dense, sexual energy that has expanded along with it will be reflected off its surface, making the persona glow. This in turn will make it easier for you to take the next step in the process—Identification.

Identification

By identifying with the persona, you will go beyond passive enjoyment to active participation with the persona and its qualities. By taking this important step, you will signify your faith in the Seven-Step Process and in the power of your authentic mind.

As soon as you identify with the qualities of the persona, it will expand upwards. This gives the persona room to express its will. It's essential that you stay centered in your authentic mind during this crucial step. If you do, more sexual energy will be reflected off the persona's surface, which will isolate it even further. By isolating the persona from the karmic baggage surrounding it, you facilitate participation, which is the next step in the Seven-Step Process. As soon as you've identified with the persona, you can move to the next step in the process—Participation.

Participation

In this step you will participate with the persona as it pursues its personal agenda. This will take you beyond an abstract relationship with the persona. By participating with the persona, you will make your relationship with the persona real by letting go of the concept of I-Thou, which is the basis of duality.

Indeed, it's only after you've embraced the persona and participated with its individual qualities—taking them on as if they're your own, while staying centered in your authentic mind—that the persona will expand forward far enough for you to become it, which is the next step in the process.

Becoming

By becoming the persona, at least temporarily, it will become your dominant persona long enough for you to use it as a tool for transcendence and to release it.

The persona will continue expanding forward during this part of the process. And sexual energy will continue to expand along with it, increasing the pressure on the persona's surface, so that it's pores continue to expand.

At this point in the process, sexual energy will be on the verge of pouring through the surface of the persona. And you will be ready for the final step in the Seven-Step Process—Permission.

Permission

It's not enough to become the persona. Without giving the persona permission to perform the activities it finds pleasurable, the persona will not continue to expand forward, beyond your energy field, into the external environment. And the sexual energy expanding along with it will not pour through the surface of the persona and release it. In fact, giving the persona permission to experience pleasure is the ultimate act of faith in Universal Consciousness, in sexual energy, and in the functions of your authentic mind.

In the final step of the Seven-Step Process, the persona you've chosen to release will expand forward beyond your auric boundary. Sexual energy will expand along with it. And when the pores in the persona's surface boundary become large enough, sexual energy will pour into the persona. Because it's impossible for sexual energy and qualified energy to occupy the same space at the same time, the persona and the non-physical beings within it will be released. You will shift into your authentic mind, and sexual energy will fill the space in your energy field that had been occupied by the persona.

The Seven-Step Process

When you're ready to begin the Seven-Step Process, choose a fantasy. An important reminder before you begin is that once you've traced the fantasy back to its persona, it's essential that you remain focused on the persona and not drift or become distracted. By letting your attention drift or by becoming distracted, you'll find that it is exceedingly difficult to refocus on your chosen persona and release it.

To begin the Seven-Step Process, find a comfortable position with your back straight, close your eyes, and breathe yogically. After two or three minutes, count backward from five to one, then from ten to one. To relax the muscles of your physical-material body, you will use the Standard Method Exercise. After you've completed the Standard Method Exercise of alternatively tensing and releasing your muscles, assert, *"It's my intent to activate and center myself in my heart chakra."* Then assert, *"It's my intent to become present in my authentic mind."* Take a few moments to enjoy the shift. Then assert, *"It's my intent to turn my organs of perception inward and follow the fantasy I have in mind back to its persona."*

Within a few moments you will become aware of the persona and at least some of its individual qualities. Stay focused, and when you're ready to use the persona as a tool for transcendence, assert, *"It's my intent to become aware of the persona I've chosen to release."* This will isolate the persona so that it begins to expand and manifest its qualities clearly.

To accept the persona, assert, *"It's my intent to accept the persona I have in mind."* By accepting the persona and suspending judgment, it will continue to expand. Continue by asserting, *"It's my intent to enjoy the persona I have in mind."* Enjoying the persona will allow it to expand downwards to the second chakra. Follow the persona as it expands downward. Then assert, *"It's my intent to identify with the persona I have in mind."* By identifying with the persona and taking on its qualities, the persona will expand upwards, making itself larger and less dense.

Continue by asserting, *"It's my intent to enjoy the qualities of the persona I have in mind."* By enjoying the qualities of the persona, you will become more receptive, and the persona will expand backward into the masculine part of your energy field. Next, assert, *"It's my intent to participate with the persona."* By participating with the persona as it pursues its personal agenda, you will make your relationship with the persona real. And the persona will expand forwards into the feminine part of your energy field.

Continue by asserting, *"It's my intent to become the persona I have in mind."* By becoming the persona, you will identify exclusively with it. With no separation between you and the persona, it will continue to expand forward and become less dense and more porous. In the final step of the process, assert, *"It's my intent to perform the activities of the persona I have in mind."* By giving yourself permission to perform the activities of the persona, it will expand forward beyond the surface of your auric field and sexual energy emerging from your energy field—particularly your chakras—will continue to expand along with the persona. As soon as the pores within the persona's surface become large enough, your sexual energy will pour through them and release the persona. You will become centered in your authentic mind, and the qualities of the persona will no longer interfere with your ability to experience transcendent sex and relationships.

Once the persona has been released, assert, *"It's my intent to fill the space occupied by the persona with sexual energy."* Then take five minutes to enjoy the shift. After five minutes, count from one to five. When you reach the number five, open your eyes. You will feel wide awake, perfectly relaxed, and better than you did before.

Chapter 6

Get Real—Expressing What You Really Feel

There are many benefits to relationships, particularly transcendent relationship. However, as long as you remain attached to your individual mind and ego—and either your dominant persona or a subordinate persona—you won't get what you seek most.

Now, before you scratch your head, I'm going to use a couple of metaphors to explain what I mean. The first is from ancient India, and the second is from modern physics. I'll start with the older of the two metaphors. The Chandogya Upanishad, one of India's great scriptures, tells the story of a boy being instructed by his father in the nature of ultimate reality. The father asks the boy to fetch him the seed of the great banyan tree under which they are sitting. When the boy brings the seed, the father asks him to break it open. Upon accomplishing that task, the father asks the boy what he sees. The boy responds that he sees nothing at all. Then, his father tells him that just as the great banyan tree springs up from the nothing at the center of the seed, so does the entire universe spring forth from ultimate reality. Thus the subtle, the seeming nothingness at the center of existence is the root of all the grosser levels of reality.

The metaphor from physics is similar. It's the metaphor of the big bang. Physics teaches us that everything in the physical-material universe emerged from one infinitely small point. This point took up no space and had no dimensions. From that point, which is called a *singularity*, the physical-material universe emerged in a big bang. It's from that moment onward, through the process of evolution, that the universe grew larger and became more diverse. What the physical sciences still haven't accepted is that a corresponding process took place within the human energy field. Remember you are an interdimensional being who exists simultaneously on all physical and non-physical dimensions.

The point I'm trying to make is that your energy field has gone through the same evolutionary process as the physical-material universe. So the foundation of your energy field is the same singularity. Some call it God or the Godhead; I prefer to call it Universal Consciousness. Regardless of what you call it, that singularity is what people are yearning to reunite with through transcendent sex and relationships.

You may ask yourself why anyone would want a relationship with Universal Consciousness if it doesn't have individual qualities such as a sense of humor or an attractive face and body. Why would anyone want the seeming nothing at the center of the banyan seed, rather than the leaves and the trunk? The answer to that question is simple: it's not individual qualities people are yearning for most from their relationships, it's universal qualities such as pleasure, love, intimacy, and joy and the freedom, truth, and unconditional love that's necessary to enjoy them.

Universal Consciousness is the source of all these qualities. It's something people know intuitively. Therefore, to get what you want most from relationships and give your partner what he or she most wants, you must be able to access those universal qualities through your own energy field. And you must be able to share them with your partner.

You may wonder why people would seek universal qualities from their partners when they are connected to Universal Consciousness and have access to those universal qualities themselves. If people want to experience pleasure, love, intimacy, and joy, the argument goes as follows: shouldn't they stay home and turn their organs of perception inward until they find them? The answer to this question goes to the crux of the human predicament and explains why in every generation the vast majority of people yearn to share universal qualities with a partner.

Although it may be true that Universal Consciousness is the source of the universal qualities people yearn for; it's also true that most people remain attached to their individual mind and ego. By remaining attached to their individual mind and ego as well as the personas within it, people are prevented from accessing the universal qualities that they seek from their own energy field.

Attachment to the individual mind and ego and the personas within them also perpetuate the idea that people are individuals and separated from Universal Consciousness. For most people, that's enough to prevent them from enjoying the benefits of their always-accessible union with Universal Consciousness and the universal qualities that emerge from it.

I'm not saying that attachment to the individual mind and ego or a specific persona can actually separate you from Universal Consciousness. The idea that you can separate yourself from Universal Consciousness is as absurd as the idea that someone in a dream could separate himself from the dreamer within whose consciousness he or she exists.

That's the good news. The bad news is that attachment to the individual mind and ego or to a specific persona can make it difficult if not impossible for you to experience the universal qualities you yearn for through relationships, particularly transcendent relationships.

Being a Surrogate

So we're left with this simple fact: people seek a human partner to use as a surrogate through whom they seek to experience the universal qualities they lost when they became attached to their individual mind and ego and to individual personas.

However, there's still more to the story, because even if you and your partner have access to Universal Consciousness and you can share universal qualities, you still won't be satisfied, because people in relationship yearn for something in addition to universal qualities. They also yearn to experience the divine masculine or feminine through their partners. And the divine masculine or feminine will emerge only after both partners are able to stay centered in their authentic minds and consistently share universal qualities with each other.

For most people in relationships, sharing universal qualities consistently is an evolutionary process that evolves in three stages. In stage one, partners learn to become present in their authentic minds and to turn their organs of perception inwards. By becoming present in their authentic minds, partners enhance their trust and integrity. In stage two, partners enhance the flow of sexual energy through their energy field and—depending on their gender—begin to experience themselves as god or goddess, the divine masculine or feminine. In stage three, partners share the divine masculine or feminine with each other by sharing energy with universal qualities such as pleasure, love, intimacy, and joy.

You may already have asked yourself what you have to do to become a god or goddess. The answer is—nothing! You may believe that you have to become more loving or radiant so that the universal qualities of a god or goddess can emerge through you. However, you don't. The truth is, you're perfect the way you are. In fact, you're already a god or a goddess. Everything you need, including Universal Consciousness and the sexual energy that you can share as pleasure, love, intimacy, and joy, are already within you. All you have to do is actualize what you already have by turning your organs of perception inward, becoming present, and sharing more energy with universal qualities with your partner. You already know how to turn your organs of perception inward and become present. And your energy field has been prepared to handle more energy. In addition, you can share more energy with universal qualities by learning to express and resolve authentic emotions spontaneously and then by substituting authentic emotions for inauthentic emotions whenever possible.

Authentic and Inauthentic Emotions

You and your partner have both authentic and inauthentic emotions. Authentic emotions are authentic for three reasons. They are composed of energy with universal qualities. They emerge from your energy system via your chakras when relationship has been disrupted. And they can be resolved by screaming, yelling, crying, or by just letting them rise upward to the organs of expression in your face.

Inauthentic emotions cannot be expressed and resolved via your energy system and your organs of expression. Regardless of how hard you try, a residue will remain in your energy field. That residue will keep you attached to either the karmic baggage and/or the external projections that support it.

You've already experienced the satisfaction that comes from expressing and resolving authentic emotions and the discomfort that comes from not being able to express and resolve them when they've been blocked. And you've already experienced the frustration that comes when you've become attached to inauthentic emotions such as jealousy, despair, and rage, which can't be expressed and resolved through your energy system and the organs of expression in your face.

To share the universal qualities of a god or goddess, you and your partner must be able to express authentic emotions spontaneously. And if you've become attached to inauthentic emotions, you must be able to substitute authentic emotions whenever possible. There are several reasons for this. Your ability to express authentic emotions spontaneously and/or to substitute them for inauthentic emotions will keep you present in your authentic mind. It will keep your sexual energy flowing and your chakras active and will allow you to experience the universal qualities of a god or goddess and share them consistently with your partner.

On the other hand, attachment to inauthentic emotions will keep you and your partner attached to your individual mind and ego. It will disrupt the flow of sexual energy through your energy field. And it will prevent you and your partner from sharing the universal qualities of the god and goddess with each other.

Authentic Emotions

There are only four authentic emotions that can be expressed and re-solved by humans via their energy system and their organs of expres-sion: anger, fear, pain, and joy. Although three of these emotions appear negative, in fact all four authentic emotions co-evolved along with your energy system and your organs of expression in your physical-material body.

Authentic emotions, in cooperation with your energy system and organs of expression, restore relationship by allowing sexual energy, which has been blocked, to move up and down through your energy system without restriction. Indeed, none of the four authentic emo-tions even feel negative when they're expressed spontaneously and resolved through your energy system and organs of expression. By working synchronistically, your four authentic emotions, your energy system, and your organs of expression are designed to restore relation-ship when it has been disrupted.

It's important to note that all four authentic emotions have several things in common. They are composed exclusively of energy with uni-versal qualities. They emerge (from the second through fifth chakras) when the flow of sexual energy through your energy system has been blocked and relationship has been disrupted. They can be expressed and resolved only through your energy system and the organs of expression in your physical-material body. And when authentic emotions are ex-pressed and resolved spontaneously, the flow of sexual energy through your energy field and your relationship will be restored.

An example will help to illustrate how this process takes place. If your partner has become attached to a persona and the karmic baggage that supports it, or an external projection that disrupts the flow of sex-ual energy through his or her second chakra, he or she can consciously or unconsciously project energy with individual qualities at your sec-ond chakra. Depending on the intent, the projection will take the form of a cord, controlling wave, or attachment field. If the projection is able to penetrate your energy field, it will disrupt the flow of sexual energy moving past your second chakra, either through your main masculine

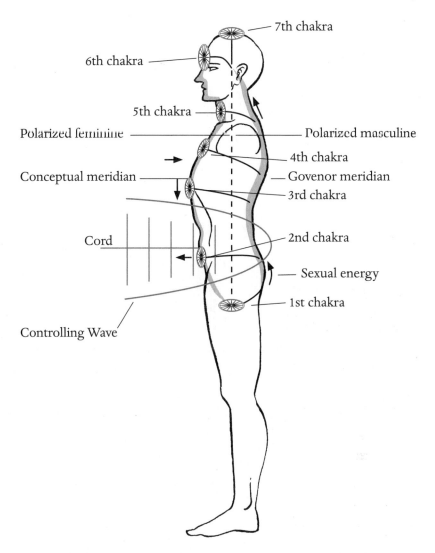

Figure 10: *Authentic Emotion: Anger (Second Chakra)*

meridian (the Governor, in your back) or down your main feminine meridian (the Conceptual, in your front; see Figure 10). In either case, the flow of sexual energy moving past your second chakra will be disrupted and so will your relationship to your partner. It's when those conditions are met that an authentic emotion will emerge.

In the case of the second chakra, the authentic emotion that emerges will be authentic anger. If the disruption takes place at your solar plexus, the flow of sexual energy by your third chakra will be blocked and the authentic emotion that emerges will be fear. If the disruption takes place by your chest or upper back, the flow of sexual energy by your fourth chakra will be disrupted, and the authentic emotion that emerges will be pain. If the disruption takes place by your shoulders, neck, and/or jaw, the flow of sexual energy by your fifth chakra will be disrupted and the authentic emotion that will emerge will be joy.

It's unfortunate, but in the modern world, projections that block sexual energy and disrupt relationships are quite common, even among partners in love, particularly in the fields regulated by the second through fifth chakras. That is why it's so important to be able to express and resolve authentic emotions spontaneously.

Inauthentic Emotions

In contrast to the four authentic emotions, there is a myriad of inauthentic emotions that can emerge from karmic baggage and external projections. When you become attached to a persona and the karmic baggage that supports it, or to an external projection, it's not unusual to experience a blizzard of inauthentic emotions.

If an emotion emerges from a position outside your personal body space, or if it's tinged with individual qualities such as blame, judgment, or belief, or if the emotion reassures you even when you're doing things that disrupt the flow of sexual energy and/or relationship, the emotion can't be authentic. If an emotion supports an inauthentic desire or makes you feel obsessive or fanatical, it cannot be authentic. And finally, if an emotion badgers you or creates confusion, chaos, and/or ambivalence, it can't be authentic.

Many emotions that seem to be authentic are not. Examples abound: insecurity, vengeance, anxiety, nervousness, sorrow—all emerge either from karmic baggage or from external projections and can't be resolved by your organs of expression. Neither can rage, melancholy, guilt, shame, envy, or jealousy.

It's worth noting that just because an emotion is inauthentic doesn't mean you won't feel it. An emotion is inauthentic for two reasons. The first reason is the particular emotion emerges from fields of energy with individual qualities (personas, karmic baggage and external projections), and the second is the emotion can't be expressed and resolved by yelling, screaming, crying, or letting the emotion rise through your energy system to the organs of expression in your face.

Why Do Inauthentic Emotions Rule?

If authentic emotions emerge from the authentic mind and are composed of energy with universal qualities, you're probably wondering why inauthentic emotions dominate people's lives. The answer is simple. Inauthentic emotions dominate because people rarely identify with their authentic mind for any length of time. In most situations, people identify with their dominant personas, subordinate personas, or external projections.

Let me give you an example. Angela had been a client of mine for several years. She had been in a committed relationship for a year, but had difficulty trusting her boyfriend. The discussion of authentic and inauthentic emotions came up in a session when Angela told me she was having difficulty trusting her boyfriend. Angela began the discussion.

"Conrad and I were having dinner in a restaurant downtown at the beginning of the week. At first, he just seemed distracted. Then I noticed that he was staring at an attractive woman at the next table. As soon as I saw what he was doing, I felt my throat tighten and my abdomen began to hurt. That's when I knew I was jealous."

"Jealousy is one of the inauthentic emotions I was talking about," I replied. *"It's no different than envy, hate, or despair. And when you*

become attached to inauthentic emotions and project them at your partner, they can be very disruptive."

"Disruptive can mean a lot of things," Angela countered.

"I know, but in this case I mean they can disrupt the flow of sexual
energy and can be used to justify a host of other inauthentic emotions
that can disrupt relationship. I'll give you an example of what I mean.
When a person becomes jealous, he or she can use jealousy to justify rage
and disappointment, and a multitude of inauthentic emotions, feelings,
and activities that can disturb relationship."

"Would you say that jealousy can poison a relationship?"

"The truth is that inauthentic emotions such as jealousy can disrupt relationship so thoroughly that once a person becomes attached to
them, a transcendent relationship can become nothing more than an
ideal they aspire to but don't expect to achieve anytime soon. Anyway,
if you're serious about transcendent sex and relationships it's essential
to recognize the difference between authentic and inauthentic emotions
and to substitute authentic emotions for inauthentic emotions whenever possible. There's another thing—because we live in a patriarchal
culture, cultural and spiritual institutions add to the problem by giving
inauthentic emotions the same weight as emotions that are authentic."

"Are you saying that our institutions support inauthentic emotions?"

"Yes, they do. And in some cases they even encourage people to substitute them for authentic emotions. The reasons for that are complex,
but it's important to recognize that by the time children have reached
puberty they've been so thoroughly indoctrinated that they probably
can't tell the difference between authentic and inauthentic emotions.
And even if they can, it's unlikely that they would know how important
authentic emotions are and how attachment to inauthentic emotions
can disrupt their relationships."

"But, as a child I think I knew the difference," said Angela.

"Maybe you did, but unfortunately by the time most children have
reached six or seven the blockages in their energy fields and attachments
to their individual minds and egos will make it difficult for them to
gain access to their authentic minds. Their loss of access will have far-
reaching consequences because access to the authentic mind and the

pleasure, love, intimacy, and joy that emerge from it will determine whether they—as adults—will be able to recognize the difference between authentic and inauthentic emotions. It might surprise you to know that in patriarchal cultures inauthentic emotions are encouraged and/or rewarded, especially if they support the agenda of the culture. In patriarchal cultures, the inauthentic emotions that are encouraged and/or rewarded most often are rage, hate, contempt, envy, and many other emotions that encourage competition and violence. That's why it's so important to give up your attachment to inauthentic emotions and to embrace authentic emotions if you want to participate in a transcendent relationship."

Angela sighed, then muttered, "How am I supposed to let go of a lifetime of attachment when I still know so little about authentic emotions?"

"I'm going to explain how you will be able to do that in a moment. However, first you will need to know how authentic emotions and chakras are related and how the Principle of Polarity influences the expression and resolution of authentic emotions. So sit back and I'll begin with the second chakra. Your second chakra regulates the sexual energy related to gender, identity, and sexual vitality. When there has been a disruption in the flow of sexual energy past your second chakra and you're unable to express your gender identity fully, or there's been a disruption in your vitality, creativity, and/or your experience of intimate relationship, the authentic emotion that emerges will be anger. Your third chakra regulates belonging, trust, comfort, satisfaction, and friendship. When there has been a disruption in the flow of sexual energy past the third chakra, and you're unable to experience trust, satisfaction, or comfort, or your sense of belonging has been disrupted, the authentic emotion that emerges will be fear. Your fourth chakra upholds your personal rights. Pain will emerge when the flow of sexual energy past the fourth chakra has been blocked and personal rights have been restricted. The authentic emotion associated with your fifth chakra is joy. Joy will emerge whenever there's been a disruption in the flow of sexual energy past your fifth chakra and your ability to express yourself authentically and spontaneously has been disrupted. When any of these

four chakras have been blocked and sexual energy has been restricted, an
authentic emotion will emerge."

Angela eventually learned to substitute authentic emotions for inauthentic emotions and to express and resolve authentic emotions spontaneously. You can learn to do the same. Like Angela, you first need to know how the Principle of Correspondence regulates the expression and resolution of authentic emotions.

Polarity and Authentic Emotions

The energetic process that allows authentic emotions to be expressed and resolved is regulated by the Principle of Polarity. The Principle of Correspondence tells us that everything is dual: everything has poles; everything has its pair of opposites; like and unlike are the same; opposites are identical in nature but different in degree; extremes meet; all truths are but half truths; all paradoxes may be reconciled.

From the Principle of Polarity we learn that everything that exists in the phenomenal universe participates in polar relationships. When it comes to your physical-material body and your energy field it means that the back of your body and your energy field is masculine in relationship to the front, which is feminine. Back/front polarity is the same for men as well as women. Both are masculine in the back and feminine in the front.

The normal flow of masculine sexual energy through your energy field is up the back of your body, through the main masculine meridian, from the first chakra at the base of your spine to the crown chakra at the top of your head, and beyond. The normal flow of feminine sexual energy is down the front of your body, through the main feminine meridian, from the seventh chakra, to the first chakra, and beyond.

Authentic emotions are always feminine because they emerge only when sexual energy—moving up your back through your main masculine meridian—has been blocked and forced forward through either the second, third, fourth, or fifth chakra, into the front half of your energy field, which is feminine.

When the flow of masculine energy up the back remains undisturbed, no authentic emotion will emerge, because energy that originates at the base of the spine, in the first chakra, will flow upward to your crown, or seventh chakra, freely. It's only when attachment to personas or external projections have blocked the flow of sexual energy through the main masculine meridian that an authentic emotion will emerge.

If you turn your attention to Figure 10, you can see that the main masculine meridian, the Governor, passes through the back of the seven traditional chakras. If a persona or an external projection disrupts the flow of sexual energy up the main masculine meridian, it will have no place to go but forward, through a chakra, into the front of your energy field, which is polarized feminine. It's when the sexual energy has reached the middle of a chakra, and its polarity has been reversed— from masculine to feminine—that an authentic emotion will emerge.

As long as the sexual energy flowing through the Governor meridian continues to move upward, it can feel warm or cold, can vibrate, or can produce a glowing sensation. However, it won't generate an authentic emotion, because the back half of your energy field is masculine in relationship to the front, which is feminine, and authentic emotions emerge only after sexual energy has entered the feminine half of your body.

If the emotion is expressed spontaneously, once it has entered the front half of your body, it will be pulled back into the Governor meridian and will continue to flow upward until it gets resolved by the organs of expression in your face. If it's not expressed spontaneously it will continue to flow, through the front of your chakra, into your auric field, where it will get trapped along with the karmic baggage already there.

By restoring a healthy flow of sexual energy, authentic emotions serve as safety valves. These safety valves evolved along with your organs of expression to restore relationship when it is disrupted by personas and external projections.

Before we move on, it's worth mentioning that emotions are a function of polarity rather than of gender. This means that emotions are feminine—that's all! It doesn't mean that women are inherently more emotional than men. Women may be subject to different hormonal and cultural influences than men, but there's nothing in their energy fields that makes them inherently more emotional. All we can say with confidence is that when sexual energy that has been forced forward through the second through fifth chakra, enters the front half of your energy field, an authentic emotion will emerge.

Exercise: Expressing and Resolving Authentic Emotions

To help you express and resolve authentic emotions spontaneously so that you can substitute authentic emotions for inauthentic emotions, I've included four meditations at the end of this chapter. All four meditations require the same skills, so by mastering one you'll be able to master them all.

Before you begin, it's important to note that to express and resolve authentic emotions you must abandon judgment and blame. Indeed, to express and resolve anger or any other authentic emotion, you can't judge or blame anyone, especially yourself. If you're judging and/or blaming yourself for your authentic emotions, particularly when they're in conflict with other people's expectations or one of your own personality patterns, you need to stop. Then you need to recognize that you have the right to express and resolve your authentic emotions spontaneously and nobody, not even your individual mind and ego, has the authority to take that right away from you.

The first meditation you will perform is the Authentic Anger Meditation. It's designed to help you to express anger spontaneously, whenever a persona or an external projection has disrupted the flow of sexual energy passing through your second chakra. In Figure 10 you can locate your second chakra as well as the other six traditional chakras in your energy system.

Exercise: The Authentic Anger Meditation

To begin the Authentic Anger Meditation, find a comfortable position, with your back straight. Then close your eyes and breathe yogically. After two or three minutes, count backward from five to one, then from ten to one. To relax the muscles of your physical-material body you will use the Standard Method Exercise. After you've completed the Standard Method Exercise, of alternatively tensing and releasing your muscles, assert, *"It's my intent to activate and center myself in my heart chakra."* Then assert, *"It's my intent to become present in my authentic mind."* Take a few moments to enjoy the shift. Then assert, *"It's my intent to activate my second chakra."*

Once your second chakra is active, assert, *"It's my intent to activate my third chakra."* Continue in the same way by activating your fifth and sixth chakras (you've already activated your fourth chakra). After you've activated your second through sixth chakras begin to chant the appropriate tone, which will create a sympathetic resonance in your second chakra.

The second chakra resonates at the frequency of A in the musical scale. And you will chant *"oh,"* as in the word "how." As soon as you begin chanting, the back of the chakra will glow more actively. And as the chakra becomes more active, sexual energy will flow upward, from the second chakra, causing the back of the third chakra to glow more vigorously. As soon as your third chakra begins to glow, shift the tone you're chanting to *"aw,"* as in the word "awe," to match the resonance of the third chakra, which will be a B, in the musical scale. Continue in the same way, spending about two minutes chanting from each chakra, from the second to the sixth chakra.

The tone for the fourth chakra, at the center of your breastbone, is C. And you will find C easily if you chant *"ah,"* as in the word "ha." The tone for the fifth chakra, at the throat, is D. And you will find D easily if you chant *"eh,"* as in the word "hey." The tone for the sixth chakra, at the brow, is E. And you will find E easily if you chant *"ee,"* as in the word "eel."

After you've chanted from the second through sixth chakras take ten more minutes to enjoy the meditation. Then count from one to five and open your eyes. You will feel wide awake, perfectly relaxed, and better than you did before.

Exercise: The Authentic Fear Meditation

The Authentic Fear Meditation is designed to enhance your ability to express authentic fear spontaneously. Authentic fear emerges whenever the third chakra has been blocked and sexual energy could not pass it without being disrupted. For the location of the third chakra refer to Figure 10.

To begin the Authentic Fear Meditation, find a comfortable position, with your back straight. Then close your eyes and breathe yogically. After two or three minutes count backward from five to one, then from ten to one. To relax the muscles of your physical-material body you will use the Standard Method Exercise. After you've completed the Standard Method Exercise, of alternatively tensing and releasing your muscles, assert, *"It's my intent to activate and center myself in my heart chakra."* Then assert, *"It's my intent to become present in my authentic mind."* Take a few moments to enjoy the shift. Then assert, *"It's my intent to activate my third chakra."* Once your third chakra has become active, continue by asserting, *"It's my intent to activate my fifth chakra"* (you already activated your fourth chakra). Then activate your sixth chakra in the same way.

Once your third through sixth chakras are active, begin chanting from your third chakra. To match the resonance of the third chakra, you will chant *"aw,"* as in the word "awe." Continue in the same way, spending about two minutes chanting from each chakra, from the third to the sixth chakra. The tone for the fourth chakra will be *"ah,"* as in the word "ha." The tone for the fifth chakra will be *"eh,"* as in the word "hey." The tone for the sixth chakra will be *"ee,"* as in the word "eel."

After you've chanted from your third through sixth chakras, take ten minutes to enjoy the effects. After ten minutes count from one to five. When you reach the number five, open your eyes. You will feel wide awake, perfectly relaxed, and better than you did before.

Exercise: The Authentic Pain Meditation

The Authentic Pain Meditation is designed to enhance your ability to express authentic pain spontaneously. Without the ability to express and resolve authentic pain, sexual energy can be blocked by the fourth chakra, your personal rights can be compromised, and your ability to share love can be disrupted.

It is important to note that authentic pain does not emerge when there has been a loss of fortune or opportunity—only when there has been a disruption of relationship. For the location of the fourth chakra, refer to Figure 10.

To begin the Authentic Pain Meditation, find a comfortable position, with your back straight. Then, close your eyes and breathe yogically. After two or three minutes count backward from five to one, then ten to one. To relax the muscles of your physical-material body you will use the Standard Method Exercise. After you've completed the Standard Method Exercise of alternatively tensing and releasing your muscles, assert, *"It's my intent to activate and center myself in my heart chakra."* Then assert, *"It's my intent to become present in my authentic mind."* Take a few moments to enjoy the shift. Then assert, *"It's my intent to activate my fifth chakra."* Continue by asserting, *"It's my intent to activate my sixth chakra."*

After you've activated your fourth through sixth chakras, begin to chant from each chakra for two minutes, beginning with your fourth chakra. The tone for the fourth chakra will be *"ah,"* as in the word "ha." The tone for the fifth chakra will be *"eh,"* as in the word "hey." The tone for the sixth chakra will be *"ee,"* as in the word "eel."

After you've chanted from your fourth through sixth chakras, take about ten minutes to enjoy the meditation. After ten minutes, count from one to five. When you reach the number five, open your eyes. You will feel wide awake, perfectly relaxed, and better than you did before.

Exercise: The Authentic Joy Meditation

The Authentic Joy Meditation is designed to enhance your ability to express authentic joy spontaneously. Without the ability to express and resolve authentic joy, sexual energy can become blocked by your fifth chakra and your ability to express yourself authentically can be compromised. For the location of the fifth chakra, refer to Figure 10.

To begin the Authentic Joy Meditation, find a comfortable position with your back straight. Then close your eyes and breathe yogically. After two or three minutes, count backward from five to one, then from ten to one. To relax the muscles of your physical-material body, you will use the Standard Method Exercise. After you've completed the Standard Method Exercise of alternatively tensing and releasing your muscles, assert, *"It's my intent to activate and center myself in my heart chakra."* Then assert, *"It's my intent to become present in my authentic mind."* Take a few moments to enjoy the shift. Then assert, *"It's my intent to activate my fifth chakra."* Continue in the same way, by activating your sixth chakra.

Once your fourth through sixth chakras are active, begin to chant for two minutes from each chakra beginning with your fifth chakra. The tone for the fifth chakra will be *"eh,"* as in the word "hey." The tone for the sixth chakra will be *"ee,"* as in the word "eel."

After you've chanted from your fifth and sixth chakras, take about ten minutes to enjoy the meditation. After ten minutes count from one to five. When you reach the number five, open your eyes. You will feel wide awake, perfectly relaxed, and better than you did before.

Authentic Emotions and Sexual Ecstasy

Now that you've mastered the meditations to express and resolve authentic emotions spontaneously, you can enhance the flow of sexual energy up your back through your main masculine meridian and down your front through your main feminine meridian. By doing that, you will shift your orientation so that you will be able to substitute authentic emotions for inauthentic emotions whenever possible.

It will take two meditations to shift your orientation. In the first meditation you will activate your seven traditional chakras and fill your energy field, on those dimensions, with sexual energy. In the second meditation, you will activate your first through thirteenth chakras and fill your energy field, on those dimensions, with sexual energy.

By activating the seven traditional chakras and the first six chakras above personal body space and filling your energy field on those dimensions with sexual energy, you will become more detached from personas and external projections. And that will make it easier for you to substitute authentic emotions for inauthentic emotions.

Exercise: Activating the Seven Traditional Chakras

To activate your seven traditional chakras, find a comfortable position, with your back straight. Then, close your eyes and breathe yogically. After two or three minutes, count backward from five to one, then from ten to one. To relax the muscles of your physical-material body, you will use the Standard Method Exercise. After you've completed the Standard Method Exercise, of alternatively tensing and releasing your muscles, assert, *"It's my intent to activate and center myself in my heart chakra."* Take a few moments to enjoy the shift. Then assert, *"It's my intent to activate my first chakra."* Continue in the same way and activate your second, third, fifth, sixth, and seventh chakras.

Once you've activated the seven traditional chakras, assert, *"On the levels of my first through seventh chakras it's my intent to turn my organs of perception inward."* Then assert, *"It's my intent to fill my energy field on those dimensions, with sexual energy."* Take about fifteen minutes to enjoy the changes you experience. Then count from one to five. When you reach the number five, open your eyes. You will feel wide awake, perfectly relaxed, and better than you did before.

Exercise: Activating the First Through Thirteenth Chakras

Once you can activate your seven traditional chakras, you can make it even easier to substitute authentic emotions for inauthentic emotions by activating your first through thirteenth chakras. In Figure 11 you can see that the eighth through thirteenth chakras are located directly above your crown chakra.

To begin the exercise, find a comfortable position, with your back straight. Then close your eyes and breathe yogically. After two or three minutes count backward from five to one, then ten to one. To relax the muscles of your physical-material body you will use the Standard Method Exercise. After you've completed the Standard Method Exercise of alternatively tensing and releasing your muscles, assert, *"It's my intent to activate and center myself in my heart chakra."* Take a few moments to enjoy the shift. Then assert, *"It's my intent to activate my first chakra."* Continue in the same way by activating your second, third, fifth, sixth, and seventh chakras.

Take a few moments to enjoy the effects. Then continue in the same way by activating your eighth, ninth, tenth, eleventh, twelfth, and thirteenth chakras. After you've activated all thirteen chakras, assert, *"On the levels of my first through thirteenth chakras it's my intent to turn my organs of perception inward."* Then assert, *"It's my intent to fill my energy field on those dimensions with sexual energy."*

Take fifteen minutes to enjoy the changes you experience. Then count from one to five. When you reach the number five, open your eyes. You will feel wide awake, perfectly relaxed, and better than you did before.

By practicing this exercise regularly you will find it easier to remain detached from personas and external projections. That will make it easier for you to express and resolve authentic emotions. And because the eighth through thirteenth chakras regulate the higher aspects of consciousness and Shakti (sexual energy), you will be able to substitute authentic emotions for inauthentic emotions. And that will bring you one step closer to making the transition to transcendent sex and relationships.

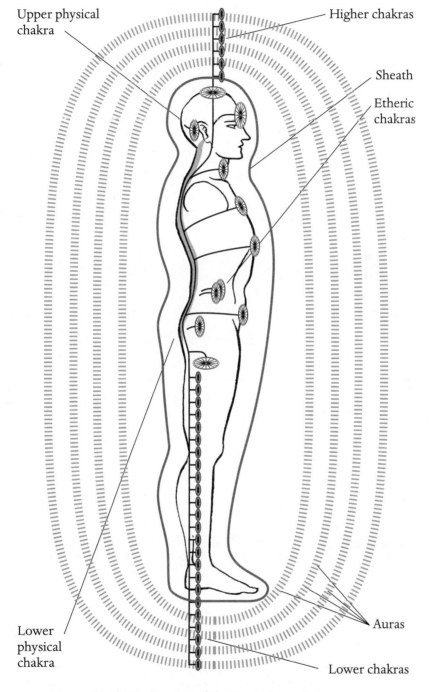

Upper physical chakra

Higher chakras

Sheath

Etheric chakras

Lower physical chakra

Auras

Lower chakras

Figure 11: *Structure of the Human Energy System*

Chapter 7

Sex Is an
Inter-Dimensional Sport

At the singles bar, Mark watches Mandy, a beautiful woman, whom he has selected out of the crowd of attractive females. When Mandy spots Mark approaching, she smiles, giving him approval. Mark in turn senses this and introduces himself. Within an hour Mark Mandy are having sex together.

Nancy and Jim have known each other for a month. Their sex life is still passionate, but they have also started to open up emotionally to each other, allowing themselves to become increasingly vulnerable and truthful about their feelings. From time to time Nancy and Jim argue about things.

Ron and Sharon have been married for decades. There is a silent understanding between them and they can speak to each other as if they were thinking out loud. They still argue, but it is rare.

Indra and Rani have been married only a few months, but they are both sincere devotees of meditation. They meditate together morning and evening. After meditation they relax in each other's arms into a long, luminous hug in which they form one perfect circle of bliss. Indra and Rani have never had a real argument. And if we could see into their future, we would see that they never will, because they always put the other, and the relationship, first.

Interactions between people in relationships invariably evolve through four stages, as the partners mature: meeting, relating, traditional relationship, and transcendent relationship. In each stage of relationship, human beings have the opportunity to become more authentic by embracing authentic desires and emotions and by emerging with greater authenticity on more dimensions.

A meeting is the most superficial form of a human interaction. Mark and Mandy enjoy this type of human interaction. In meetings, people interact primarily through the individual mind and ego. During meetings, authentic interactions generally produce pleasure, whereas inauthentic interactions generally don't. Some people can associate with one another over extended periods and never connect more deeply than they did when they first met. In fact, their interactions may remain rooted exclusively in patterns that emerge from their individual mind and ego. Of course, it doesn't have to be that way. The more authentic people are capable of being during their initial meeting, the more pleasure they will experience during and after the meeting and the more likely their future interactions will reach the next stage of interaction, which is relating.

When people relate they will be authentic at least part of the time. And the desire to experience pleasure and love will overcome the need to look good, compete, control, and/or make an impression. As pleasure increases, so will the flow of sexual energy. With more sexual energy available, the human heart will become more active. And that can lead to strong feelings of love. In fact, when there is chemistry or mutual interest, or when people are in extreme situations, meetings can be so abbreviated that it can appear that people initiate their association by relating rather than meeting. Jim and Nancy enjoy this stage of relating.

A traditional relationship is designed to support the family unit. That will be its highest goal, and it will use pleasure, love, and periodic intimacy to achieve that goal. Ron and Sharon enjoy traditional relationship.

In order to advance beyond relating to traditional relationship, inauthentic desires, emotions, and activities, which emerge from personas and external projections, must be replaced—at least some of the time—by authentic desires, emotions, and activities that emerge from the authentic mind. When partners make the transition to traditional relationship, their commitment to each other will keep them centered in their authentic mind, at least part of the time. And because they can stay centered in their authentic mind part of the time, they will be able to share pleasure, love, and periodic intimacy.

In a transcendent relationship, the traditional needs of partners have been subordinated to a higher purpose, transcendence. Indra and Rani enjoy a transcendent relationship. Partners who've made the transition to transcendent relationship will be authentic all the time. By remaining authentic, they will experience an uninterrupted flow of sexual energy. And they will advance beyond periodic intimacy to permanent intimacy and joy. Those who've made the transition to transcendent relationship are easy to spot. Their feelings and emotions emerge spontaneously from their authentic mind and they're able to empathize with the authentic desires, feelings, emotions, and goals of other people.

Partners who've made the transition from traditional sex to transcendent sex experience many of the same challenges and benefits as partners who've made the transition to transcendent relationship.

In one of her last sessions, Tracy, a thirty-three-year-old designer, described the difficulties she had making the transition to transcendent sex and relationship with her boyfriend, Bob. It was on a Tuesday afternoon, and Tracy had been crying. After she hung up her coat, she sat down and wiped her eyes. Then Tracy looked at me and declared,

"I still don't see how I'm supposed to overcome all my sexual taboos and have Bob respect me in the morning."

"I know it's not easy. If it were easy everyone would be experiencing transcendent sex and relationships. And most of the world's relationship problems would have been solved long ago. But what I have to say may help. You already know that interactions between people go through four stages: meeting, relating, traditional relationship, and transcendent relationship. In each stage, people have an opportunity to become more authentic and to experience more of the benefits of a transcendent relationship. A similar

process goes on in your sexual relationship. Your sexual relationship goes through four stages. In the first stage sexual interactions will be the most superficial because the primary goal of both partners will simply be to experience pleasure. And it doesn't matter whether partners are engaged in petting, having intercourse, or doing something more extreme."

Tracy asked, *"You're talking about Eros, aren't you?"*

"You can call it Eros, although it's important to remember that even Eros strives for a basic form of human love that will emerge if partners—who are sexually intimate—share universal qualities with one another at least some of the time."

"So, you're saying that in the first stage, people interact through their individual mind and ego, most of the time?"

"That's right. But the more authentic people are capable of being, the more pleasure they will experience, and the more likely future interactions will reach the next stage. In stage two, partners go beyond the pursuit of pleasure for its own sake. Sexual pleasure will still be there, but it will serve a higher purpose. It will serve as a stepping stone to physical love."

"Does that mean sex becomes less pleasurable?"

"No, not at all. In stage two, pleasure will increase along with authentic contact. And it's precisely because partners experience more pleasure and authentic contact that they can make the transition to physical love."

"But they won't reach the third stage—sexual relationship—until they're both authentic, at least part of the time," said Tracy.

"That's right. In order to advance to the third stage, inauthentic desires and emotions, and the activities that emerge from them, must give way to authentic desires, emotions, and activities, at least some of the time. Only then will partners trust each other enough to share their authentic sexual desires and secrets. The truth is that once partners have made the transition to the third stage, their commitment to be authentic will keep them centered in their authentic minds at least some of the time. And that will enable them to overcome the limitations imposed on their sexual expression by personas and external projections, at least temporarily."

"And taboos ... ?"

I nodded. *"Those, too."*

"So, let me get this straight. You're saying that in stage three, the more authentic I become, the more fun I'll have in bed."

"That's part of it. However, I'm also saying that being authentic part of the time will enable you to trust your partner more and share more sexual energy. That will enable you to surrender to pleasure, share physical love, and experience periodic sexual intimacy. Of course, if you and your partner expect to make the transition to a transcendent sexual relationship, you will need to make sexual intimacy permanent so that you can share sustained joy and orgasmic bliss with one an-other." To bring home my point I added, *"Tracy, you already know that in a traditional sexual relationship partners don't share perma-nent intimacy, orgasmic bliss, or sustained joy with one another, be-cause they believe the primary function of sex is to procreate and to keep the family unit together. By embracing that belief, partners will block their sexual energy from radiating freely. And they will prevent themselves from staying centered in the authentic mind long enough to make the transition to a transcendent sexual relationship. The fact is that to make the transition to a transcendent sexual relationship, you and your boyfriend, Bob, must overcome your fears and the limitations of your belief systems, and you must use sex as a vehicle for transcen-dence. Only then will periodic sexual intimacy give way to permanent sexual intimacy."*

"If I do all that, will I be able to overcome my sexual taboos and make the transition to transcendent sex?"

"That will happen naturally as soon as you and Bob learn to use the organs of your energy system to share more pleasure, love, intimacy, and joy with each other."

I took a moment to gauge Tracy's reaction, then I added, *"So, if you're ready to make the transition ..."*

"I'm ready and willing. And I've already made my choice. I want to experience transcendent sex and I want it to be part of a transcendent relationship with Bob."

Like Tracy, everyone can take the appropriate steps to experience a transcendent sexual relationship. The first step you must take is to learn as much as possible about your energy system because it's the condition of your energy system that will determine whether you will be able to experience sustained sexual intimacy and joy.

Structure of the Human Energy System

Your energy system is composed of four major groups of organs. They function synergistically with one another to promote the flow of sexual energy through your energy field. The four groups are the chakras, auras, meridians, and minor energy centers located throughout your energy field (see Figure 12). The human energy system, as a structural and functional unit, can be thought of as a power plant and grid of substations and power lines that transmute consciousness into sexual energy and sexual energy from one frequency into another.

In this chapter, we are concerned primarily with the sexual potential of the chakras and minor energy centers. Throughout your energy field, there are one hundred and forty-four chakras and a large number of minor energy centers that are linked to the chakras by streams of sexual energy known as *meridians*.

Eleven chakras are located within your body: the seven traditional chakras as well as two etheric chakras and two physical chakras. Seventy chakras are located below your body space and sixty-three additional chakras are located above it.

The main function of the chakras is to keep you connected to Universal Consciousness so that you can participate in transcendent sex and relationships. To perform that function, the chakras serve as vortices through which consciousness will be transmuted into sexual energy and through which sexual energy can be used to nourish your energy bodies, sheaths, and auras.

Once consciousness has been transmuted into sexual energy, this energy must be transmuted into the exact frequency needed by your energy bodies, sheaths, and auras on each dimension. The chakras perform that function. They transmute sexual energy into the complete

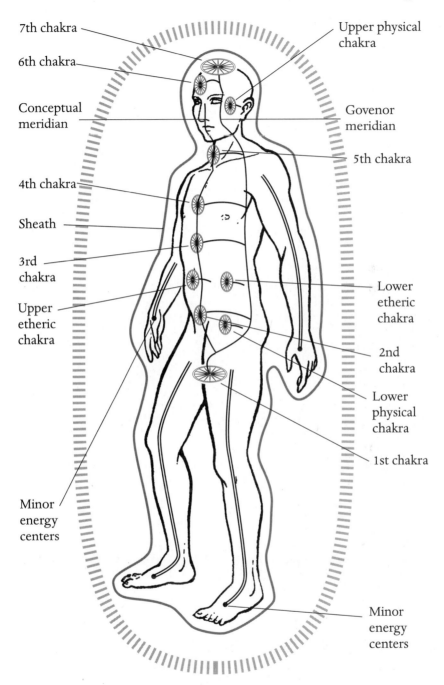

Figure 12: *Organs of the Human Energy System*

range of frequencies necessary for your energy field to function health-fully and for you to participate in transcendent sex and relationships.

In addition to transmitting and transmuting sexual energy, your chakras, along with your auric fields, serve as sensors that allow you to sense fields of non-physical energy in both your internal and external environment. Only when you're able to sense fields of non-physical energy will you be able to discern if the energy of any specific field has universal or individual qualities. And it's only by sensing energy fields that you will be able to discern the difference between desires and emotions that are authentic and those that are not.

The more active your chakras are, and the more energy they can transmit, the more sexual energy you will have and the less reactive you will be to external projections.

The Seven Traditional Chakras

From yoga and tantra we learn that the first seven chakras are responsible for regulating life on the dimensions dedicated to feeling, emotion, finite human consciousness, and psychic well-being. In order to fulfill their functions so that you can make the transition to a transcendent sexual relationship, these chakras must function healthfully.

The Muladhara Chakra

The first chakra in your body is called Muladhara. In Sanskrit, *mula* means "root" and *adhara* "to support." The Muladhara chakra emerges from the Governor meridian at the base of your spine, directly behind your sexual organs, at a point corresponding to the perineum. From that point, it curves downward in a semi-circle and emerges six inches (fifteen centimeters) below the perineum, at a point midway between your thighs.

When your first chakra, Muladhara, is functioning properly, you will feel secure and comfortable in the physical-material world. Pleasure will emerge spontaneously, and you won't feel compelled to justify your existence or lean on others for support.

In contrast, the disruption of your first chakra by karmic baggage and/or external projections will make life on earth a trial because sexual energy radiating through your first chakra will be blocked and pleasure will be restricted.

The most powerful source of sexual energy in the human energy system is Kundalini Shakti, which emerges from the Muladhara chakra. When Kundalini Shakti is blocked, the transmission and transmutation of sexual energy will be disrupted, boundaries will be weakened, and relationships will suffer. In fact, when the functions of the first chakra have been disrupted long enough, life can become an ongoing struggle for survival, which will leave little time or space for transcendent sex and relationships.

The Svadhistana Chakra

The second chakra has its point of origin in the Governor meridian, about three and a half inches (nine centimeters) above your first chakra. In Sanskrit, *svad* means "that which belongs to itself" and *dhisthana* means "its actual place." From its point of origin in the Governor meridian, the chakra extends forward to a point in the Conceptual meridian that is two and one-half inches (nine centimeters) below your navel. The second chakra, Svadhistana, regulates sexual function and gender identity as well as creativity and vitality. When this chakra is active, you will be able to express your creativity through your relationships, and pleasure will emerge spontaneously.

When the flow of sexual energy through the second chakra has been disrupted, vitality and creativity will be affected. In some cases this will lead to depression, which can start as an acute problem, but will become chronic if the chakra is burdened by an inordinate amount of karmic baggage or is being influenced by external projections.

In some cases, the disruption of the second chakra can also lead to sexual dysfunction and gender confusion in both men and women. This in turn can lead to sudden outbursts of anger, periods of depression, or a pattern of passive-aggressive behavior.

The Manipura Chakra

The third chakra has its origin within the Governor meridian, directly behind your solar plexus. It is called Manipura, which means "city of jewels." From its point of origin, the Manipura chakra extends forward to a point in your Conceptual meridian that corresponds to your solar plexus.

The Manipura chakra is concerned primarily with people, places, and things. Belonging, trust, contentment, the ability to remain calm during times of duress, as well as status, comfort, and satisfaction, are all regulated by your third chakra.

When the chakra is functioning healthily you will feel content and there will be no compulsion to compromise your personal integrity in order to participate in relationships. Relationships will be based on mutual trust, the ability to share intimacy and joy, and not on dependency, need, control, or manipulation.

When the flow of sexual energy by your third chakra has been disrupted, you will feel alienated from your body and your partner. Satisfaction will diminish as well as your sense of belonging and contentment.

When the flow of sexual energy through your third chakra has been blocked, fear will emerge. When fear becomes chronic, trust will be diminished, and that will make shared empathy and intimacy difficult to sustain.

The Anahata Chakra

The fourth chakra is the heart chakra. It emerges from the Governor meridian at a point that corresponds to the eighth cervical vertebra. In Sanskrit it is called *Anahata*, which means "unstuck." From its point of origin the Anahata chakra extends forward to a point in the Conceptual meridian that corresponds to the center of your breastbone.

Your heart chakra upholds your personal rights, even when there is internal (from the individual mind and ego) and/or external (from people, institutions, and your restrictive belief system) opposition. Among these rights are the right to share pleasure, love, intimacy, and joy without fear, shame, or guilt; the right to feel, express, and resolve authentic emotions; the right to experience, feel, and act on desires that emerge from your authentic mind and, of course, the right to experience transcendent sex and relationships.

The emotion regulated by the heart chakra is pain. If the flow of sexual energy through the heart chakra has been blocked, pain will emerge, and that can lead to a disruption of intimate relationship.

The Visuddha Chakra

The fifth chakra emerges from a point in the Governor meridian that corresponds to the third cervical vertebra, just below the medulla oblongata, the base of your brain. From its point of origin, the Visuddha chakra extends forward to a point in the Conceptual meridian that corresponds to the center of your throat, just below the Adam's apple. In Sanskrit, it's called *Visuddha* which means "pure."

The fifth chakra is called "pure" because it transmutes sexual energy passing through it into joy. The chakra also regulates self-expression. This includes verbal expression and the expression of authentic feelings and emotions.

The fifth chakra's ability to function healthfully will determine whether you can occupy your personal space fully and express yourself honestly.

When the functions of the fifth chakra have been disrupted, it's not unusual for people to compensate for this by attaching themselves to beliefs and personas that emerge from the individual mind and ego.

The Ajna Chakra

The sixth chakra emerges from a point in the Governor meridian directly above your upper palate. From its point of origin the Ajna chakra curves up and then forward until it joins the Conceptual meridian in the center of your brow. In Sanskrit it's called *Ajna*, which means "command."

Will and intent are important functions of the sixth chakra as well as your ability to visualize, to imagine and conceptualize, to reason deductively, and to use your intuition and extrasensory abilities, which include discernment—the ability to sense subtle energy fields.

The sixth chakra has an important influence on memory, including the memory of energetic interactions. When the sixth chakra is functioning healthily you will remember events by re-experiencing the energetic fields associated with them. For adults, the memory of energetic interactions can provide much-needed continuity with childhood.

There is no emotion associated with the Ajna center. However, when the functions of the chakra have been disrupted, your ability to express will and intent and to use them both to solve problems will also be disrupted.

The Sahasrara Chakra

The seventh chakra emerges from the Governor meridian at a point three quarters of an inch (two centimeters) above your sixth chakra. From its point of origin the Sahasrara chakra extends directly upward to a point at the top of your head. In Sanskrit it's called *Sahasrara*, which means "thousand-petaled lotus."

The seventh chakra serves as a bridge between the chakras within your body and those above it. In fact, it's only after the seventh chakra has become active that you will be able to function with conscious awareness on the higher dimensions (the dimensions associated with your higher chakras) and to participate fully in transcendent sex and relationships.

There is no emotion associated with the Sahasrara chakra. However, when the seventh chakra has become active, there will be a sense of completion and/or satisfaction, which coincides with the recognition that limitations imposed by the individual mind and ego and restrictive belief systems are to be overcome and not accepted with resignation.

Etheric and Physical Chakras

In addition to the traditional seven chakras, there are four additional chakras in your body; the upper and lower etheric chakras, and the upper and lower physical chakras. The upper etheric chakra is located by the spleen (on the left side of your abdomen), between your second

Upper physical chakra

Upper etheric
chakra

Lower etheric
chakra

Lower physical
chakra

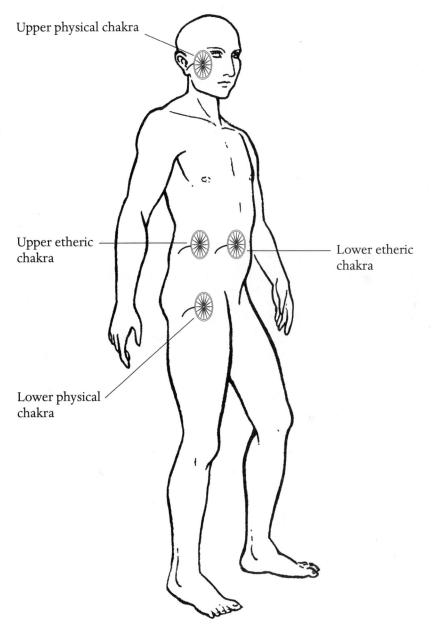

Figure 13: *The Etheric and Physical Chakras*

and third chakras. The lower etheric chakra is located directly across from it (see Figure 13).

Etheric chakras regulate feelings. Feelings vibrate at lower frequencies than emotions and are less precise. Although there are only four authentic emotions, there are hundreds of authentic feelings, ranging from comfort and satisfaction to fatigue and enthusiasm.

The upper physical chakra is located in the head, just above and behind the back of your sixth chakra. The lower physical chakra is located in the middle of your pelvis, just in front and two inches (five centimeters) below the back of your second chakra (see Figure 13). Structurally, the etheric and physical chakras are identical to the seven traditional chakras, except for their length: they're about 40 percent shorter.

Together with your etheric chakras, your physical chakras bridge the gap between your authentic mind, which includes your energy bodies, sheaths, and energy system, and your nervous system and organs of expression and perception, which are located in your physical-material body. By working together with your nervous system and organs of expression and perception, your etheric and physical chakras allow you to share the universal qualities of the god or goddess with your partner in both the physical and non-physical universe.

When both your etheric and physical chakras are active, you will be grounded in the physical-material world. The importance of being grounded cannot be overstated. Being grounded allows you to experience physical pleasure and sexual intimacy without disruption. It also provides an anchor that will keep you from drifting, without the ability to remain present in the physical-material universe.

The Chakras' Sexual Potential

All one hundred and forty-four chakras in your energy field have an effect on your ability to experience transcendent sex. However, the eleven chakras in your body have the most influence. You've already learned to activate your seven traditional chakras in order to enhance your ability to express and resolve authentic emotions. By giving special attention to the feminine pole of those chakras, you can enhance their sexual potential.

The following exercise, known as Chakra Boosting, is designed specifically to enhance the sexual potential of the seven traditional chakras. At first you will practice the exercise on your own. Then you can practice a simple variation with your partner.

To perform Chakra Boosting, you will use the palm of your assertive (masculine) hand to stimulate the front end (the feminine pole) of each chakra. That's your right hand if you're right-handed or your left hand if you're left-handed. Both palms contain minor energy centers that radiate sexual energy (see Figure 14). The sexual energy emerging through the energy center in your masculine palm will activate the feminine pole of a chakra if you place your masculine hand in the auric field directly above it.

You will find that Chakra Boosting works best if you keep the palm of your hand about six inches (fifteen centimeters) above the chakra that you wish to activate.

In Chakra Boosting you will begin with your seventh chakra, at the crown, and work down, stimulating the female pole of each chakra until you reach your first chakra, at the base of your spine.

As soon as you place the palm of your masculine hand over the female pole of a particular chakra it will become active and begin to vibrate. The vibration will continue even after you've removed your palm.

You may also experience sensations that are unique to the chakra you've stimulated. The sensations you experience could be anything from a sense of security, if it's the first chakra, to contentment and/or comfort if it's the third chakra. You will find a list below indicating the location of the seven traditional chakras and the sensations, feelings, and emotions associated with them.

First Chakra: Base of the spine—security, self-confidence, body image, connection to the earth and the life-force that emerges from it.

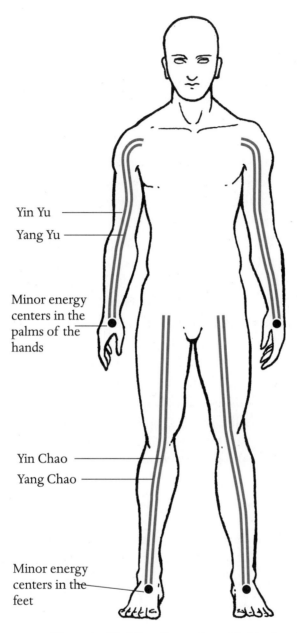

Yin Yu

Yang Yu

Minor energy
centers in the
palms of the
hands

Yin Chao

Yang Chao

Minor energy
centers in the
feet

Figure 14: *The Minor Energy Centers in Hands and Feet*

Second Chakra: Four finger widths below the navel—vitality, gender identity (masculinity or femininity), creativity, sexual joy, and the power of shakti to procreate.

Third Chakra: Solar plexus—belonging, trust, comfort, satisfaction, empathy, and intimacy.

Fourth Chakra: Center of the breast bone—self-awareness, personal rights (including the right to be aware of your internal and external environment on all physical and non-physical dimensions, the right to radiate and resolve your authentic feelings and emotions, and the right to experience transcendent sex and relationships).

Fifth Chakra: Half inch below the Adam's apple—integrity, self-expression, and the experience of unconditional joy.

Sixth Chakra: Center of the brow—human awareness, personal will, memory, intuition, reasoning, and rational thought.

Seventh Chakra: Crown of the head—transcendental awareness and relationship.

Exercise: Enhancing Your Chakras' Sexual Potential

To enhance the sexual potential of the seven traditional chakras begin by finding a comfortable position, with your back straight. Then, close your eyes and breathe yogically. After two or three minutes, count backward from five to one, then from ten to one. To relax the muscles of your physical-material body, you will use the Standard Method Exercise. After you've completed the Standard Method Exercise of alternatively tensing and releasing your muscles, assert, *"It's my intent to become present in my authentic mind."*

Once you're centered, open your eyes but keep them slightly unfocused. Then use your masculine hand to make clockwise circular motions about six inches (fifteen centimeters) above the feminine pole of each chakra, beginning with your seventh chakra at the top of your head. Your palm should be facing the chakra while your fingers are slightly extended. Hold your hand steady above the chakra and continue to make clockwise motions (at a moderate pace) until you feel that the chakra begins to vibrate.

Once your crown chakra has begun to vibrate, move your hand to your sixth chakra, at your brow, and repeat the process. Continue in the same way, making clockwise motions above each chakra, until you reach your first chakra, at the base of your spine. After you've stimulated all seven traditional chakras, close your eyes and take ten minutes to enjoy the effects. Then count from one to five. When you reach the number five open your eyes. You will feel wide awake, perfectly relaxed, and you will experience the residual glow that comes from the enhanced sexual potential of your chakras.

Exercise: Chakra Cleansing

Once you are confident that you can enhance the sexual potential of your chakras, you can use a simple variation to do the same for your partner. To begin the exercise known as Chakra Cleansing, have your partner lie on his or her back with his or her arms at the sides. Once your partner is relaxed, next close your eyes and begin to breathe yogically. After two or three minutes, count backward from five to one, then from ten to one. To relax the muscles of your physical body, you will use the Standard Method Exercise. After you've completed the Standard Method Exercise of alternatively tensing and releasing your muscles, assert, *"It's my intent to become present in my authentic mind."*

Once you're present, open your eyes and keep them slightly unfocused. Rub your hands together for ten seconds. This will polarize your hands and enhance the flow of sexual energy through your palms. Once your hands are polarized, you will make the first of seven strokes, with your positive hand, over your partner's seven traditional chakras.

You will find it best if you keep your palm about six inches (fifteen centimeters) above the surface of your partner's physical body and trail your fingers behind your palm on each stroke. Each stroke will begin at your partner's crown and end at the base of his or her spine (see Figure 15). At the beginning of each stroke, inhale through your nose and hold your breath until you've completed the stroke. At the end of each stroke you will exhale through your mouth. Inhale once again through your nose and hold while you make the next stroke. Repeat until you've made seven strokes.

After you've completed the seven strokes, continue to keep your eyes open but slightly unfocused while you breathe through your nose. Then use your masculine hand to make clockwise circular motions above your partner's crown chakra, at the top of his or her head. Continue for two minutes at a moderate speed, with your hand three to four inches (eight centimeters) above the chakra. After two minutes, move your hand to your partner's sixth chakra and repeat. Continue in the same way with your partner's fifth, fourth, third, second, and first chakra (see figure 16).

After working individually on all seven traditional chakras, rub your hands together again, and make seven more strokes through your partner's energy field, with your positive (masculine) hand.

When you're finished, close your eyes and give your partner five minutes to enjoy the benefits of chakra cleansing. After five minutes, count out loud from one to five. When you reach the number five, open your eyes and tell your partner to do the same. Your partner will feel wide awake and will enjoy the benefits of having the sexual potential of his or her chakras enhanced.

Companion Chakras

To enhance the sexual potential of your chakras even further, you can boost the flow of sexual energy in companion chakras. Companion chakras are two chakras with complementary functions. When the functions of one companion in a chakra pair has been blocked and sexual energy cannot flow through it, symptoms will appear in it and its companion. If the blockage is severe enough, the afflicted chakra will become numb, but its companion will develop acute symptoms, such as pressure, aches, and sharp pain, which cannot be hidden so easily.

Many sexual and relationship issues are not successfully treated, even by energy practitioners, because symptoms in the area regulated

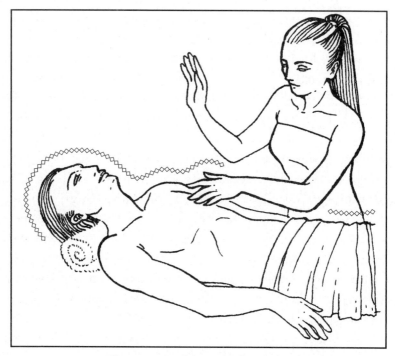

Figure 15: *Stroking and Polarization*

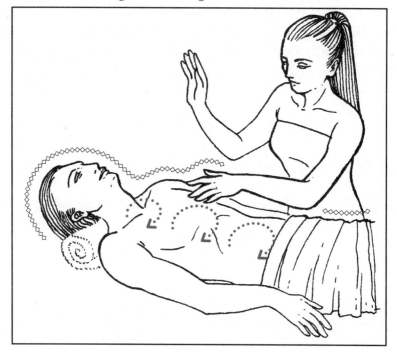

Figure 16: *Hand in Circular Motion*

by one chakra—tension in the musculature, discomfort and/or pain, and so on—may mask a deeper problem in its companion.

By becoming aware of which chakras function in pairs and by enhancing the functions of both chakras, you will enhance their sexual potential and correct many untreated energy problems. The chakra pairs that function as companions are the first and third chakras, the second and fifth chakras, the fourth and sixth chakras, and the first and seventh chakras.

The First Pair

The first chakra pair consists of the first and the third chakras. Their partnership is based on the complementary roles they play in security and relationship. The first chakra regulates the frequencies of energy related to body image, vitality, and the confidence that comes from knowing that you have the inalienable right to exist.

The third chakra regulates the frequencies of energy related to belonging. This includes status and the security that comes from being a member of a group as well as the satisfaction, comfort, trust, and empathy that are all normal functions of relationship and group affiliation. When the third chakra is functioning healthfully, you will feel secure and satisfied, and you will enjoy the fruits that come from empathy, intimacy, and mutual trust.

The Second Pair

The second chakra pair consists of the second and fifth chakras. Their partnership is based on the complementary roles they play in regulating self-expression and joy—including sexual joy—which is regulated by the second chakra, and unconditional joy, which is regulated by the fifth chakra.

The second chakra regulates the frequencies of sexual energy responsible for self-expression on the most fundamental level: the expression of gender identity, gender orientation, libido, vitality, and creativity.

The fifth chakra regulates the full spectrum of self-expression. It also regulates the frequencies of sexual energy responsible for unconditional joy, which you will experience during transcendent sex and relationships.

Unconditional joy is an authentic emotion. In your physical-material body it can be expressed authentically by your organs of expression. On the non-physical dimensions you can express it authentically by sharing sexual joy and orgasmic bliss.

The Third Pair

The third chakra pair consists of the fourth and sixth chakras. Their partnership is based on the complementary roles they play in securing your human rights. These rights include the right to experience and express authentic desires; the right to express and resolve authentic feelings and emotions; the right to express the will, desire, and intent of your authentic mind; and the right to participate freely in transcendent sex and relationships.

The fourth chakra secures your rights, because it serves as a gateway into your authentic mind as well as your center of awareness—at least until you consciously experience union with Universal Consciousness.

The sixth chakra plays a direct role in securing human rights through personal will. Will can emerge in two ways: when you embrace authentic desires, and when you engage in authentic activities that support transcendent sex and relationships.

When your personal will supports authentic desires and/or authentic activities, your personal rights will be secure. When your personal will supports your individual mind and ego, the functions of your authentic mind can be blocked or even usurped by your individual mind and ego.

Retaining your personal rights is so important for transcendent sex and relationships that it's never appropriate to surrender them or to give them away by default. Sometimes surrender is disguised as openness. However, any form of openness that demands the forfeiture of personal rights will disrupt the flow of sexual energy through your energy field and prevent you from sharing sexual energy with your partner through transcendent sex and relationships.

The Fourth Pair

The fourth chakra pair consists of the first and seventh chakras. Their partnership is based on the complementary roles they play regulating pressure in the human energy system. Like the circulatory system in the physical-material body, the organs of the human energy system function under pressure in a closed system. Pressure facilitates the movement of sexual energy through the chakras, auras, and meridians. Also, pressure maintains a healthy balance of polarity and gender throughout the entire energy system.

The first and seventh chakras also connect the chakras within your body with the chakras above and below it, which deal with issues of transcendence. Those within your body deal with physical and psychic survival. The first and seventh chakras integrate these seemingly unrelated human functions.

In the meditations that follow, you will enhance the function of the four chakra pairs. This will enhance the flow of sexual energy between each pair, coordinate their activities, and enhance their sexual potential.

Exercise: First-Pair Meditation

The First-Pair Meditation is designed to enhance the flow of sexual energy between your first and third chakras. It helps to coordinate their activities and to enhance their sexual potential. To begin, find a comfortable position, with your back straight. Then begin breathing yogically. Use the Standard Method Exercise to relax the muscles of your physical-material body. Then assert, *"It's my intent to become present in my authentic mind."* Once you're present, assert, *"It's my intent to activate my first chakra."* Take a moment to experience the vibration of your first chakra. Then assert, *"It's my intent to activate my third chakra."* Once both chakras are active, assert, *"It's my intent to turn my organs of perception inward on the levels of the first and third chakra."*

Take about fifteen minutes to enjoy the enhanced sexual potential of your first and third chakras. Then count from one to five. When you reach the number five, open your eyes. You will feel wide awake, perfectly relaxed, and better than you did before.

Exercise: Second-Pair Meditation

The Second-Pair Meditation is designed to enhance the sexual potential of your second and fifth chakras. To begin, find a comfortable position, with your back straight. Then begin to breathe yogically. Use the Standard Method Exercise to relax the muscles of your physical-material body. Then assert, *"It's my intent to become present in my authentic mind."* Continue by asserting, *"It's my intent to activate my second chakra."* Then assert, *"It's my intent to activate my fifth chakra."* Once both chakras are active, assert, *"It's my intent to turn my organs of perception inward on the levels of the second and fifth chakras."*

Take about fifteen minutes to enjoy the meditation. Then count from one to five. When you reach the number five, open your eyes. You will feel wide awake, perfectly relaxed, and better than you did before.

Exercise: Third-Pair Meditation

The Third-Pair Meditation is designed to enhance the sexual potential of your fourth and sixth chakras. To begin, find a comfortable position, with your back straight. Then begin to breath yogically. Use the Standard Method Exercise to relax the muscles of your physical-material body. Then assert, *"It's my intent to become present in my authentic mind."* Continue by asserting, *"It's my intent to activate my fourth chakra."* Then assert, *"It's my intent to activate my sixth chakra."* Once both chakras are active, assert, *"On the levels of my fourth and sixth chakras it's my intent to turn my organs of perception inward."* Take fifteen minutes to enjoy the meditation. Then count from one to five. When you reach the number five, open your eyes. You will feel wide awake, perfectly relaxed and better than you did before.

Exercise: Fourth-Pair Meditation

The Fourth-Pair Meditation is designed to enhance the sexual potential of the first and seventh chakras. To begin, find a comfortable position, with your back straight. Then begin to breath yogically. Use the Standard Method Exercise to relax the muscles of your physical-material body. Then assert, *"It's my intent to become present in my authentic mind."* Continue by asserting, *"It's my intent to activate my first chakra."* Then assert, *"It's my intent to activate my seventh chakra."* Once both chakras are active, assert, *"On the levels of my first and seventh chakras it's my intent to turn my organs of perception inward."* Take fifteen minutes to enjoy the meditation. After fifteen minutes count from one to five. When you reach the number five, open your eyes. You will feel wide awake, perfectly relaxed, and better than you did before.

Chapter 8

Your Energy Field Is a Love Machine

A mong Jewish mystics, the physical and subtle bodies, as well as the sheaths of partners who experience transcendent sex, "are regarded as altars or tabernacles ... sanctified by the presence of the Shekinah" (*Shekinah* is the indwelling of Universal Consciousness). That they are considered tabernacles implies that we should revere them. Reverence to what is true and powerful rewards us, and that reverence is reflected back into our lives. A simple story from ancient China illustrates this fundamental truth. There was once an area in southern China that had received no rain for many months. All the plants were withered, the ground was cracked, and in the intense heat of summer thousands of flies buzzed around everyone's eyes. The governor of the area heard of a Taoist sage who had a magical umbrella that would bring the rain. The governor asked the old sage to pray for rain. Immediately it rained and the entire earth rejoiced. The governor asked the old man what he had done. *"Nothing special,"* the old man answered. *"I simply fast on the first and fifteenth days of every month and worship deeply the gods of heaven and earth. When I go to the toilet, I place the umbrella over my head so that the sun and moon and stars above me will not be offended by what they would otherwise see."* All the people of the region then understood that by showing respect for what is above and below as well as for all that is in between, one's prayers will be heard and one's life will be blessed by divine energy.

This chapter is an exploration in revering and integrating what is below and what is above.

Given that so many long for transcendent sex and relationships today, it's noteworthy that centuries ago the ancients recognized that your physical body and your subtle bodies and sheaths were designed to do one thing perfectly—to be vehicles through which you can experience transcendent sex and relationships. This makes both your physical and non-physical bodies and sheaths part of a vast inter-dimensional love machine.

Unfortunately, even though you should be the beneficiary of everything the machine is capable of doing, you weren't given a user manual when you were born nor when you came of age. So you're probably unaware of all your physical and non-physical bodies and sheaths and of what they're capable of doing. In this chapter you will learn what your physical and non-physical bodies and sheaths can do, and how you can use them to get the most pleasure, love, intimacy, and joy out of your sexual relationship.

However, before we begin, you must recognize that as an inter-dimensional being, you have more than one physical body. You have a physical-material body composed of flesh and bone. This body must eat and drink to survive. It reproduces sexually and it ages as it evolves through time-space. In addition to your physical-material body, you have two subtle physical bodies, with sheaths that interpenetrate them. In addition, you have two etheric bodies, with sheaths that interpenetrate them as well.

Although your physical-material body receives the bulk of its nourishment from the air you breathe and the food you eat, your physical and etheric bodies and their respective sheaths are nourished by sexual energy radiating through your physical and etheric chakras.

Your upper physical body and its sheaths get the nourishment they need from your upper physical chakra, located in your head, whereas your lower physical body and its sheaths receive the nourishment they need from your lower physical chakra, located in your pelvis.

Your upper etheric body and its sheaths are nourished by your upper etheric chakra, on the left side of your abdomen. Your lower etheric body and its sheaths are nourished by the lower etheric chakra, on the right side of your abdomen.

In addition to your physical and etheric bodies and sheaths, you have subtle energy bodies and sheaths on the dimensions of spirit, intellect, and soul. They allow you to be present, to express yourself, and to engage in relationships.

The energy bodies and sheaths in the field of spirit have the highest frequency. The energy bodies and sheaths in the fields of intellect, soul, and on the etheric levels and physical levels, have progressively lower frequencies. All subtle bodies and sheaths, however, have a higher frequency than your physical-material body. There is a simple reason for that. Unlike your subtle non-physical bodies, your physical-material body is part of the field of Maya. The field of Maya contains your individual mind and ego as well as your physical-material body. Maya is the only field subject to change and that evolves through time-space.

Structure of Your Subtle Bodies and Sheaths

All your subtle bodies, including your etheric and your physical bodies, have the same size and shape as your physical-material body. Under normal conditions, your subtle bodies interpenetrate your physical-material body. This means they occupy (on their dimension) the same space as your physical-material body.

Although they have the same size and shape as your physical-material body, your subtle bodies are quite different in their anatomy. Instead of physical organs, your subtle bodies are composed of large internal cavities surrounded by porous surface boundaries designed to maintain their shape and structural integrity.

At the back of each subtle body—in your neck, about three finger widths below the back of the fifth chakra—is an organ that connects the body to the space it should normally occupy. This space is known as *personal body space*. Some esoteric schools call the connector "the silver cord." This silver cord, if necessary, can stretch like a rubber band if the body it's connected to has been pushed out of its normal position in personal body space. The silver cord has one purpose: to keep its body connected to personal body space.

Sheaths have a less precise structure and, unlike subtle bodies, they extend several finger widths beyond the surface of personal body space.

Sheaths are vehicles of expression and communication, and they extend themselves whenever you express yourself, communicate, radiate power, or have the intent to learn more about your external environment. Like energy bodies, sheaths are composed of inner cavities and surface boundaries that surround the cavity. Your sheaths are also connected to personal body space by a silver cord, which will stretch as far as necessary if a sheath is pushed out of its normal position.

Surrounding each of your subtle bodies and sheaths is an auric field. On each dimension, your subtle bodies, sheaths, and auras work together as one functional unit so that you can remain present and participate in transcendent sex and relationships.

Each auric field has two parts: an internal cavity, which is egg-shaped, and a surface boundary which surrounds it. The internal cavity serves as a reservoir of sexual energy that the body and sheath can draw on in times of need. The surface boundary is porous and is designed to maintain the aura's shape and structural integrity and also to allow toxins to exit. When your auras are functioning healthily, their surface boundaries will deflect external projections that could disrupt your ability to participate in transcendent sex and relationships.

Auric fields interpenetrate one another and extend your energy field beyond personal body space, from as little as half an inch (one centimeter) to as much as twenty-six feet (eight meters).

Function of Your Subtle Bodies

All energy bodies and sheaths are composed of energy with only universal qualities. This allows them to serve as vehicles through which you can experience transcendent sex and relationships. However, to serve in such a way, your subtle bodies and sheaths must be fully integrated in personal body space. Only when they are fully integrated will they be able to radiate orgasmic bliss, which emerges from Universal Consciousness, and provide the sexual energy you must have in order to experience and share pleasure, love, intimacy, and joy.

Unfortunately, stress, shock, and trauma caused by the penetration of external projections into your energy field, as well as attachment to personas, can prevent your subtle bodies and sheaths from remaining fully integrated. When they're not fully integrated, your energy field can become fragmented. And fragmentation—which is caused by the full or partial ejection of one or more energy bodies or energetic vehicles (sheaths and auras)—can prevent you from radiating sexual energy freely and from experiencing the benefits of a transformative relationship.

Fragmentation

Fragmentation can take place on any dimension, at any time, during any phase of your life, including the nine months between conception and birth.

Fragmentation is most commonly caused by the penetration of an external projection into your energy field. However, it can also be caused by personas, which usurp the functions of your authentic mind. When fragmentation takes place on one of the subtle physical or etheric dimensions, the flow of sexual energy will be disrupted, and your ability to enjoy or even experience physical sensations will be disrupted. This can lead to problems in sexual performance, including impotence or premature ejaculation in men and orgasmic dysfunction in women. The truth is that almost any type of aversion to normal sexual stimulation and pleasure can be traced back to fragmentation in a person's energy field on the subtle physical and/or etheric dimensions.

When the effects of fragmentation become too great a burden on the physical or etheric dimensions, a person may become angry, and lash out at loved ones in a vain effort to gain some control over oneself and the flow of their sexual energy in his or her physical and etheric bodies, sheaths, and auras. When verbal outbursts offer no relief, a person may become physically violent.

Violent outbursts can be externalized (assertive) or internalized (passive), or shift erratically between the two. When violent outbursts are passive, they can be played out ritualistically through sado-masochistic sexual activities. When they're assertive, they can become explosive and can be played out through sexual abuse and/or physical violence.

For those who internalize their anger, fragmentation can give rise to a host of addictive patterns and activities that can disrupt the flow of sexual energy. This in turn can disrupt the production of pleasure-producing compounds in the brain. The disruption of body chemistry can then lead to sexual addiction or physical dependency, particularly if the afflicted person is unable to reintegrate the physical or etheric body, sheath, or auric field that has become fragmented.

When attachment to a persona or the penetration of an external projection is temporary, the fragmentation will also be temporary. In this case, the fragmented body, sheath, or aura will return on its own and will be reintegrated. However, fragmentation will become a permanent condition if the external projection remains in a person's field, if a persona permanently usurps the functions of the body or energetic vehicle that has been ejected, or if one or more of the conditions cited below becomes permanent:

1. If the penetration of an external projection is part of a pattern that makes a person feel chronically insecure.

2. If the penetration of an external projection causes a fundamental breakdown in trust and/or disrupts a person's worldview to the extent that he or she begins to distrust his or her perceptions, gut feelings, and/or intuition.

3. If there is conscious intent behind the external projection and the perpetrator wants to permanently control, have, and/or change his or her victim.

4. If a person identifies with a persona and makes its goals, needs, and/or desires his or her own.

Fragmentation and its collateral effects have become common, especially among people who've been victims of violence and/or abuse, who have been in relationships with substance abusers, or with people who seek to control them, change them, or manipulate them. However, overcoming fragmentation is essential if a person hopes to experience transcendent sex and relationships.

Exercise: The Body Integration Mudra

Because your subtle bodies have a strong and enduring connection to your personal body space through their connector, they will be—even when they're ejected—drawn back to your energy field and will be reintegrated unless one of the conditions cited above has been met or the functions of the connector have been blocked by karmic baggage or external projections.

In order to help the connector to function properly—so that your energy bodies and energetic vehicles stay integrated in your energy field and those that have been ejected can be brought back and reintegrated—I've developed an exercise called the Body Integration Mudra. If you practice the Body Integration Mudra regularly, you will strengthen the bond between your energetic vehicles and their connectors. This will keep your vehicles integrated and help those that have been ejected to quickly find their way back home.

Begin the Body Integration Mudra by placing the tip of your tongue behind your upper teeth at the point where they meet the flesh. Next put the pads of your thumbs together so that they're touching from the tips to the first joint. Then place the outside of your remaining fingers together from the second joint to your knuckles. Keep your hands for ten minutes in this position, with your fingers comfortably apart, while you sit with your back straight and breathe yogically (see Figure 17).

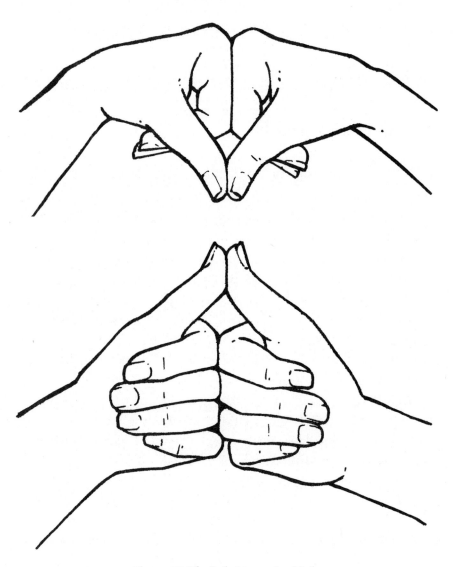

Figure 17: *The Body Integration Mudra*

The Truth About
Feelings and Sensations

Although all your subtle bodies, sheaths, and auras collectively make transcendent relationships possible, it's your subtle bodies, sheaths, and auras on the etheric and physical levels that make it possible for you to experience transcendent sex. They do that by connecting your energy field—and its bodies, sheaths, and auras—with your physical-material body.

By connecting your energy field to your physical-material body, your physical and etheric bodies, sheaths, and auras allow sexual energy emerging from your energy field to enhance your libido, stimulate your physical-material body, and intensify your sexual excitement.

When your physical and etheric bodies, sheaths, and auras are integrated properly, they also allow you to experience and share authentic feelings and sensations with your partner. They do this by allowing you to feel and express feelings and sensations emerging from your etheric and physical bodies, sheaths, and auras through your organs of expression in your physical-material-body: eyes, mouth, and facial musculature.

Though it may run counter to your personal experience, neither feelings nor sensations emerge directly from your physical-material body. Feelings emerge from your etheric bodies, sheaths, and auras. Sensations emerge through your physical bodies, sheaths, and auras.

Although emotions and feelings are often lumped together, feelings have a lower frequency than emotions. Because they vibrate at a lower frequency, feelings are less precise than emotions. In fact, many sexual disorders linked to emotional stress are caused by a disruption of sexual energy on the etheric levels, which means most sexual disorders are more closely related to blocked feelings than to blocked emotions.

It's also worth noting that intuitive insight—which you commonly experience as a gut feeling or vague perception of the truth—will emerge into your awareness on the etheric and physical levels. Unfortunately, if the buildup of karmic baggage is too great on either the etheric or physical dimensions, or if you are being influenced by external projections on these dimensions, it will become increasingly difficult for you to experience intuitive insight because your ability to experience your authentic feelings and sensations will be diminished. Because the condition of your energy field on the etheric and physical dimensions also influences your ability to experience transcendent sex, it's essential that you find a way to counteract the effect of karmic baggage and external projections on the etheric and physical dimensions.

To counteract their effect I've included exercises at the end of this chapter that will help you to reintegrate your etheric and physical bodies, sheaths, and auras if they're not already fully integrated.

Before you begin, it's worth noting that centuries ago yogic and tantric masters recognized that transcendence is a process of integration, which requires that you integrate the functions of your energy bodies, sheaths, and auras with those of your physical-material body.

Your Etheric and Physical Chakras

To reintegrate your etheric bodies, sheaths, and auras, you must first increase the amount of sexual energy that's available to them. You can do this by activating your etheric and physical chakras.

As you know, you have eleven chakras in personal body space: the seven traditional chakras in addition to two etheric and two physical chakras. Your upper etheric chakra is located by your spleen, which is on the left side of the abdomen, between your second and third chakras. The lower etheric chakra is located on the other side of your abdomen, directly across from it.

Your upper physical chakra is located in your head, just above and behind the back of your sixth chakra. The lower physical chakra is located in the middle of your pelvis, one inch (two centimeters) in front and below the back of your second chakra (see Figure 13).

Exercise: Activating Your Etheric Chakras

In the exercise that follows, you will activate your upper and lower etheric chakras and experience their unique resonance.

To begin, find a comfortable position with your back straight. Begin breathing yogically. Count from five to one, then from ten to one. Use the Standard Method Exercise to relax the muscles of your physical-material body. Then assert, *"It's my intent to activate and center myself in my heart chakra."* Once you're centered in your heart chakra, assert, *"It's my intent to activate my upper etheric chakra."* Take a few moments to experience the shift. Then assert, *"It's my intent to activate my lower etheric chakra."* Once both your etheric chakras have become active, assert, *"On the level of my two etheric chakras, it's my intent to turn my organs of perception inward."* Take fifteen minutes to enjoy the meditation. Then count from one to five. When you reach the number five, open your eyes. You will feel wide awake, perfectly relaxed, and better than you did before.

Exercise: Activating Your Physical Chakras

In this exercise you will activate your upper and lower physical chakras. To begin, find a comfortable position with your back straight. Begin breathing yogically. Count from five to one, then from ten to one. Use the Standard Method Exercise to relax the muscles of your physical-material body. Then assert, *"It's my intent to activate and center myself in my heart chakra."* Once you're centered in your heart chakra assert, *"It's my intent to activate my upper physical chakra."* Take a few moments to experience the shift. Then assert, *"It's my intent to activate my lower physical chakra."* Once both your physical chakras have become active, assert, *"On the level of my two physical chakras, it's my intent to turn my organs of perception inward."* Take fifteen minutes to enjoy the meditation. Then count from one to five. When you reach the number five, open your eyes. You will feel wide awake, perfectly relaxed, and better than you did before.

Prepare to Get Grounded

You've already learned a great deal about the importance of your etheric and physical bodies, sheaths, and auras. What you may not know is how important it is to activate and integrate the functions of your etheric and physical chakras with your etheric and physical bodies, sheaths, and auras.

When your etheric chakras are active and you've integrated their functions with your etheric bodies, sheaths, and auras, you will be able to empathize with your partner and you will be able to get grounded the right way.

Empathy can be defined as the ability to experience another person's feelings by experiencing the condition of his or her energy field. When your etheric chakras are active and they've been integrated with your etheric bodies, sheaths, and auras, you will be able to discern the condition of your partner's energy field and empathize with his or her condition. You will also be fortified against the judgment of the individual mind and ego, which condemn and/or disrupt normal human activities such as eating, working, trusting your intuition, and empathizing with another person.

When your physical chakras are active and they've been integrated with your physical bodies, sheaths, and auras, you will experience a wider spectrum of physical sensations and you will feel them with greater intensity, particularly sensations related to sexual pleasure. You will also be more creative, and the more creative you can be, the more you will be able to share with your partner through transcendent sex and relationships.

Your physical and etheric chakras, bodies, sheaths, and auras also share another important function: they work together to keep you grounded. By being grounded, you're able to maintain a healthy connection to the earth. When grounded, you will be able to share uninterrupted pleasure, love, intimacy, and joy with your partner on the etheric, physical, and physical-material dimensions.

People use various techniques to ground themselves, but unless your etheric and physical chakras have become active and you've integrated them with your bodies, sheaths, and auras on the physical and etheric levels, there will be no true grounding, and the foundation necessary for experiencing pleasure, love, intimacy, and joy through sex will not be properly laid.

You will learn to ground yourself in steps. In step one, you will activate your upper physical chakra. After you've activated your upper physical chakra, you will become present on the upper physical dimension. Then you will perform the Body Integration Mudra.

The integration process is a natural one. And if there isn't any resistance from karmic baggage or external projections, your upper physical body, sheaths, and auras will be reintegrated almost instantaneously.

If there is resistance, it will take more time. In either case, be patient, because once you've activated your upper physical chakra and performed the Body Integration Mudra, it's just a matter of time before your upper physical body, sheaths, and auras have been reintegrated into your energy field.

Once you've integrated your upper physical body, sheaths, and auras, you will repeat the same process with your lower physical chakra. Then you will repeat the same process with your upper and lower etheric chakras and their bodies, sheaths, and auras.

Exercise: Reintegrating a Subtle Vehicle

To begin the reintegration process on the upper physical dimension, find a comfortable position, with your back straight. Begin to breathe yogically. Count from five to one, then from ten to one. Use the Standard Method Exercise to relax the muscles of your physical-material body. Then assert, *"It's my intent to activate and to center myself in my heart chakra."* Once you're centered in your heart chakra, assert, *"It's my intent to activate my upper physical chakra."* Then assert, *"It's my intent to become present on the upper physical dimension."*

Take a few moments to experience the shift into the authentic mind. Then perform the Body Integration Mudra, which has been described earlier in this chapter (see Figure 17).

Take a few moments to follow the reintegration of your upper physical body, sheaths, and auras. However, be careful not to interfere with the process. When all the vehicles have been reintegrated, you will experience a feeling of completion that will be accompanied by a feeling of relief and/or satisfaction.

If there are no blockages, the body, sheaths, and auras will quickly reintegrate themselves. If there are blockages, the process of return will take longer. In some cases blockages in the form of karmic baggage and external projections will be strong enough to delay the process for some time. In that case, bring yourself out of the exercise and repeat it again daily for several days or until you're satisfied that all three vehicles have been reintegrated.

You will repeat the same process with your lower physical body, sheaths, and auras. Then you will repeat the process with your energetic vehicles on the upper etheric and lower etheric dimensions. When you have completed the process with all your physical and etheric vehicles you will be ready for getting grounded.

Exercise: Getting Grounded the Right Way

To get grounded the right way, you must first activate your physical and etheric chakras. Then you must become present in your energy field and turn your organs of perception inward on the levels of your physical and etheric bodies, sheaths, and auras. Once you're present, you will perform the Body Integration Mudra and hold it for ten minutes.

To begin, find a comfortable position, with your back straight. Breathe yogically. Count from five to one, then from ten to one. Use the Standard Method Exercise to relax the muscles of your physical-material body. Then assert, *"It's my intent to activate and center myself in my heart chakra."* Once you've activated and centered yourself in your heart chakra, assert, *"It's my intent to activate my upper etheric chakra."* After you've activated your upper etheric chakra assert, *"It's my intent to activate my lower etheric chakra."* Take a few moments to enjoy the shift. Then assert, *"It's my intent to activate my upper physical chakra."* Continue by asserting, *"It's my intent to activate my lower physical chakra."* Once all four chakras are active, assert, *"It's my intent to become present on my etheric and physical dimensions."*

To make sure that all your etheric and physical bodies, sheaths, and auras are perfectly integrated, you will perform the Body Integration

Mudra. Continue to perform the mudra while you assert, *"It's my intent to turn my organs of perception inward on the levels of my physical and etheric bodies, sheaths, and auras."* Once you've turned your organs of perception inward, you will be grounded the right way. With your etheric and physical chakras active, each sensation will seem richer and more real.

Continue to hold the mudra while you stay grounded for ten more minutes. Then release the mudra and count from one to five. When you reach the number five, open your eyes. You will feel wide awake, perfectly relaxed, and better than you did before.

Only after grounding yourself the right way will you realize how much you've lost. It's not just empathy and transcendent sex that are disrupted. Being ungrounded will disrupt clarity, dull your senses, and obscure the childlike joy that is your birthright.

The Importance of Touch, Taste, and Smell

You may not be aware of it, but your ability to sense the physical world through your organs of perception—sight, hearing, taste, smell, and touch—are regulated by the organs of your energy field, particularly your chakras. With that in mind, it comes as no surprise that by activating the appropriate energy centers you can enhance the function of your senses and then use them as tools to enhance your experience of transcendent sex.

Unfortunately, karmic baggage and external projections can dull your senses and can make you overly reactive to sensations that emerge from karmic baggage and external projections. Both karmic baggage and external projections are able to dull your senses by alienating you from your etheric, physical, and material environment.

In order to counteract the dulling of your senses, we can use the potential of the chakras in personal body space along with the corresponding chakras below personal body space to enhance your sense of touch, taste, smell, sight, and hearing, especially during sex.

Chakras Above
and Below Body Space

You already learned in chapter 7 that in addition to the eleven chakras within personal body space there are chakras above and below personal body space. The claim that there are chakras above and below personal body space is not entirely new. Some ancient texts refer to seven chakras below personal body space, which regulate the baser functions of human nature. Other texts refer to six more chakras above personal body space. Unfortunately, none of the ancient texts offer much detail concerning the chakras' structure and function.

More recent research indicates that the chakras above personal body space are located above the seventh chakra, beginning one and a half inches (four centimeters) above it. From that point they extend approximately eighteen feet (six meters) above the top of the head.

The chakras below personal body space begin their descent downward, just below your first chakra at the base of your spine. The first chakra below personal body space is located three inches (eight centimeters) below the perineum, and the remaining chakras extend downwards approximately eighteen feet (six meters; see Figure 18).

The structure of the chakras above and below personal body space is almost identical to the chakras within personal body space, except for their length. They are about 40 percent shorter.

It's the first six chakras below personal body space that we will look at now because, along with your chakras in personal body space, they have the most influence on your five senses.

Indeed, tantric texts are very clear that to make the transition to transcendent sex you and your partner must enjoy touching, tasting, smelling, hearing, and seeing one another. The best way to do that is by activating all the chakras that are responsible for regulating each of your five senses.

You've already activated your eleven chakras in personal body space and begun to wake up your senses by getting grounded the right way. In the following series of exercises you will wake up each of your five senses by activating the two chakras that regulate them. Then you will

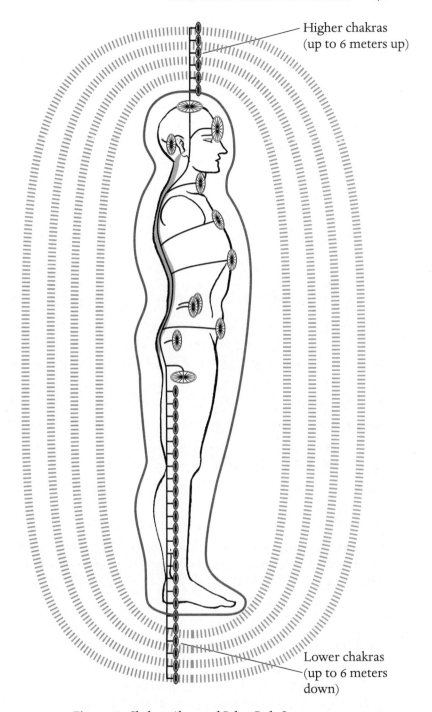

Higher chakras
(up to 6 meters up)

Lower chakras
(up to 6 meters
down)

Figure 18: *Chakras Above and Below Body Space*

become present on the dimension regulated by the two chakras you've activated.

You will wake up your sense of touch by activating your third chakra and your third chakra below body space and then becoming present on the dimensions regulated by those chakras. You will wake up your sense of smell and taste by activating your fifth chakra and fifth chakra below body space and becoming present on the dimensions regulated by those chakras. And you will wake up your senses of sight and hearing by activating your sixth chakra and sixth chakra below body space and becoming present on the dimensions regulated by those chakras. After you've awakened your five senses, you will use them to enhance your sexual pleasure, love, intimacy, and joy.

Exercise: Awakening Your Sense of Touch

To awaken your sense of touch, you will activate your third chakra and your third chakra below body space. Then you will become present on the two dimensions regulated by these chakras. The dimensions I'm referring to are the third dimension and the third dimension below body space. Once you are present, you will turn your organs of perception inward on these two dimensions.

To begin, find a comfortable position, with your back straight. Breathe yogically. Count from five to one, then from ten to one. Use the Standard Method Exercise to relax the muscles of your physical-material body. Then assert, *"It's my intent to activate and center myself in my heart chakra."* Once you're centered in your heart chakra, assert, *"It's my intent to activate my third chakra."* Once your third chakra has become active, assert, *"It's my intent to activate my third chakra below body space."* Take a minute or two to enjoy the shift. Then assert, *"It's my intent to become present on the levels of my third chakra and third chakra below body space."* Once you're present, assert, *"It's my intent to turn my organs of perception inward on the levels of my third chakra and third chakra below body space."*

Take fifteen minutes to enjoy the meditation. Then count from one to five. When you reach the number five, open your eyes. You will feel wide awake, perfectly relaxed, and you will experience the benefits that come from enhancing your sense of touch.

Exercise: Awakening Your Senses of Smell and Taste

Your senses of smell and taste are closely related. To awaken them both, you will activate your fifth chakra and your fifth chakra below body space. Then you will become present on the two dimensions regulated by the chakras of the fifth dimension and the fifth dimension below body space. Once you are present, you will turn your organs of perception inward on both dimensions.

To begin, find a comfortable position with your back straight. Breathe yogically. Count from five to one, and then from ten to one. Use the Standard Method Exercise to relax the muscles of your physical-material body. Then assert, *"It's my intent to activate and center myself in my heart chakra."* Continue by asserting, *"It's my intent to activate my fifth chakra."* Then assert, *"It's my intent to activate my fifth chakra below body space."* Take a minute or two to enjoy the shift. Then assert, *"It's my intent to become present on the levels of my fifth chakra and fifth chakra below body space."* Once you are present, assert, *"It's my intent to turn my organs of perception inward on the levels of my fifth chakra and fifth chakra below body space."*

Take fifteen minutes to enjoy the meditation. Then count from one to five. When you reach the number five, open your eyes. You will feel wide awake, perfectly relaxed, and will experience the benefits that come from enhancing your sense of smell and taste.

Exercise: Awakening Your Senses of Sight and Hearing

To awaken your senses of sight and hearing, you will activate your sixth chakra and your sixth chakra below body space. Then you will become present on the two dimensions regulated by these chakras: the sixth dimension and the sixth dimension below body space. Once you are present, you will turn your organs of perception inward on these two dimensions.

To begin, find a comfortable position, with your back straight. Breathe yogically. Count from five to one, and then from ten to one. Use the Standard Method Exercise to relax the muscles of your physical material body. Then assert, *"It's my intent to activate and center myself in my heart chakra."* Once you're centered in your heart chakra, assert, *"It's my intent to activate my sixth chakra."* Once your sixth chakra has become active, assert, *"It's my intent to activate my sixth chakra below body space."* Take a minute or two to enjoy the shift. Then assert, *"It's my intent to become present on the levels of my sixth chakra and sixth chakra below body space."* Once you are present, assert, *"It's my intent to turn my organs of perception inward on the levels of my sixth chakra and sixth chakra below body space."*

Take fifteen minutes to enjoy the meditation. Then count from one to five. When you reach the number five, open your eyes. You will feel wide awake, perfectly relaxed, and will experience the benefits that come from enhancing your sense of sight and hearing.

Chapter 9

The Problem of Past-Life Lovers

Remaining centered in the authentic mind and experiencing sustained intimacy and joy can be such a powerful tonic that it can keep partners from becoming reactive, even in the most extreme situations. The following story is from the Yoga Vasishtha, and it illustrates the powers partners will enjoy if they remain authentic.

Ahalya, the queen of an ancient kingdom, fell in love with a man named Indra. The King became very angry. He had them both cast into the cold water of a tank in mid-winter. However, neither Ahalya nor Indra showed the least sign of pain. They kept smiling together as if they were in blissful merriment. Next, the jealous King had them thrown into a large frying pan kept on fire. They remained unhurt and said, "O King! We rejoice at the delight of our souls in thinking of each other." They then were trampled down by elephants, but did not show the least symptom of pain. They simply smiled and laughed. The King was wonder-struck. He asked Indra and Ahalya, "How is it that you both do not experience any pain when you are tortured?" They gave the following reply: "O King! No torture can separate us from each other. We see our beloved in every shape and form. We are in the enjoyment of bliss. We do not experience any pain." The King realized the truth of their statements. In order that they might enjoy themselves freely, the King banished them from his kingdom to dwell forever in a foreign country.[4]

Although this parable lacks literary realism, it does illustrate two essential facts about energetic interactions. Partners can continue to experience pleasure, love, intimacy, and joy during periods of distress by engaging exclusively in authentic energetic interactions. And authentic energetic interactions are the foundation of transcendent sex and relationships.

Although energetic interactions between energy fields with universal qualities support transcendent sex and relationships, all interactions between human beings include an exchange of energy that has either universal or individual qualities. Energetic interactions between energy fields with universal qualities—such as those between Ahalya and Indra—enhance pleasure, love, intimacy, and/or joy, and promote transcendent sex and relationships. Energetic interactions between fields with individual qualities—such as those between the king and Ahalya—will disrupt transcendent sex and relationships by disrupting the flow of sexual energy between partners. That in turn will alienate partners from one another.

Energetic interactions between partners take place in all physical and non-physical fields of activity, including the fields of spirit, intellect, soul, and the etheric and physical fields. In each field you and your partner have energetic bodies, sheaths, and auras. All these permit you to be present, express yourselves, and interact with other living beings via energetic interactions.

This community of bodies, sheaths, and auras—as well as the energy system that supports it—is composed exclusively of energy with universal qualities (sexual energy). They emerged via the tattvas. And along with your organs of perception and expression, they create a structural and functional community known as the authentic mind.

In yoga and tantra, an energetic field is authentic if it remains the same "in the beginning, the middle, and the end," which means it doesn't evolve or change through time.

Once your authentic mind emerged, a second hierarchy of fields emerged, which has only the appearance of being authentic. This field is known as the field of Maya. The field of Maya cannot be authentic because it consists of a hierarchy of energetic fields with individual qualities, and unlike the authentic energy fields, they evolve through time. The field of Maya includes your individual mind and ego and your physical-material body.

Because human beings are interdimensional beings and exist and participate in relationships on all physical and non-physical dimensions, the vast majority of interactions between people are not physical interactions. Instead, they're energetic interactions. Therefore it comes as no surprise that partners must be centered in their authentic minds to engage in transcendent sex and relationships. Furthermore, their energetic interactions must be between authentic fields of energy with only universal qualities.

The Principle of Field Dominance

All energetic interactions—whether they're between energy fields with individual or universal qualities—are regulated by the Principle of Field Dominance. The Principle of Field Dominance teaches us that all fields of energy interact. Fields with a higher vibration will have a greater impact and/or effect than will fields with a lower vibration. In all field interactions, fields with a higher vibration dominate and/or displace fields with a lower vibration. For instance, the love between Ahalya and Indra was of such a high vibration that it was able to dominate the cold, heat, and pain they were subjected to while the king was torturing them.

If we apply the Principle of Field Dominance, we learn that when Universal Consciousness interacts directly with subordinate energy fields, it will dominate all energetic interactions. Indeed, yoga and tantra teach that subordinate energy fields have no influence over Universal Consciousness, whereas Universal Consciousness can influence, control, transmute, or release subordinate energy fields with either universal or individual qualities.

When subordinate fields of energy interact with each other, the Principle of Field Dominance dictates that energy fields with universal qualities will influence, dominate, control, transmute, or release energy fields with individual qualities, and that fields with a higher vibration will dominate fields with a lower vibration.

The Principle of Field Dominance explains how partners who interact through their authentic minds can overcome the influence of personas and external projections in order to experience transcendent sex and relationships.

Indeed, partners who remain centered in their authentic minds won't be dominated by individual qualities that emerge from personas and external projections. Such people will experience sustained intimacy and joy in their relationship. However, most couples do not remain centered in their authentic minds. Thus, their energetic reactions can take on lower qualities.

Energetic Interactions with Dead People

It's important to note that not all energetic interactions take place between people. Energetic interactions can take place between humans and animals, humans and non-physical beings, or even humans and independent fields of energy. In fact, you don't have to be in physical contact with another being for energetic interactions to take place. People can continue to interact energetically when one person thinks about another, has strong feelings about him or her, or has the desire to change, manipulate, or control the other. Energetic interaction can even continue between old friends and former partners after the relationship has "ended." In fact, you've lived many times and you can still be interacting energetically with people you knew in former lives. That means you can be participating in energetic interactions with past-life lovers, even if you don't have a relationship with them in this life.

Some people are so attached to the feelings of satisfaction, love, or sexual pleasure they experienced in a past life that they are actively searching for their past-life lover or yearning for a particular quality they miss or that excites them sexually.

For some people, it's a quality they can't get from their present partner. Their yearning can produce feelings of dissatisfaction and resentment. In some cases, energetic interactions with past-life lovers are so compelling that they can interfere with healthy energetic interactions and disrupt partners' abilities to share pleasure, love, intimacy, and joy with one another through transcendent sex and relationships.

Like many people, you may insist that there's no proof that energetic interactions can take place between people who are living and those who are dead. However, there's a great deal of anecdotal evidence to suggest that people incarnate more than once and that they can be influenced by past-life relationships. For instance, there's the yearning people have for a soulmate, someone they haven't met in this life but whose qualities they desperately seek. And there's even more compelling evidence than that. Some people remember their past lives and the people with whom they interacted. The following case illustrates what I mean:

> Titu was born in northern India. When he was about three, he began to talk about his former life. He told his family that he'd lived in the northern city of Agra and had been the owner of an electronics shop that sold TVs, radios, and videos. His former name, he told them, had been Suresh Verma. At the time of his death he'd been married to a woman named Uma, who had given birth to two children. He went on to explain that he'd died of a gunshot wound and had subsequently been cremated. At first he wasn't taken seriously. However, Titu's older brother was intrigued by the story and traveled to Agra to check his brother's account.
>
> To his surprise, he found a video shop called Suresh Radio, run by a widow named Uma, whose husband had been shot and subsequently cremated. After hearing about Titu and his claims, Uma decided to pay the young boy a visit. When she arrived, Titu recognized her immediately and asked her about their children. He went on to describe additional details about his life in Agra, which were corroborated by the Suresh family.[5]

Titu's story is an intriguing one. However, it's not unique. It's one of many you'll find if you consult the research on past lives. However, when it comes to intimate relationship, the important thing to remember is that you carry the legacy of your past lives and of your energetic interactions with your past-life lovers in your energy field—in the form of karmic baggage. That karmic baggage can still attach you to your past life lovers through cords, controlling waves, and attachment fields.

Cords, Controlling Waves, and Attachment Fields

As you learned in chapter 2, cords are projections of energy with individual qualities. Structurally, they closely resemble thin tubes that have a consistent diameter along their entire length.

A cord will remain active as long as the person who projected it holds on to the false impression that he or she needs or desires something, even if it's just contact from his or her target. Once the person abandons that idea, the cord will become dormant, and qualified energy will no longer flow through it. However, even if a cord has become functionally dormant, it will remain structurally intact and keep the target connected to the perpetrator, in some cases for lifetimes after the initial projection.

Even dormant cords can be disruptive. There is a simple explanation for this. Energy that has been projected through the cord can polarize the host's energy field, making it more feminine and receptive and therefore more reactive, particularly to energetic interactions between energy fields with individual qualities. Again, as you learned in chapter 2, controlling waves are projections of energy with individual qualities. When controlling waves emerge from a person's energy field, they will be wedged shaped, with the narrow end facing their target. Once the wave enters the target's energy field, it will quickly expand to fill a large portion of the field on the dimension on which it has been projected.

What you may not know is that if the desire, need, or intent of the perpetrator is strong enough, the controlling wave can push energy bodies or energetic authentic vehicles out of your energy field.

The perpetrator's motivation for projecting a controlling wave is usually complex. She or he may want to influence you, but may not know that the desire and/or need to change, control, manipulate, connect, belong to, or harm you is enough to cause a projection. In addition, the perpetrator may not be aware that a projection of qualified energy in the form of a thought, emotion, feeling, and/or desire can disrupt your energy field for years or even lifetimes.

The truth is that controlling waves can attach you to the perpetrator for years or even lifetimes, if their needs or desires remain unrequited. This means that a controlling wave can remain in your energy field lifetimes after your physical relationship with the perpetrator ended.

An attachment field is another type of external projection that can attach you to a past life lover for lifetimes. As you know, an attachment field normally has a long rectangular shape, and will be extremely dense and sticky. It's because of these qualities, particularly its density, that an attachment field can disrupt the flow of sexual energy through your energy field and make it difficult for you to engage in transcendent sex and relationships.

Because an attachment field acts like a computer virus, the perpetrator doesn't have to be conscious for it to remain intact. This explains why lifetimes after it was projected, an attachment field can still produce powerful sensations, feelings, emotions, and thoughts that can prevent you from remaining present in your energy field and from sharing pleasure, love, intimacy, and joy with your partner.

Past-Life Lovers

By now it should be clear that you carry the legacy of your past-life relationships in your energy field in the form of karmic baggage (cords, controlling waves, and attachment fields). This means that energetic interactions with past-life lovers—whether you're conscious of them or not—can be interfering with your ability to share pleasure, love, intimacy, and joy with your present partner.

It may help you to know that past-life lovers (who aren't presently incarnated) aren't permanently dead and gone. People are interdimensional beings. When they die, they don't just disappear along with the karmic baggage they've collected. People continue to exist and interact through their physical and non-physical bodies—and the karmic baggage they carry in their energy field—even when they're dead. That means you can be unconsciously in love with a dead lover or yearning for one of his or her qualities. Of course, if your lover is dead, you won't find him or her. Even if he or she is incarnated, the lover is probably the wrong age or living on the other side of the world. It's also possible that you may not want him or her anymore—even if you found him or her—because the two of you have evolved in different directions. In any case, remaining attached to a past-life lover and/or one of his or her qualities will cause problems in your present relationship.

Overcoming Past-Life Attachments

Fortunately, even if you don't remember your past-life lover, you can overcome your attachment to him or her, or one of his or her qualities, by severing the cord, controlling wave, or attachment field that connects you two together.

You may wonder how you can overcome your attachment to someone who's dead and whom you don't remember. It's possible, in fact, you don't even have to know his or her name or what your past-life lover looked like. You don't even have to know when or where you knew him or her or exactly what kind of relationship you had. All you have to do is to isolate the quality you've been yearning for or the quality that is disrupting your ability to experience pleasure, love, intimacy, or joy with your present partner. If you do that, you'll isolate the energy your past-life lover projected into your field. When you've isolated the energy, you can sever the energetic link that attaches you to him or her. If you center yourself in your authentic mind and use your intent, it won't be difficult to do.

I've included the following conversation with Karen, a long-time client of mine, to illustrate how simple the process can be. Karen had blushed in embarrassment when I had brought up the issue of past-life lovers:

> Karen said, *"I'm sure I have a lot of past-life lovers who are still hopelessly in love with me. But really, I don't think I can do what you suggest."*

"It won't be as difficult as you think," I replied. *"What you'll be looking for is a quality you've yearned for but haven't found in a man, a quality you believe will give you a deep feeling of satisfaction or contentment."*

"That's not hard. I've always yearned to be with a man who understands me. And I always felt I would recognize him when I looked into his eyes."

"Good, it sounds as if we have a past-life attachment we can work on. So, if you're ready, get comfortable and we'll begin."

Karen sighed. Then she leaned back in her seat and closed her eyes.

"You'll begin the same way we always do, by breathing yogically and counting backward from five to one, then from ten to one. Next you'll use the Standard Method Exercise to relax the muscles of your physical-material body. Then you'll center yourself in your authentic mind and turn your organs of perception inward. The rest will be simple; just follow my instructions."

Karen did, and after she'd activated and centered herself in her heart chakra she asserted, *"It's my intent to turn my organs of perception inward and observe the energy in my energy field that makes me yearn for understanding."* Almost immediately, she felt pressure on her solar plexus, at the point where her third chakra is located.

I asked Karen, *"Do you see something that looks like a cord emerging from your third chakra or from the area around your solar plexus?"*

"I found it," Karen said breathlessly.

"Good, just stay centered. Then use your organs of perception to observe its qualities."

After a short delay, Karen said, *"Okay, I'm doing that now. I think I can feel its qualities and even sense the person on the other end."*

"You're doing great. Get ready. You'll use your intent to sever the cord by asserting, 'It's my intent to sever the cord I'm observing and to release its source and extensions.'"

After following my instructions, Karen felt an immediate shift in her energy field. The pressure on her solar plexus diminished, and she felt more centered in her authentic mind. Softer feelings began to emerge, and Karen felt a renewed sense of well-being.

"Take a moment to enjoy the shift," I added. *"Then count from one to five, and open your eyes."*

When Karen opened her eyes, she smiled brightly. *"So, what do you think? Did I sever the cord?"*

"Absolutely! You released the cord and the attachment."

"Something has definitely changed. I feel less driven and more my-self."

I couldn't help but smile. *"You'll be integrating the changes for the next few hours, so don't be concerned if you feel a little disoriented. Just remember, the cord has been cut, and now you'll be able to share more pleasure, love, intimacy, and joy with your current partner."*

Exercise: Severing a Past-Life Connection

Four steps are required to sever your attachment to a past-life lover. In step one, you will choose a feeling you yearn for or a blockage that consistently interferes with your ability to share pleasure, love, intimacy, and joy with your partner. Once you've made your choice, you must determine whether the feeling you yearn for or the blockage you've chosen to work with connects you to a past-life lover.

To determine that, find a comfortable position, with your back straight. Begin to breathe yogically. Count from five to one, and then from ten to one. Use the Standard Method Exercise to relax the muscles of your physical material body. Then assert, *"It's my intent to activate and center myself in my heart chakra."* Once you've activated and centered yourself in your heart chakra, assert, *"The blockage [yearning/feeling] I have in mind attaches me to someone I knew in a past life."* If the statement is true, it will resonate, and you will become present and experience an enhanced flow of sexual energy through your energy field.

Assuming the statement resonates, you can continue the process by asserting, *"It's my intent to become present on the dimension where the attachment is located."* Once you're present on the appropriate dimension, take a moment to observe the attachment. If it's a cord, it will be long, thin, and taut. It will extend outward from your energy field in the direction of the perpetrator. If it is a controlling wave, it will look like a cloud of energy, with well-defined edges, that fills at least part of your energy field and extends outward in the direction of the perpetrator. If it's an attachment field, it will be long and rectangular and extend outward from your field in the direction of the perpetrator. It will also be sticky, so it will be important to remain detached by remaining present in your authentic mind while you observe it.

After you've examined the projection and you've determined whether it's a cord, controlling wave, or attachment field, assert, *"It's my intent to sever the cord [controlling wave/attachment field] I'm observing and to release it and its source and extensions."*

If you can't determine whether the attachment is caused by a cord, controlling wave, or attachment field, you can still release it by asserting, *"It's my intent to sever the external projection I have in mind and its source and extensions."*

As soon as the cord, controlling wave, or attachment field has been released, you will feel a shift in your energy field. Pressure will diminish, sexual energy will flow more freely, and you will be able to remain present in your authentic mind more easily. Like Karen, you may also experience a renewed sense of well-being and softer feelings emerging from your energy field.

Once you've released the attachment, take ten minutes to enjoy the effects. Then count from one to five, and open your eyes. You will feel wide awake, perfectly relaxed, and better than you did before.

You can use the technique you just learned to release cords, controlling waves, and attachment fields on all physical and non-physical dimensions. It doesn't matter how long the cord, controlling wave, or attachment field has been in your field or even why it was projected at you.

Exercise: Ending Relationships the Right Way

It's not only an attachment to a past-life lover that can interfere with your ability to share pleasure, love, intimacy, and joy with your current partner. Your attachment to former lovers from this lifetime as well can disrupt your ability to share pleasure, love, intimacy, and joy.

Just because you've ended a relationship doesn't mean that all energetic interactions have ended and all attachments have been released. To be over, a relationship must be over on all physical and non-physical dimensions. That means a relationship isn't over until you've permanently revoked a lover's permission to engage in energetic interactions with you and you've released all energetic attachments that connect you to him or her.

If your former lover remains interested in you after your relationship has ended, energetic interactions can persist. The energy of your ex-lover can continue to affect or even interfere with your ability to share pleasure, love, intimacy, and joy. It doesn't matter if you change the nature of the relationship, even if you make your former lover a friend, business partner, or associate, the old energetic relationship will persist as long as the permission to interact with your energy field hasn't been revoked.

This means that you can remain attached to a former lover via cords, controlling waves, and/or attachment fields, even after love and intimacy have ended on your part. In fact, energetic interactions can keep you and a former lover connected indefinitely unless you revoke his or her permission to interact with you energetically. To do that, you must end the relationship the right way.

To revoke a former lover's permission to engage in energetic interactions with you, even when they're unconscious of them, you must make it clear that the original relationship is permanently over on all physical and non-physical dimensions and that there is no hope of renewing it in the future. This may seem harsh, but in the end it is far more compassionate than doing nothing, because revoking the permission will allow you and your former lover to let go and move on without energetic attachments blocking the way.

The simplest way to end a relationship the right way, so that it's over on all physical and non-physical dimensions, is to speak with your former lover. If that's not possible, then you can write him or her a short note or an e-mail.

I've included a sample note below that can be used as a blueprint to permanently end a relationship with a former lover who continues to interfere with your energy field and your relationships.

Tom [or fill in the appropriate name],

   After experiencing the blockages your projections and attachments have caused me, it's clear to me that it's not appropriate for me to participate in energetic interactions with you or to have any type of relationship with you now, or any time in the future. This is a permanent decision.

   Good bye,

   [fill in your name]

The blueprint note I've included is short, however, it includes everything necessary to permanently end a relationship with a former lover who interferes with your ability to radiate sexual energy freely and to experience transcendent sex and relationships. A word of caution: If you use the note to soothe your former lover's injured feelings, it may encourage him or her to interact with you energetically even more than before. Or, worse, it may give him or her the false hope that you still care. In either case, if your note offers your former lover hope instead of dashing it, he or she will probably continue to project at you.

Once the note has been delivered and your former lover has read it, you may experience his or her projections for a short time. However, after a few days you will feel a renewed sense of freedom and well-being, as well as an enhanced ability to share pleasure, love, intimacy, and joy with your current partner.

Some of you may object to ending a relationship abruptly—even if it has negative aspects—in the mistaken belief that forgiving your former lover will put an end to his or her projections. It will not. There is a major problem with forgiveness, and that is blame. You can only forgive someone you blame. If you forgive someone you blame, then forgiveness becomes a device to shift responsibility.

Shifting responsibility is always a bad idea because it will make it difficult for you to learn why you became involved in a relationship that restricted your ability to share pleasure, love, intimacy, and joy freely.

Without that knowledge, you will remain trapped in the blame game, and you will continue to lose power and will remain reactive to your former lover's projections. It's far better for you and your current relationship (and even for your former lover) to end the unhealthy attachment and stop the blame game by working through the karmic baggage and/or external projections that support it.

Exercise: Strengthening Your Boundaries

Severing unhealthy links to past-life lovers and to former lovers in this life can greatly enhance your well-being and your ability to share pleasure, love, intimacy, and joy with your current partner. However, there is an additional step you can take that will protect your energy field against external projections regardless of the source. You can strengthen the surface of the boundaries that surround your auric fields.

As you know, there is an auric field that surrounds your energy field on every physical and non-physical dimension. Structurally, your auric fields are composed of large internal cavities that serve as reservoirs of sexual energy. Surrounding the internal cavity is a surface boundary designed to separate your internal environment from the external environment. The surfaces of the auras are composed of sexual energy in the form of elastic fibers that criss-cross each other in every imaginable direction. This makes the surface of your auras flexible, porous, and remarkably strong.

Unfortunately, even though they're remarkably strong and they can deflect external projections, some of your auric surfaces have probably been weakened by the introduction of non-physical beings into your energy field. These beings feed on the sexual energy that emerges from your chakras and your minor energy centers.

There are hosts of creatures on the physical and non-physical dimensions that will feed on your sexual energy if they get the chance. However, all those creatures have one thing in common: their ability to disrupt the flow of sexual energy through your energy field if they are actively or passively permitted to intrude into it.

You're probably unaware of it, but many of the activities that introduce non-physical beings into the human energy field have been part of human culture since the birth of our species. I'm referring to activities such as channeling and invoking spirit guides and angels. These practices and others like them have a long tradition and were embraced by our ancestors for thousands of years through the worldwide practice of shamanism.

Shamanism was a worldwide tradition that lasted for millennia. Because you've lived many times, you must have participated in its practices in at least one or more of your past lives. That means you propitiated non-physical beings or took on their qualities by worshiping nature-spirits, elementals, power-animals, and so on. Activities such as these gave non-physical beings permission to enter your energy field. There, they became integrated into the karmic baggage you had already accumulated. That explains why the greatest density of karmic baggage in your energy field can be found around the sources of sexual energy, in your energy field, particularly around your chakras and the minor energy centers in your hands and feet and scattered throughout your energy field.

Once these non-physical beings were integrated into your karmic baggage, they added their will, finite awareness, emotions, feelings, sensations, and subtle matter to the karmic baggage you'd already collected. Of course, all this together makes it increasingly difficult for you to engage in transcendent sex and relationships.

The question you have to answer now is whether you're ready to take back control of your energy field or not. If you are, you can permanently revoke the permission you once consciously or unconsciously gave to these beings that allowed them to be inside of your energy field and to participate in your relationships. The most effective way to do that is to make three commitments to yourself, which are listed below. As soon as you make these three commitments and revoke your permission, you will strengthen your auric boundaries and liberate the sexual energy that has been blocked by these beings for lifetimes.

First commitment: *"If I have given permission or inadvertently given permission for any non-physical beings or any fields with individual qualities* to be in any of my authentic fields, anywhere, at any time, I revoke that permission now and permanently in the future."

Second commitment: "It's my desire and my will that all non-physical beings and all fields with individual qualities depart from all my authentic fields now and remain permanently outside of them in the future. I want you to leave now."

Third commitment: "All my authentic fields, everywhere at all times are my sacred space. It's my desire and my will that they are occupied solely by myself now and permanently in the future."

If you know it's appropriate for you to make the commitments and you know you'll keep them permanently, then simply read them out loud and then affirm, in a normal voice, "I agree to these three commitments."

By making these three commitments, you will strengthen your auric boundaries and liberate your sexual energy. That will make you less reactive to external projections and make it easier for you to stay centered in your authentic mind.

After you've made the three commitments, it's not unusual for layers of karmic baggage to be dislodged and pushed away from your energy field. Don't interfere with the process by concentrating on it. The process will last five or ten minutes. However, when it's over, you will have strengthened your boundaries, your energy field will have achieved a healthier balance, and you will be prepared to take the next step in the process of transcendence.

Chapter 10

Gender Is in Everything

During World War II, many U.S. troops were stationed on various islands in the South Pacific. However, probably the luckiest found themselves assigned to Bora Bora, in French Polynesia. These troops never saw any action, except from the local Tahitian girls. It seems that whenever a new contingent of troops arrived, the girls from the local village would greet them during their first South Sea evening, welcoming them with a dance performance. This turned out to be quite a problem for the U.S. commander, because the men would run off with these beauties into the tropical night for sexual activities.

So, the next time a contingent of new troops arrived, the commanding officer devised a new plan. As usual, the beautiful tropical evening arrived, and then dancing beauties from the local village. The troops became instantly infatuated. Troops and dancers intermingled. Rendezvous were planned. And then soldiers disappeared off into the jungle or off to one of the lovely beaches with one of the beauties. They next day, however, all the natives on the island were laughing. It seems that the dancers who had come for the previous evening's entertainment were a kind of third gender known as *mahu*, Tahitian men who cross-dress as women. The commanding officer had succeeded in sowing great seeds of gender confusion and suspicion among the troops.

Today, of course, not only have gender norms been changed by the feminist and men's movements, but also by lesbians, gay men, drag performers, as well as trans- and inter-sexed persons. In this chapter, we will examine the issues of gender and gender orientation and how they affect your ability to experience transcendent sex and relationships.

The Principle of Gender states that gender is in everything; everything has its masculine and feminine principles; gender manifests on all planes. The Principle of Gender determines your gender and your gender orientation. The sexual tension created by gender and gender orientation determines how much attraction you and your partner will experience for one another and what you must do to satisfy each other sexually.

For the vast majority of people, gender is a clear-cut issue. You're born either as a man or a woman, and you're attracted to the opposite sex. However, the issue of gender orientation can be much more complicated. Maleness and femaleness—gender orientation—will not be the same for everyone. Some men will be more masculine than other men. Some women will be more feminine than other women. Gender orientation is determined by the interaction of male and female, by the Yin and Yang forces in each person's energy field.

The more extreme a person's gender orientation is, the more extreme is the solution he or she must find in order to achieve balance and sexual satisfaction. An inordinately masculine person will seek an inordinately feminine person who is often an extremely receptive partner to balance his gender orientation and achieve sexual satisfaction. An inordinately feminine person will seek an inordinately masculine person who is often an extremely assertive partner, to balance her gender orientation and achieve sexual satisfaction.

Gender orientation remains a lifelong issue for most people. In fact, it's only when a person has transcended the individual mind and ego and can remain centered in his or her authentic mind that he or she will find a permanent solution to the problem created by his or her gender orientation.

Gender and gender orientation are of special importance to us because on the physical-material plane, gender and gender orientation play a direct role in the way people express themselves sexually. Sexuality on the grossest level is the principle that causes male and female to unite for the purpose of procreation.

In the East, gender is represented by the Yin and Yang symbol. The symbol represents the polar relationship between masculine (Yang) and feminine (Yin) energies, which are inherent in everything. A person's gender orientation will be determined by the particular balance of the Yin and Yang forces in his or her energy field.

Yin and Yang

The Taoists tell us that before the manifest universe came into existence there was nothingness. Within the nothingness was *Ching Shing Li*: cosmic energy (also known as chi). At that moment of conception, this cosmic force split into two halves, which came to be known by the Chinese as Yin and Yang. Nothing, however, is completely Yin or Yang, and no one is completely masculine or feminine. Everyone has elements of both. Indeed, the balance in the universe and in your energy field is the product of the relationship of opposites.

Human sexuality cannot be understood outside the concept of Yin Yang, and your sexual activities cannot be considered as events separate from the other events in the phenomenal universe. Because events are really points of energetic interactions between energy fields with different concentrations of Yin and Yang, sexuality is a mirror of cosmic relationships.

In Plato's *Symposium*, the god Hephaestus poses a simple question to two lovers: "What do you people want of one another?" This question goes to the core of what we all intuitively sense about gender and the issue of gender orientation. When the lovers cannot formulate a response, Hephaestus responds, *"Is it not perhaps this for which you long, a perfect mutual fusion so that you will never be sundered from each other by day or night? If this is what you wish, I am ready to melt you and weld you together with fire into one and the same individual so as to reduce you to one single being instead of the two which you were beforehand; in this way you may live united to each other for the whole of your lives."*

Alice Bailey echoed this passage two millennia later by writing, *"It must be remembered that this separation fosters a powerful impulse toward fusion, and this urge to blend we call sex. Sex is, in reality, the instinct toward unity—first of all, a physical unity. It is the innate (though much misunderstood) principle of mysticism, which is the name we give to the urge to unite with the divine."*

Gender creates the appearance of separation. However, the sexual excitement sparked by gender orientation creates a strong desire to unite and transcend separation by experiencing intimacy with another person and with Universal Consciousness.

Unfortunately, the buildup of karmic baggage and your attachment to personas and external projections can confuse your gender orientation, by disrupting the flow of sexual energy between your etheric and physical bodies and your physical-material body. The result of this is that you feel more or less masculine or more or less feminine than you normally would if your sexual energy flowed more freely.

To restore your normal gender orientation, you must enhance the flow of sexual energy between your etheric, physical, and physical-material bodies. Once you've restored the flow of sexual energy to healthy levels in these fields and your gender orientation has returned to its natural state, you and your partner will be one step closer to achieving balance. In addition, you will be one step closer to finding a permanent solution to the issue of gender orientation. The permanent solution I'm referring to, of course, is sustained intimacy and joy, which you can experience only after you've experienced transcendent sex and relationships.

Enhancing the Flow

The normal flow of sexual energy is upwards through the Governor meridian, from the first to seventh chakra and above, and downwards through the Conceptual meridian, from the crown chakra to the first chakra and below. As sexual energy radiates through your energy field, some of it will be transmuted by your etheric and physical chakras for the use of your etheric and physical bodies. Excess sexual energy not needed by your etheric and physical bodies will be transmuted into the full spectrum of energy necessary to maintain the health and well-being of your physical-material body.

Unfortunately, the disruption of sexual energy flowing into your physical-material body is a common problem. It's one of the leading causes of sexual dysfunction in society today.

Sexual dysfunction normally begins to manifest at puberty and is found more often in women than men because society puts more restrictions on a woman's sexual freedom and her flow of sexual energy. Many women, out of fear, confusion, or because they don't want to attract the wrong kind of attention, restrict the flow of sexual energy into their physical-material body.

Unfortunately, when a woman restricts the flow of sexual energy into her physical-material body, she will restrict the very energy she needs to experience sexual excitement and sexual satisfaction. She will also diminish her vitality, creativity, and femininity. That will make it difficult for her to attract the kind of partner who would balance her natural gender orientation.

Men often disrupt the flow of sexual energy into their physical-material body by indulging in sex and using it like a drug. Rather than simply restricting the flow of sexual energy, this will distort it. That will make it difficult for a man to attract the kind of partner who would balance his natural gender orientation. When a man distorts the flow of sexual energy that enters his physical-material body, he can become more sexually aggressive and less responsive and/or sensitive to his partner and to the forces of polarity and gender that would normally compel him to seek gender balance and transcendence.

The Quest for More Desire (Sexual Energy)

The yearning to achieve balance and to solve the problem of gender orientation is related to Kama. In Hindu cosmology, Kama represents the god of lust and sexual passion. Kama is sent to awaken Shiva's lust for his future wife, Parvati (Shakti). To arouse Shiva, Kama uses sounds, scents, and intoxicating objects, as well as the sexual tension created by gender orientation.

In your energy field, Kama may emerge as a desire for more sexual energy, to be sexier, or to balance your gender orientation by uniting with your partner. In its impure form, when Kama has been contaminated by inauthentic desires emerging from personas and external projections, it can manifest as the desire for sex of any kind.

However, Kama is too powerful and to important for transcendent sex and relationships to be ignored because Kama motivates people to enhance the flow of sexual energy through their physical-material body, experience sexual excitement, and achieve gender balance. Indeed, studies done at universities suggest that Kama and the need to balance gender orientation are inherent in people and their energy fields, and that the sexual activities that balance gender orientation are the most intense way Kama can be expressed by partners in relationships.

Researchers have also gathered considerable evidence that suggests that in order to achieve orgasm, partners must remain stimulated long enough for sexual energy to be transmuted into frequencies that can be used by the physical-material body.

Indeed, the need to enhance the flow of sexual energy through your physical-material body and to restore your gender orientation to its natural state to satisfy Kama is so important that I've included a series of physical exercises and mudras that will enhance the flow of sexual energy between your etheric and physical bodies and your physical-material body. With more sexual energy flowing into your physical-material body, you will experience more sexual excitement, balance your gender orientation, and get ready for the next step in transcendent sex and relationships.

Sweet Surrender

The exercises that follow form a six-day program that can be done prior to an evening of lovemaking. You should do the exercises in a comfortable environment, and you can accompany them all with music to enhance your enjoyment.

Exercise: Creating Flexibility

To create flexibility in your physical-material body and increase the flow of sexual energy between your etheric, physical, and physical-material body, you will first activate and center yourself in your heart chakra. Then you will become present in your authentic mind. Once you're present, you will fill your joints with sexual energy by bringing your attention to them, and, on each exhalation, breathing sexual energy into them. By exhaling into your joints and by replacing qualified energy with sexual energy, at least temporarily, you will begin to reestablish your normal gender orientation.

To begin the Creating Flexibility Exercise, lie down on your back. Then close your eyes and begin to breathe yogically. Once you're relaxed, count from five to one, and then from ten to one. Use the Standard Method Exercise to relax the muscles of your physical-material body. Then assert, *"It's my intent to activate and center myself in my heart chakra."* Once you're centered in your heart chakra, assert, *"It's my intent to become present in my authentic mind."* Once you're present, focus your attention on the vertebrae that connect your neck to your head. Then fill your neck, throat, and shoulders with sexual energy by exhaling through your nose, on each breath, into this area.

Continue to breathe into the vertebrae for two or three minutes while you remind yourself to let go of any inauthentic desire or emotions that have restricted the free flow of sexual energy through your neck, throat, and shoulders. After you've filled the area with sexual energy, you'll be able to turn your neck and head more freely.

Next, bring your attention and breath to your shoulders and the bones, tendons, and muscles that connect them to your arms. Breathe into each shoulder joint for two or three minutes while you remind yourself to let go of any inauthentic desire or emotions that have restricted the free flow of sexual energy through them. When you're finished, shake your shoulders loose and let go of any residual heaviness. Repeat the process with your right and left elbows.

The rib cage is an important area of your body. You will bring sexual energy into your rib cage by exhaling into it on each breath. Continue for two or three minutes while you remind yourself to let go of any inauthentic desire or emotions that have restricted the free flow of sexual energy through it.

To continue, bring your mental attention to your hips and abdomen. Place one hand on your lower abdomen and the other opposite it, and begin to move your hips. With your hands in this position, you will experience the forward, backward, right, and left movements of your hips and pelvis. Then bring sexual energy into your hips by exhaling into them on each breath. Continue for two or three minutes while you remind yourself to let go of any inauthentic desire or emotions that have restricted the free flow of sexual energy through them.

Next bring your mental attention to your knees. Try different ways to move them. Bring sexual energy into your left knee by exhaling into it for two or three minutes while you remind yourself to let go of any inauthentic desires or emotions that have restricted the free flow of sexual energy through it. Repeat the same process with your right knee. Continue in the same way with your ankles, feet, toes, arms, wrists, hands, and fingers.

Then bring your mental attention to your spine. Make snake-like movements by undulating it from top to bottom. Then bring sexual energy into your spine by exhaling into the vertebrae. Begin at your coccyx and move upward. Continue for two or three minutes while you remind yourself to let go of any inauthentic desires or emotions that have restricted the free movement of sexual energy through it. By the time you're done, you'll feel the enhanced flow of sexual energy radiating up your spine from the first through seventh chakras. For two or three minutes, follow the movement of sexual energy with your mental attention.

After you've isolated your joints and filled them with sexual energy, begin to put your body parts together. Begin by bringing your mental attention to your toes and feet. Then add your ankles and your knees. From your knees add your hips and so on until you can feel the enhanced flow of sexual energy radiating through your entire body.

Continue to enjoy the enhanced flow of sexual energy for five minutes. Then count from one to five. When you reach the number five, open your eyes. You'll feel wide awake, perfectly relaxed, and better than you did before.

Exercise: The Pelvic Thrust
(to be accompanied by rhythmic music)

In the Pelvic Thrust Exercise, you will look at the parts of your belief system that restrict the flow of sexual energy through your physical-material body, particularly through your pelvis.

To begin the Pelvic Thrust Exercise, listen to the music while standing in a relaxed position with your knees slightly bent. Then bring your arms up over your head and start moving your pelvis to the rhythm of the music. Bring your attention to the area around your pelvis. Pay attention to how your pelvis can be pushed forward and up and then tilted back. It's helpful to put your hands on the front and back of your pelvis to feel how it moves.

Accompany the thrusting movements with sounds. Be sure that the sounds you make reflect authentic desires and emotions and that they resonate through your physical-material body—particularly your pelvis. If you synchronize the sounds you make with your authentic desires and emotions, you will become present in your authentic mind, old attachments will become weaker, and you will be able to enjoy the enhanced flow of sexual energy through your pelvis.

Continue to move your pelvis and to make the appropriate sounds for five minutes. By performing the Pelvic Thrust Exercise, your physical-material body will relax, and more sexual energy will radiate through your pelvis. After you've completed the exercise, lie down on your back with your eyes closed for five minutes and pay attention to how you feel mentally, emotionally, and physically. Then count from one to five. When you reach the number five, open your eyes. You will feel wide awake, perfectly relaxed, and better than you did before.

Exercise: The Running Cat
(accompanied by rhythmic music)

Begin the Running Cat Exercise on your hands and knees. Once you're in position, begin to breathe yogically. Then arch your spine upward (like an angry cat), tuck your chin into your chest, and push your pelvis forward. On your next exhalation, stick your tongue out as far as you can and arch your spine downward. Then tilt your pelvis back and bring your head up as far as you can without straining. Execute the entire movement slowly at first.

Now quicken the pace. Let the movements become as fast as possible and continue them as long as you can without straining. Then gradually slow down the pace until you finally stop. After you stop, lie down on your stomach with your arms at your sides, for about five minutes. Breathe yogically again while you pay attention to the changes you experience mentally, emotionally, and physically.

The Running Cat Exercise will help you to release blockages that restrict the flow of sexual energy through your physical-material body, particularly your solar plexus. By releasing blockages in your physical-material body, you will enhance the flow of sexual energy through it. That, in turn, will make it easier for you to experience your natural gender orientation.

Exercise: The Snake Push

To begin the Snake Push Exercise, lie down on your back with your knees up and your feet as close to your buttocks as possible. Your feet should be flat on the floor and your arms at your sides. Begin to breathe yogically. Then slowly push your pelvis up and lift your spine off the floor, vertebrae by vertebrae. As you lift your pelvis, you will feel the muscles of your thighs and lower abdomen stretch and become more elastic. Make sure the rest of your body is completely relaxed as you stretch the muscles of your legs and abdomen.

When you finish the movement, all your weight will be supported by your feet and shoulders, and your back will be fully arched. If possible, hold the pose for at least thirty seconds. Then release the pose very slowly by rolling your spine back onto the floor, beginning with your neck and moving downward.

Repeat this exercise three times. Then lie on your back with your arms at your sides for five minutes and pay attention to how you feel physically, emotionally, and mentally.

The Snake Push Exercise is designed to strengthen the muscles of your abdomen and lower back, and to enhance the flow of sexual energy between your physical and physical-material bodies. That, in turn, will make it much easier for you to accept your natural gender orientation.

Exercise: Yes Mudra: To begin the Yes Mudra, lie on your back, legs together with knees bent and feet on the floor, as close to your buttocks as possible. Your arms should be at your sides with your palms up. Inhale deeply through your nose and, while you exhale, loudly say, "Yes." Continue to silently repeat "Yes" to yourself, then slowly let your legs fall apart.

Put the soles of your feet together after your legs are on the floor. Then bring the tip of your tongue to the point where your upper teeth meet the gum. Continue by bringing your legs up slowly until your knees are back together and your feet are flat on the floor. Keep your tongue in the same position. Then bring the tips of your thumbs to the insides of your middle fingers, by the first joint (see Figure 19).

Relax in this position for five minutes while you enjoy the changes you experience physically, emotionally, and mentally. Then release the mudra, and count from one to five. When you reach the number five, open your eyes. You will feel wide awake, perfectly relaxed, and better than you did before.

Exercise: Becoming Honest

The goal of this exercise is to bring you to the point where you can honestly share your gender orientation and sexual identity with your partner. To begin the Becoming Honest Exercise, take some time to lie down and to relax. While you are relaxing, ask yourself these questions: "Am I experiencing my natural gender orientation?" "Am I expressing my sexual identity honestly with my partner?" These questions (and the answers to them) are important because your ability to be honest about your gender orientation and your sexual identity will determine whether you can be sexually open and honest with your partner. Without this basic trust in yourself (and your partner) as a foundation, all

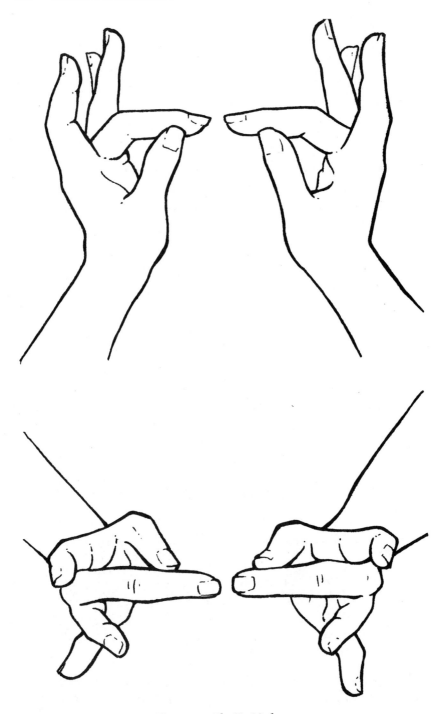

Figure 19: *The Yes Mudra*

your sexual communication, verbal and nonverbal, will be tainted with ideas, attitudes, emotions, and feelings that emerge from your individual mind and ego. That will disrupt your ability to share universal qualities freely with your partner.

This doesn't mean you should immediately dump on your partner everything you've been storing up. The point of this exercise is to be honest with yourself so that you can experience your natural gender orientation and sexual identity and then share them with your partner.

You can express yourself by writing a letter (which is never mailed). Another effective way is to imagine your partner sitting in front of you. When you get a mental picture of him or her, you can express the feelings you have about your natural gender orientation and sexual identity.

This is an exercise you do on your own; it's not a partner exercise. When it comes to sharing the truth about your gender orientation and sexual identity, remember the importance of timing. To sum up Ecclesiastes 3:1: "There's a time for everything under the sun." When it comes to your sexuality, there is an appropriate time to share intimate truths. Normally, it's the time when you and your partner can use the information to enhance your process of transcendence.

If you're not sure if it's appropriate to share the truth about your natural gender orientation or sexual identity with your partner, you can check if sharing it resonates. You can do that by becoming present in your authentic mind. Then you can assert, *"It's appropriate to share the truth about my gender orientation and sexual identity with my partner— now."* Repeat the affirmation three times. Then assert the opposite three times, *"It's inappropriate to share the truth about my gender orientation and sexual identity with my partner—now."* If sharing the truth resonates, then share it. If it doesn't resonate, wait.

Once you've completed the six-day regimen and you've enhanced the flow of sexual energy between your etheric, physical, and physical-material bodies, you're ready to use your hands and feet as tools for transcendent sex and relationships.

Exercise: Activating the Energy Centers in Your Hands and Feet

To share universal qualities with your partner through your hands and feet during sex, you must be able to activate the minor energy centers in your extremities. Along with your chakras, you have four minor energy centers in your hands and feet that have sexual potential. These energy centers complement the functions of your chakras, particularly your etheric and physical chakras and the meridians that connect them.

The energy centers in your hands and feet shouldn't be confused with the chakras, because they're not vortices. They're centers of activity created by the functional interaction of major meridians (one masculine and one feminine) located in the palms and soles. In the palms the energy centers are created through the interaction of the Yang Yu and Yin Yu meridians. In the soles they are created through the interaction of the Chao Yang and the Chao Yin meridians (see Figure 14).

Before you enhance the sexual potential of the energy centers in your hands and feet, it's important to recognize that these energy centers have important functions that contribute to the health of your relationship. Along with the chakras and meridians, the energy centers in your hands and feet help to distribute sexual energy through your energy system. They do this by regulating pressure within your energy field. If the energy centers in your hands and feet are functioning healthfully, sexual energy will radiate through the meridians in your arms and legs, and then the meridians will distribute it throughout the rest of your energy system.

The energy centers in your hands allow you to manifest creativity and the intent of your authentic mind in the physical-material universe.

The energy centers in your feet provide you with the sexual energy you need to make sustained progress. The same energy centers provide you with a solid foundation in the physical-material world.

Only after the minor energy centers in your hands and feet are functioning healthfully will you be able to share sexual energy through them all by touching, caressing, or stroking your partner.

The two exercises that follow are designed to activate the minor energy centers in your hands and feet so that sexual energy can radiate through them freely and they can fulfill their sexual potential.

Exercise: Expressing Sexual Energy Through Your Hands

To enhance the sexual potential of your hands, you will activate the energy centers in your right and left palms. To begin, find a comfortable position, with your back straight. Then breathe yogically. Continue by counting from five to one, then from ten to one. Use the Standard Method Exercise to relax the muscles of your physical-material body. Next, assert, *"It's my intent to activate and center myself in my heart chakra."*

Continue by asserting, *"It's my intent to activate my upper physical chakra."* Then assert, *"It's my intent to activate my lower physical chakra."* Continue by asserting, *"It's my intent to turn my organs of perception inward on the levels of my upper and lower physical chakras."* After you've turned your organs of perception inward, assert, *"It's my intent to activate the energy center in my right palm."* Then assert, *"It's my intent to activate the energy center in my left palm."* Once the energy centers in your hands are active, take fifteen minutes to enjoy the enhanced flow of sexual energy through them.

After fifteen minutes, count from one to five. When you reach the number five, open your eyes. You will feel wide awake, perfectly relaxed, and better than you did before.

Exercise: Expressing Sexual Energy Through Your Feet

To enhance the sexual potential of your feet, you will activate the minor energy centers in your right and left soles. To begin, find a comfortable position, with your back straight. Then breathe yogically. Continue by counting from five to one, then from ten to one. Use the Standard Method Exercise to relax the muscles of your physical-material body. Then assert, *"It's my intent to activate and center myself in my heart chakra."*

Continue by asserting, *"It's my intent to activate my upper physical chakra."* Then assert, *"It's my intent to activate my lower physical chakra."* Continue by asserting: *"It's my intent to turn my organs of perception inward on the levels of my upper and lower physical chakras."* After you've turned your organs of perception inward, assert, *"It's my intent to activate the energy center in my right sole."* Then assert, *"It's my intent to activate the energy center in my left sole."* Once the energy centers in your feet are active, take fifteen minutes to enjoy the enhanced flow of sexual energy through them.

After fifteen minutes count from one to five. When you reach the number five, open your eyes. You will feel wide awake, perfectly relaxed, and better than you did before.

Chapter 11

Spiritual Foreplay

I magine that television's *Star Trek* starship *Enterprise* could impregnate a lovely planet with life. First, the environment would need to be made safe for such a sacred and sexy mission. The starship would need to scan the planet's energy field for any disruptive fields being projected toward it. The *Enterprise* would need to neutralize those. The *Enterprise* would also need to make sure that all its own energy fields are operating in a healthy fashion. Then it would need to stimulate new life on the planet by sending down a long laser of life-giving light. Similar energetic preparations can vastly augment the joy lovers share in sacred embrace.

Now that you've learned to restore your gender orientation to its natural state and to enhance the sexual potential of your hands and feet, you can begin to share more pleasure, love, intimacy, and joy with your partner through spiritual foreplay.

However, before you get started, it's important to note that the activities that constitute spiritual foreplay aren't something that can be choreographed in the same manner as a dance. To attempt to do so through a rigid structure of exercises and rituals can stifle creativity, disrupt gender orientation, and inhibit the flow of sexual energy between partners.

Fortunately, with the tools you've developed and your enhanced flow of sexual energy, you're now ready to make the transition from traditional sexual foreplay to spiritual foreplay.

When it comes to spiritual foreplay, two things must be kept in mind. First, before you and your partner engage in spiritual foreplay, it's essential to create an environment conducive to shared intimacy. Second, while you and your partner are engaged in spiritual foreplay, you must take your time and stay centered in your authentic mind so that you and your partner can fully enjoy what you're doing.

Being in an environment that is uncomfortable or that inhibits you and your partner from expressing yourselves freely will not be conducive to spiritual foreplay. And moving too quickly from foreplay to coitus won't leave enough time for you to make the energetic shifts necessary to experience the full spectrum of pleasure, love, intimacy, and joy possible in spiritual foreplay.

Setting the External Conditions

According to the tantric texts, the best time for foreplay and coitus is from 7:00 in the evening to midnight. The tantras advise that lovemaking should never take place in total darkness. The room you use should be prepared beforehand. It should be clean, pleasing, and airy. A number of symbolic articles should be laid out on an elegant cloth beforehand. These include two glasses and a pitcher of cold drinking water, a decanter of wine or any favorite alcoholic beverage, two candles in holders, and essence of musk, incense, or any good perfume.

Music, lighting, and pleasing objects can be used to enhance the environment for lovemaking. You can use them to create a pleasing effect as well as to increase the mutual excitement you and your partner experience.

Both men and women must prepare themselves for spiritual foreplay. Nothing should be left to chance. Things that promote transcendent sex should be enhanced. Those that don't should be avoided. Both men and women should give special attention to how they look, what they wear, and how they smell. Special attention can also be given to personas, especially those that lead to enhanced sexual excitement. Because the tongue is the most unruly organ of your body, it's important to recognize that foolish talk can undermine trust and receptivity and inhibit the flow of sexual energy. Avoid the compulsion to bring up contentious issues or to talk about personal defects, especially physical defects. Both men and women should avoid asking questions such as "Do I look fat?" or "Do I turn you on as much as your ex-lover?"

Each partner finds certain activities erotic and/or exciting. And during spiritual foreplay it's important to trust yourself enough to love what gives you and your partner pleasure. If your partner wants you to do something he or she finds stimulating, then find a way to do it. If your lover wants you to wear something that excites him or her sexually or wants to hear you say stimulating things, what's the problem? Let go of your inhibitions and enjoy yourself. Remember, spiritual foreplay is supposed to be fun.

Because foreplay is one of the primary ways that men and women experience intimacy, it may surprise you to know how little time most people spend engaged in foreplay of any kind. Data from the Kinsey studies indicate that in 11 percent of marriages foreplay lasted a mere three minutes. In 36 percent of marriages, foreplay lasted anywhere between four and ten minutes. In 31 percent of marriages, foreplay lasted between eleven and twenty minutes, and in only 21 percent of marriages did foreplay last more than thirty minutes. It is speculated that in such hurried sexual encounters "the natural chemicals that accompany touch and sexual arousal don't have enough time to be released into the bloodstream, which then short-circuits the general sense of well-being that usually accompanies lovemaking ... In other words, when sex is 'hasty,' the man and woman are not able to exchange sexual energy and harmonize with each other, and may even drain each other of energy."[6]

However, when foreplay is given enough time, it can bring partners into an energetic condition that allows them to experience all the benefits of transcendent sex.

How Flexible Are You?

Besides creating a pleasant physical environment and staying centered in your authentic mind, you must also be flexible in order to engage in spiritual foreplay. This means you must discard rigid ideas about sex and the sexual roles of men and woman.

A man isn't always dominant and assertive. A woman isn't always receptive and submissive. Roles change, so do feelings and the energy that supports them. The truth is that you must be flexible and change as your internal and external environment changes. This can mean many things. It can mean that a normally dominant woman submits to her partner's enhanced masculinity. It can mean that a normally assertive man agrees to accept a more passive role, so that his female partner can act out a scenario she finds sexually exciting.

It also can mean that the rhythm of lovemaking changes during foreplay and intercourse. In one phase, foreplay may be passionate. In another, it may be gentle and loving. Passion can be interrupted by periods of conversation. And conversation can extend to topics that demand greater intimacy and trust.

Partners may want to look at each other for a while or to explore each other's body, through their sense of smell, taste, and/or touch. Flexibility may also mean that partners are willing to go beyond their traditional limits and to experiment with new feelings and new activities.

So, when it comes to foreplay, be flexible, and if you're frightened or embarrassed, talk to your partner. You'd be amazed at how much can be accomplished by just talking honestly about sex with someone you trust.

Traditional Sexual Foreplay

Although you may not be able to define sexual foreplay, you certainly know it when you've experienced it or when you've seen it played out on the movie screen or in a novel you've read.

What you may not know is that sexual foreplay is a powerful tonic. Sexual foreplay lowers inhibitions and increases the emotional comfort of partners who engage in it. It stimulates a man and woman's physical body by enhancing a man's ability to achieve and sustain an erection and by making a woman's clitoris erect and increasing vaginal lubrication.

Dr. Lasse Hessel, a noted sexologist, explains that sexual foreplay is part of a complex sexual dance that emerges in phases. In the first phase of foreplay, Hessel asserts that "couples excite and prepare each other for having sex, using their own rituals or sexual code. This happens at a more mental and emotional level. In the next phase, couples sexually stimulate each other by touching, kissing, or any other way that gets their bodies sexually aroused so that the blood flow to the genitals increases. In the third phase, the blood flow increases to such a degree that genitals are fully engorged with blood—for the woman, her vagina and clitoris are enlarged and aroused; for the man, his penis has become erect and his scrotum swells or lifts. The fourth phase is orgasm and the fifth and last phase is relaxation ..."[7]

Sexual foreplay has more to do with motivation and the energy partners radiate than where and how partners touch each other. In fact, just because you're touching someone, hugging them, or holding their hand doesn't mean you are engaged in sexual foreplay. You're engaged in sexual foreplay only if you and your partner are motivated by sexual desire and your intent is to engage in sexual activities that lead to orgasm.

For human beings, sexual foreplay is universal, although what constitutes foreplay can differ depending on age, culture, and religion. Sexual foreplay is often subtle in its initial stages. Even before partners are together, they can engage in sexual foreplay by selecting and creating a particular environment and bringing themselves into a particular state of mind. A romantic, intimate, or overtly sexual atmosphere can be considered as a gesture of foreplay.

The truth is that in many instances it's difficult to tell when sexual foreplay has begun. It can begin with non-physical behavior that signals sexual availability. When initiated verbally, foreplay may include sexual compliments, subtle comments with double entendre, and intimate conversations. Non-verbally, foreplay can include provocative clothing, preening gestures, licking or biting one's lips, standing inside a partner's personal space, and holding a gaze longer than is acceptable for casual acquaintances. In the final analysis, sexual foreplay can include any activity, either physical or non-physical, which when reciprocated will lead to the experience of sexual pleasure and orgasm.

Spiritual Foreplay

There is a variation to normal sexual foreplay that is called spiritual foreplay. It includes many of the same activities as sexual foreplay, such as stroking, gazing, and entering another person's personal space or comfort zone. However, spiritual foreplay differs in one essential way: the goals of spiritual foreplay aren't restricted to the experience of sexual pleasure and intercourse. The ultimate goal of spiritual foreplay is the experience of transcendent sex and relationships.

Although most people remain unaware that spiritual foreplay exists, some people recognize its importance intuitively. In *The Hite Report on Male Sexuality* one interviewee declared, "When I'm making love to my wife, I like it to go on for a while. There's an awful lot of pleasure in the arousal period, so why get it over with? Touching, caressing, caring, being close—are all pleasurable experiences … What's the big hurry about ejaculating anyhow? It will eventually come, and in the meantime you can have a lot of fun, and get a lot of pleasure out of expressing love to the other person. Besides, when I have taken much more time, the ejaculation which I eventually got was much more pleasurable and lasted about twice as long."[8]

Spiritual foreplay accentuates the universal over the personal. In spiritual foreplay, partners use their sexual energy, as well as the words and activities that accompany it, to share universal qualities through physical and non-physical contact.

In Hindu mythology, the shift from sexual to spiritual foreplay is illustrated by Parvati, Shiva's consort and a manifestation of the goddess Shakti, and her challenging courtship with Shiva. The events surrounding the divine couple's courtship took place at the time when Aryan gods Brahma (the creator of the universe) and Vishnu (the preserver of the universe) began to assert their influence over the pre-Aryan peoples of India. High on their list of priorities was the domestication of Shiva, a pre-Aryan god of India who later became the third member of the Hindu godhead.

The problem faced by the Aryan gods was that Shiva had been personified by the indigenous people of India as an eccentric yogi who vehemently refused to take a mate. In order to rectify this situation so that Shiva could take his rightful place in the pantheon of Hindu gods, Brahma and Vishnu implored the god Himalaya to betroth his beautiful daughter Parvati to him.

There was only one hitch in the plan hatched by Vishnu and Brahma. Shiva, the consummate yogi and "bad boy" of the Hindu pantheon, was completely disinterested in women and household affairs. From the Shiva Puranas we learn that Shiva preferred the company of goblins and creatures of the underworld to the joys of domestic life. In fact, he spent much of his time practicing yogic *tapas* (austerities and penance) in graveyards and other unsavory places.

Despite Shiva's reputation, Parvati did her best to entice him. However, given Shiva's eccentric ways and lack of interest, it wasn't surprising that Parvati's initial attempts failed. Shiva's interest was aroused only after she abandoned the traditional method of seduction and began practicing yogic tapas so that she could unlock her sexual power and share the universal qualities of the goddess (Shakti) with Shiva through spiritual foreplay. The passage below describes Parvati's transformation and Shiva's joyful response.

Convinced that Siva [Shiva] could be achieved by means of penance, (tappas) Parvati become glad and decided to perform penance ... Parvati was engaged in penance ... a long time ... but Siva [Shiva] did not appear ... when Brahma and the other Gods had gone back to the respective abodes, Siva, [Shiva] entered into spiritual contemplation in order to test her penance. After completing her spiritual practice and being tested by various gods and even himself, Shiva declared: "... O Parvati ... you have been tested by me in various ways. Let guilt be excused in following this worldly game. Even in the three worlds I do not see a beloved like you. O Parvati, in every respect I am subservient to you. You can fulfill all your desires. O beloved, come near to me. You are my wife. I am your bridegroom. I shall immediately go to my abode—the excellent mountain, along with you ...” When the lord of the gods spoke in this way, Parvati rejoiced. Whatever distress she had felt during penance she cast off as something old ... her weariness subsided.[9]

It's clear that Parvati embraced energy with universal qualities and was rewarded for her efforts. You can also embrace universal qualities through spiritual foreplay, and, like Parvati, you can experience the same rewards.

It doesn't matter how long you've been attached to the individual mind and ego or how long you've practiced sexual foreplay. None of this matters if you're willing to engage in spiritual foreplay and share universal qualities with your partner. In fact, once you choose spiritual foreplay, all your sexual activities will be motivated by authentic desires, which means that everything you do with your partner during foreplay will lead you closer to the experience of transcendent sex.

Transcending Duality

In order to engage in spiritual foreplay, your sexual activities must be motivated by the desire to share universal qualities. Unfortunately, most people are attached to the dualistic belief that they must be good and must not do things that are taboo or that compromise their sense of right and wrong. Remaining attached to such restrictive beliefs at the expense of pleasure, love, intimacy, and joy will keep you centered in your individual mind and ego. And it will prevent you from sharing the universal qualities of a god or goddess with your partner.

In order to overcome your attachment to good/bad notions and the taboos of your society, you must overcome the effect that duality had on your energy field. To do that you will activate the Kundalini Shakti. Activating the Kundalini Shakti will keep blockages that are connected to restrictive beliefs and taboos from restricting your ability to participate in spiritual foreplay.

The Kundalini Shakti

The Kundalini Shakti is the greatest repository of sexual energy in your energy field. It emerged from Shakti, via the tattvas, along with you and everything else in the phenomenal universe. The Kundalini Shakti comes in two forms: structural Kundalini, and the serpent energy. Both forms influence your ability to engage in spiritual foreplay.

Structural Kundalini provides structure to your energy field and enables it to function on all dimensions of the physical and non-physical universe. Without structural Kundalini, energy with universal qualities wouldn't flow through your chakras and meridians or fill your auric fields. And without structural Kundalini there would be no energetic link between your authentic mind and Universal Consciousness, or between your authentic mind and the physical-material universe. The fact is that no activities or energetic interactions between sentient beings would be possible without the participation of the structural Kundalini.

Complementing the functions of structural Kundalini is the serpent energy. In most cases, the serpent energy lies dormant by your first chakra, at the base of your spine. Tantric texts explain that as long as the serpent energy lies dormant, it will have a feminine polarity and will resemble a snake with its head facing downward. However, once the serpent energy has been aroused, its polarity will be reversed and the head will turn to face upward. It's only then, after it has been aroused, that it will begin to move upward.

The serpent energy is closely related to sexual energy but differs in several important ways. It emerges from a specific point or points, and moves in predictable ways. Its traditional route takes it through the Governor, the main masculine meridian in your back, to the crown chakra and beyond. As it moves up the Governor, the serpent energy activates the seven traditional chakras and fills your energy field.

However, there are two other routes that the serpent energy can take to reach the crown chakra. It can rise the short distance from the back of the heart chakra through the Governor meridian up to the crown chakra. And it can rise from the front of the heart chakra through the Conceptual meridian, up to the crown chakra.

The route the Kundalini Shakti takes will be determined by the condition of your energy system and the quality and quantity of energy with individual qualities that affects it. As the serpent energy moves upward and grows stronger, it will become a powerful ally. It will help you to overcome the blockages in your energy field that prevent you from consistently engaging in spiritual foreplay.

The Problem of Qualified Energy

Much has been written in yogic and tantric literature about arousing the serpent energy and about the effects it will have when it has begun to rise. From the ancient texts we learn that your ability to arouse the Kundalini Shakti and its ability to move upward is directly affected by the condition of your energy system as well as your attachment to personas and external projections.

If energy with individual qualities intrudes into the path of the serpent energy by blocking the Governor or Conceptual meridians or disrupting the function of the chakras in personal body space, your ability to arouse the serpent energy and it's ability to move upward will be blocked.

Attachment to restrictive beliefs and taboos—which emerges from karmic baggage and external projections as well as cords, controlling waves, and attachment fields—has the ability to prevent the serpent energy from being aroused and/or rising to the crown chakra and beyond. Indeed, for the serpent energy to be aroused and to rise without disruption, all karmic baggage, cords, controlling waves, and attachment fields dense enough to disrupt it's movement must be released, at least temporarily.

Exercise: The Five-Step Method– Arousing the Serpent Energy

In the following Five-Step Method, you will learn to arouse the serpent energy. In step one, you will become present in your energy field, turn your organs of perception inward, and scan your energy field to determine if there is anything that will interfere with the natural movement of the Kundalini Shakti.

In step two, you will release all cords, controlling waves, and/or attachment fields that have blocked the path of the serpent energy. You can do that by using the technique you've learned in chapter 9.

In step three, you will also remove temporary blockages that can disrupt the movement of the serpent energy. You will do that by making an appropriate apology.

In step four, you will activate the front and back of the seven traditional chakras by filling your energy field with sexual energy. You can do that by using the Self-Love Meditation you've learned in chapter 3.

You will begin step five after you've removed the external projections and karmic baggage that have the potential to interfere with the movement of the serpent energy, and immediately after you have activated the backs and fronts of the seven traditional chakras. Then, in step five, you will perform *Mulabandha*, the Root Lock, so that the serpent energy can begin to move upward through the Governor meridian, to your crown chakra and beyond.

This entire process will take time, particularly step two, which requires you to release the cords, controlling waves, and attachment fields that have the potential to block the serpent energy. It is advisable to practice steps one and two for several days before you move on to step three. When you are confident that the most disruptive cords, controlling waves, and attachment fields have been released, you can continue by practicing steps one through three for several days until your energy field can support an enhanced level of sexual energy without difficulty. Once you've reached that stage, you can complete the process by practicing all five steps on a daily basis until the serpent energy is aroused and rises to your crown chakra and beyond.

Step One: Scanning

In step one, you will check your energy field by becoming present and scanning it. During the scan you must attempt to answer the following questions:

1. Is there an inordinate buildup of karmic energy on the path of the serpent energy that will prevent it from rising to my crown chakra and beyond?

2. Are there cords, controlling waves, or attachment fields that will interfere with the activity of my seven traditional chakras or the function of my Governor and/or Conceptual meridian?

3. Is there something I've done that has blocked the flow of sexual energy through my energy field and disrupted intimacy with someone I love?

4. Am I attached to restrictive beliefs or social taboos that would prevent the serpent energy from being aroused and rising to my crown chakra and beyond?

If your answer to any of these questions is yes, it's important that you correct the condition before you attempt to arouse the serpent energy and go beyond the third step in the five-step process.

Exercise: Step One–Scanning Your Energy Field

The first step in arousing the serpent energy is to scan your energy field. Once you are familiar with the questions that must be answered, find a comfortable position, with your back straight. Then breathe yogically. Continue by counting from five to one, then from ten to one. Use the Standard Method Exercise to relax the muscles of your physical-material body. Then assert: *"It's my intent to activate and center myself in my heart chakra."* Continue by asserting, *"It's my intent to become present in my authentic mind."* Take a few moments to enjoy the shift. Then assert, *"It's my intent to turn my organs of perception inward and to observe the blockages in my field, which have prevented the serpent energy from rising."* As soon as you've made the last assertion, you will see a large cavity.

If there are any blockages blocking the serpent energy, they will be in the cavity or pushing up against it from the outside. Cords will be thin and taut and extend outward from your energy field. Controlling waves will fill a portion of the cavity and extend outward. Attachment fields will look like loose clouds that partially or completely fill the cavity. Karmic baggage will be layered like bricks or look like individual lumps of energy.

Each type of blockage will have its own set of qualities that differentiate it from other blockages in your energy field. Most won't move, although a few may shift slightly when you focus your attention on them. Make a mental note of what you observe; you can write it down later. Then count from one to five. When you reach the number five, open your eyes. You will feel wide awake, perfectly relaxed, and better than you did before.

Exercise: Step Two–Releasing Blockages from the Serpent Energy

Once you know what is blocking the serpent energy, you can begin to release the cords, controlling waves, and attachment fields that are in the way by using the technique you learned in chapter 9.

To release blockages, find a comfortable position, with your back straight. Begin to breathe yogically. Count from five to one, and then from ten to one. Use the Standard Method Exercise to relax the muscles of your physical-material body. Then assert, *"It's my intent to activate and center myself in my heart chakra."* Once you've activated and centered yourself in your heart chakra, assert, *"It's my intent to become present on the dimension where the blockage is located."* Once you're present on the appropriate dimension, take a moment to observe the blockage. It will be important to remain detached by remaining present in your authentic mind while you observe it.

After you've examined the blockage and you've determined whether it's a cord, controlling wave, or attachment field, assert, *"It's my intent to sever the cord [controlling wave/attachment field] I'm observing and to release it and its source and extensions."* However, if you can't determine whether the blockage is caused by a cord, controlling wave, or attachment field, you can still release it by asserting, *"It's my intent to sever the blockage I have in mind and its source and extensions."*

As soon as the blockage has been released, you will feel a shift in your energy field. After fifteen minutes, count from one to five. When you reach the number five, open your eyes. You will feel wide awake, perfectly relaxed, and better than you did before.

To remove more recent blockages, which also disrupt your intimacy but haven't been integrated into your karmic baggage yet, you can make an appropriate apology, which is step three.

Exercise: Step Three–An Appropriate Apology

Whenever you've consciously or unconsciously projected energy with individual qualities at your partner or at another person with whom you are intimate, you will block intimacy and make it more difficult for the serpent energy to be become active and rise to your and your partner's crown chakra and beyond.

As long as the other person has not integrated the energy by becoming attached to it, you can restore intimacy and remove the energy blockage, in both your energy fields, by making an appropriate apology. Of course, you may not want to apologize because at the time you projected you felt that you were the injured party and that you should weather the storm or fight harder to prove you're right and they're wrong.

However, neither of the last two alternatives will help the serpent energy to rise because neither of them will remove the projection that has disrupted intimacy and blocked the movement of the Kundalini Shakti.

So, in step three, apologize, not because you're wrong, but because an appropriate apology will remove the blockage that has disrupted intimacy and blocked the movement of the Kundalini Shakti. For an apology to restore intimacy and remove the projection that has blocked the movement of the serpent energy, it must be given freely and it must have two parts.

The first part of an appropriate apology must accurately describe the action or inaction that disrupted intimacy. The second part must express the sincere regret you feel for harming the other person energetically, first by projecting qualified energy at him or her, and then by disrupting intimacy and interfering with the movement of Kundalini Shakti through his or her energy field.

An appropriate apology sounds something like this: *"I'm sorry for projecting my anger, jealousy, blame, or insecurity at you and harming you and your energy field."*

Once the apology has been given, intimacy will be restored and the energy blocking the movement of the serpent energy will be removed.

Exercise: Step Four–Activating the Front and Back of the Seven Traditional Chakras

After you've scanned your energy field, released blockages, and made the appropriate apologies, you're ready to begin step four. In step four, you will activate the front and back of your seven traditional chakras.

To activate the front and back of the seven traditional chakras, begin by finding a comfortable position with your back straight. Then breathe yogically. Continue by counting from five to one, then from ten to one. Use the Standard Method Exercise to relax the muscles of your physical-material body. Then assert, *"It's my intent to activate and center myself in my heart chakra."* Take a few moments to enjoy the shift. Then assert, *"It's my intent to activate the back of my first chakra."* Continue in the same way, working upward until the backs of all seven traditional chakras have been activated, including the back of your heart chakra.

Once you've activated the back of the seven traditional chakras, take a few moments to experience the changes you feel. Then assert, *"It's my intent to activate the front of my seventh chakra."* Continue in the same way, working downward until the fronts of all seven traditional chakras have been activated, including the front of your heart chakra.

After you've activated the backs and fronts of the seven traditional chakras, assert: *"It's my intent to turn my organs of perception inward on the levels of my seven traditional chakras."* Then assert, *"It's my intent to become present on the level of the seven traditional chakras."* Take fifteen minutes to enjoy the experience. After fifteen minutes, count from one to five. When you reach the number five, open your eyes. You will feel wide awake, perfectly relaxed, and better than you did before.

Once you've activated the front and back of the seven traditional chakras, the next step will be to perform the Root Lock. The Root Lock is designed to temporarily release blockages that have forced the muscles by your first chakra to contract. Once you've released the blockages, the area will relax and it will become far easier for the serpent energy to become active and to rise to your crown chakra and beyond.

Exercise: Step Five–The Root Lock

The Root Lock is known as *Mulabandha* in Sanskrit. It's advisable to perform the Root Lock directly after you've activated the front and back of the seven traditional chakras. It's performed either standing or sitting in a comfortable position with your back straight.

In the first part of the Root Lock, you will contract the anal sphincter and draw it in, the same way you would to hold in a bowel movement. Then you will pull in your sexual organs so that there is a contraction along the urinary tract and in the lower trunk. In the second part, you will draw in your lower abdomen, at the navel, pulling it back toward your spine. This draws your rectum and sexual organs up and back toward your lower back.

To begin, close your eyes and breathe yogically. Count backward from five to one, then from ten to one. When you're ready, inhale deeply through your nose. On the exhalation, contract your anal sphincter and draw it in. Hold it for a count of five, and then release it for a count of five. Repeat this three times. After the third repetition, exhale completely and relax. Continue to breathe yogically, with closed eyes, for five minutes more while you pay attention to your first chakra and the movement of the serpent energy as it becomes aroused. After five minutes, count from one to five. When you reach the number five, open your eyes. You will feel wide awake and better than you did before.

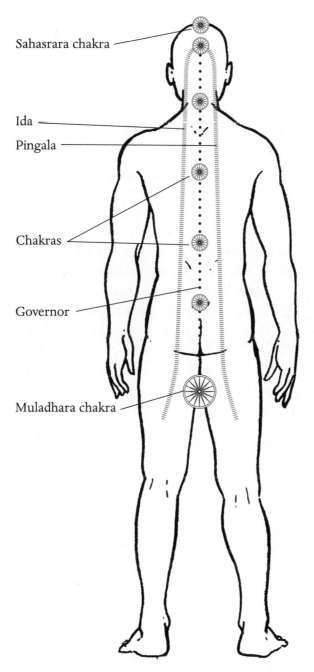

Figure 20: *The Governor, Ida, and Pingala Meridians*

After the Kundalini Shakti Has Been Aroused

Yoga and tantra both teach that once the serpent energy has reached the crown chakra, the Governor and Conceptual meridians will merge with two other meridians, the Ida and Pingala, to create one large channel of sexual energy that extends up and down, from the center of your energy field to the surface of your auric fields (see Figure 20).

Although these four meridians will eventually merge, don't expect to have the complete Kundalini experience all at once. It's more common for the chakras along the route of the serpent energy to become active one at a time and for the serpent energy to rise in fits and starts for weeks or even months before it reaches the crown chakra.

You will learn that working with the Kundalini Shakti is a process that takes time to complete. Discipline and perseverance will help. However, having the desire to transcend your attachments is also important. Remember, you get what you want most, and if you sincerely want the serpent energy to rise and you apply yourself by practicing the exercises you just learned, it's only a matter of time until you experience the benefits of having aroused the Kundalini Shakti in your energy field and relationships.

Exercise: Enhancing Your Gazing

You can begin spiritual foreplay by practicing the Gazing Exercise. In the sixth chapter of Matthew we are told that "The light of the body is in the eye." People who radiate energy through their eyes are usually admired because of the strength of their gaze. In fact, a strong steady gaze, fueled by sexual energy, can be used to enhance transcendent sex and bring you and your partner closer.

You can use your eyes to convey the desire, will, and intent of your authentic mind. And you can use them to share universal qualities with your partner.

However, to actualize your eyes' sexual potential, you must strengthen your gaze and learn to focus it. To do that you will need a large mirror. Place the mirror about three feet (one meter) in front of you so that you can see your whole face clearly.

To begin to use the Gazing Exercise as a tool for transcendence, sit comfortably in front of the mirror with your back straight. Then close your eyes and breathe yogically. Continue by counting from five to one, then from ten to one. Use the Standard Method Exercise to relax the muscles of your physical-material body. Then assert, *"It's my intent to activate and center myself in my heart chakra."*

Continue by asserting, *"It's my intent to activate my upper physical chakra."* Take a few moments to enjoy the shift. Then assert, *"It's my intent to become present in my authentic mind, on the level of my upper physical chakra."* Once you're present, open your eyes (keep them slightly unfocused), and make eye contact with yourself in the mirror. Once you've made contact, assert, *"It's my intent to turn my organs of perception inward on the level of my upper physical chakra."* As soon as you've turned your organs of perception inward, you will experience dual awareness.

Take a moment to enjoy the shift. Then assert, *"It's my intent to radiate sexual energy through my eyes."* Don't do anything after that. Don't try to understand what's happening or to give the sexual energy you're radiating an extra push. Just enjoy the enhanced flow of sexual energy radiating through your eyes while you continue to make eye contact. Continue for ten minutes. Then count from one to five, release eye contact, and bring yourself out of the exercise.

Once you're confident that you can radiate sexual energy through your eyes without the interference of your individual mind and ego, you can substitute your partner for the mirror and practice mutual gazing.

Exercise: Mutual Gazing

The Mutual Gazing Exercise is a variation of the Gazing Exercise. By practicing mutual gazing, you will be able to share universal qualities with your partner and actualize the sexual potential of your eyes. Shakespeare poetically described the pleasure lovers get through gazing at each other in his Sonnet 24:

Mine eyes have drawn thy shape, and thine for me
Are windows to my breast, where-through the sun
Delights to peep, to gaze therein on thee.

It's important to remember that when you practice the Mutual Gazing Exercise, you and your partner shouldn't be staring at one another. Instead, you will be sharing universal qualities with one another by gazing while you're both centered in your authentic minds.

In the Mutual Gazing Exercise, you and your partner will sit three feet (one meter) apart and face each other. To begin, breathe yogically. Continue by counting from five to one, then from ten to one. Use the Standard Method Exercise to relax the muscles of your physical-material bodies.

To continue, you and your partner will assert, *"It's my intent to activate and center myself in my heart chakra."* Then assert, *"It's my intent to activate my upper physical chakra."* Take a few moments to enjoy the shift. Then assert, *"It's my intent to become present on the level of my upper physical chakra."* Once you're both present, assert, *"It's my intent to turn my organs of perception inward on the level of my upper physical chakra."* As soon as you've both turned your organs of perception inward, you will experience dual awareness.

When you're ready to continue, assert, *"It's my intent to radiate sexual energy to my partner through my eyes."* Don't do anything after that. Don't watch yourself or give the sexual energy you're radiating an extra push. Just enjoy the enhanced flow of sexual energy, and the universal qualities you're sharing with your partner. Continue gazing at one another for another five minutes. Then release your gaze, count from one to five, and bring yourselves out of the exercise.

Exercise: Gazing from Your Chakras

Once you and your partner have practiced the Mutual Gazing Exercise, you can gaze at one another from one of your seven traditional chakras. This exercise will allow you to choose the universal quality that you want to share with one another, and will allow you and your partner to experience more variety and excitement during spiritual foreplay. Below is a list of universal qualities you can share with your partner from your seven traditional chakras.

First chakra: Authentic power, pleasure, security.

Second chakra: Vitality, creativity, natural gender orientation, sexual love.

Third chakra: Satisfaction, trust, and belonging.

Fourth chakra: Freedom to be authentic, intimacy.

Fifth chakra: Joy, freedom of expression.

Sixth chakra: Authentic will, awareness.

Seventh chakra: Transcendent sex and relationship, self-knowledge.

In the following Gazing from Your Chakras Exercise, you and your partner will gaze at one another from your second chakra. Once you master this exercise, you will be able to gaze at each other from any of your traditional seven chakras.

To begin, sit three feet (one meter) apart, facing each other. Begin to breathe yogically. Continue by counting from five to one, then from ten to one. Use the Standard Method Exercise to relax the muscles of your physical-material bodies.

When you're ready to continue, assert, *"It's my intent to activate and center myself in my heart chakra."* Then assert, *"It's my intent to activate my upper physical chakra."* Take a few moments to enjoy the shift you experience. Then assert, *"It's my intent to become present on the level of my upper physical chakra."*

Continue by asserting, *"It's my intent to activate my second chakra."* Then assert, *"It's my intent to turn my organs of perception inward on the level of my second chakra."*

As soon as you've both turned your organs of perception inward, you will experience dual awareness.

When you're ready to continue, assert, *"It's my intent to radiate sexual energy from my second chakra to my partner through my eyes."* Take five minutes to share the energy of your second chakra with your partner. Then release your gaze, count from one to five, and bring yourselves out of the exercise.

Chapter 12
Celebrating the Goddess

Once you've aroused the serpent energy and mastered gazing, you can take spiritual foreplay one exciting step further by celebrating the goddess (Shakti) in her human form. Celebrating the goddess as a woman is central to the religions of many cultures. It will bring you into union with her universal qualities so that you can enjoy them and share them with your partner.

This may seem alien if you've grown up in a patriarchal culture. However, whether you're aware of it or not, your life is a celebration of the goddess. In fact, by celebrating the universal qualities of the goddess—alone or with your partner—you will affirm the truth that "Women are Gods, women are life, women are adornment."[10] These words of Dr. Jonn Mumford in *Ecstasy Through Tantra* were attributed to the Buddha.

It's worth noting that celebrating the goddess is so natural that children must be taught not to do it. In the New Testament, Jesus declares, "Lest you be like a little child you shall not enter the kingdom of heaven." The spontaneity, vitality, and creativity of children are, in fact, the outer manifestation of this celebration.

From the study of yoga we learn that children, until they reach the age of seven, naturally celebrate the goddess.

Children are able to celebrate the goddess because the "I" hasn't been fully developed. And because the "I" hasn't fully developed, children remain much less attached to personas and external projections. However, as they grow older, the natural celebration of the goddess can be disrupted as they become more attached to personas and to the intrusion of external projections. The emergence of personas tied to past-life karma and the intrusion of external projections contribute to the formation of the "I" and to a greater identification with the individual mind and ego, which focuses the "I" into the external environment.

It's attachment to the "I" that makes people feel separate from Universal Consciousness and ultimately alone in the universe. Although attachment to the "I" is a gradual process, once a child reaches the age of seven, attachment to the "I" is usually complete. It's after the process is complete that children become more aware of the limitations karma imposes on them and their free range of activities, both internal and external. At the same time, they begin to experience a more fixed personality and rigid orientation toward themselves and their relationships. It's also during this period that children become increasingly prone to intrusions of dense qualified energy, particularly from adults who exercise authority over them.

Fortunately, by celebrating the goddess in her human form, you can regain the childlike joy you lost when you became attached to the "I" and to your individual mind and ego. By celebrating the goddess, you embrace Shakti's creative role in the universe. In doing so, you will be able to experience and share with your partner more of the universal qualities that emerge from her.

There are three ways you can celebrate the goddess. You can create space in your energy field sacred to the goddess. You can activate the parts of your energy field that are polarized feminine (both men and women can do this), and you can engage in transcendent sex with your partner.

Exercise: The Yoni Mudra

In tantra, there is a mudra designed specifically to create space in your energy field sacred to the goddess. It's called the Yoni Mudra, and it creates sacred space by helping you to accept your natural sexual identity (regardless if you're a man or a woman) and the sexual energy emerging from your primary sexual center, your second chakra.

The Yoni Mudra represents the goddess in her fullness, both as the archetype of the divine feminine and as the source of creative sexual energy. Both men and women who practice the Yoni Mudra will experience the benefits that come from creating space within their energy field sacred to the Goddess.

Yoni is a Sanskrit word that means "divine passage" or "place of birth." On the physical-material level, it corresponds to a woman's vagina. In a wider context, "yoni" also means "origin, fountain, or sacred space." To perform the Yoni Mudra, find a comfortable position, with your back straight. Then bring your hands together, palms open and facing each other, at a slight angle. Interlock your pinkies together at the first joint. Then cross your ring fingers behind your middle fingers. Your middle finger should be fully extended and touching at the tips. Your ring fingers will be held down by the index fingers. Your thumbs will be curled into the palms (see Figure 21).

If you perform the Yoni Mudra for ten minutes a day, you will not only create a sacred space in your energy field, you will also celebrate the goddess by allowing her universal qualities to radiate through your energy field.

You can perform a variation of Yoni Mudra with your partner as part of spiritual foreplay. To perform the variation, sit on the floor, facing your partner. Once you're both comfortable, bring the soles of your feet together so that your right foot is touching your partner's left foot and your left foot is touching your partner's right foot. After your soles are touching, close your eyes and begin to breathe yogically. Continue for two or three minutes. Then, activate and center yourselves in your heart chakras. Once you're both centered, assert, *"It's my intent to become present in my energy field."* Once you're both present, you can perform the Yoni Mudra.

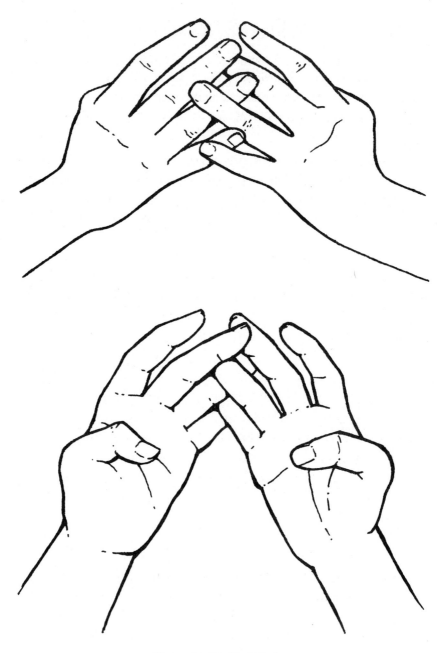

Figure 21: *The Yoni Mudra*

Both partners will perform the mudra for ten minutes with closed eyes. After ten minutes, release the mudra, and count from one to five. Then open your eyes. You can keep your feet together for another two or three minutes while you and your partner enjoy the effects of celebrating the goddess.

In addition to the benefits mentioned above, those of you who perform the Yoni Mudra will experience more pleasure when you're sexually stimulated. You will have more intense orgasms, and the afterglow of your coitus will last longer and be more satisfying.

Exercise: The Ohm Technique

The Ohm Technique is another exercise you can do with your partner that will celebrate the goddess. In the Ohm Technique, partners will sit directly in front of one another with their legs intertwined. Both partners should breathe yogically and then activate and center themselves in their heart chakras. As soon as both partners have activated and centered themselves in their heart chakras, the female partner will slide forward until she is sitting on her partner's lap. Partners should then embrace each other with their arms and legs intertwined.

The male partner will lean his head against the right side of his partner's head next. Then he will inhale deeply, and on the exhalation chant softly in the tone of C, the frequency of the heart chakra. He will find C easily if he chants "*ah*," as in the word "ha."

Chanting in C will enhance the activity of the male's heart chakra, particularly in the front, which is feminine. While the male partner is chanting, he must allow the vibration, which comes from his heart chakra, to flow freely into his partner's energy field. No effort is required for this transfer. It will take place naturally as long as both partners remain centered in their heart chakras and continue to embrace each other.

The male partner will continue to chant for three or four minutes. Then he will move to the left side of his partner's head, and continue in the same way, for three or four more minutes. After he has finished, the female partner will begin to chant in the same way, first on the right side of her male partner's head, then on the left.

After both partners have completed the Ohm Technique, they should continue to embrace for several minutes while they share the universal qualities of the goddess.

Exercise: Celebrating the Yoni

Another way for men to celebrate the goddess is to give pleasure directly to the yoni, without the expectation that it will be reciprocated. Each woman manifests the universal qualities of Shakti through her yoni. By pleasuring the yoni, the male will unselfishly be celebrating his female partner and her relationship to Shakti in one of the most direct ways possible.

In the following exercise, the male, who will represent Shiva, will pleasure his partner—who represents Shakti—by activating her yoni.

Partners should first undress. Then they should sit in front of each other and breathe yogically. After two or three minutes, partners will activate and center themselves in their heart chakras. Then they will perform the Orgasmic Bliss Mudra.

To perform the Orgasmic Bliss Mudra, each partner will place the tip of his or her tongue on the upper palate, then bring it straight back until it comes to rest at the point where the hard palate rolls up and becomes soft. Once the tip of the tongue is in that position, each partner will put his or her feet together, so that the soles are touching. Then each partner will bring his or her hands in front of the solar plexus, with the inside tips of the thumbs together.

To complete the Orgasmic Bliss Mudra, each partner will bring the outside of his or her index fingers together, from the tips to the first joint. Next, they will bring the outsides of the middle fingers together, from the first to the second joint. Then each partner should curl his or her fourth and fifth fingers into their palms (see Figure 1).

Partners should hold the mudra for five minutes. Then the female partner will spread her legs so that the yoni is exposed. After viewing the yoni for a few moments, the male partner must release the mudra and move forward until his head is directly in front of the yoni. Once his head is directly in front of the yoni, the male partner will inhale deeply through his mouth, hold his breath for a count of five, and exhale sexual energy through his nose directly into the yoni.

The yoni has been described as a furnace. By blowing sexual energy into the yoni, while in orgasmic bliss, the male partner will be stoking the yoni like a blacksmith stokes his fire.

As sexual energy pours into the yoni, the creative power of Shakti will radiate through the female's legs and from the base of her spine to the top of her head. Under ideal conditions, a woman who participates in this celebration will take on the character of Shakti and will be able to share Shakti's universal qualities with her partner through spiritual foreplay and transcendent sex.

Exercise: Empowering the Goddess

Now that you've celebrated the goddess by practicing the Ohm Technique with your partner, you can empower the goddess by enhancing the flow of sexual energy through her three most important meridians: the Ida, the Pingala, and the Governor. These three meridians are known as Trishira. In Sanskrit *tri* means "three" and *shira* means "that which carries."

Meridians are streams of energy that connect chakras to one another and transmit sexual energy through the human energy field. There are thousands of them, large and small, although there is disagreement on just how many there are. One ancient yogic text tells us that there are 72,000 meridians. Other texts tell us there are over 350,000.

The disagreements in the ancient texts shouldn't concern us too much because among the thousands of meridians that carry sexual energy, there are ten major meridians. Among these ten, the Ida, the Pingala and the Governor are of particular importance.

Although the meridians are often compared to the veins and arteries of the circulatory system, which distributes blood and life nutrients through the physical-material body, structurally they closely resemble currents of water and/or air found in the earth's oceans and in the atmosphere. In fact, meridians are streams of sexual energy whose size, shape, and carrying capacity are regulated by the quantity of energy they carry, the condition of the energy centers in the hands and feet, and variations in pressure exerted by fields of qualified energy (blockages) in their immediate environment.

The energy that radiates through Trishira (Ida, Pingala, and the Governor) has its origin at the base of the spine, in the coiled serpent energy. Many of the practices of yoga and tantra are aimed at enhancing and balancing these three currents of energy. Indeed, once the Kundalini Shakti has risen to your crown chakra, the Governor, Ida, and Pingala will merge into one massive channel of sexual energy and your entire energy field will become a celebration of the goddess's creative power.

Although raising the Kundalini Shakti to the crown chakra and beyond is a process that takes time, you can empower the goddess, even during this process, by enhancing and balancing the flow of sexual energy through the three meridians that make up the Trishira.

You can do this alone or with a partner. When you empower the goddess with a partner, the two of you will sit facing each other, six feet (two meters) apart.

In either case, to empower the goddess, you must enhance the pressure in your energy system by activating your first and seventh chakras. Then you must perform the Trishira Mudra (description below), and stimulate the minor energy centers along the three meridians that compose the Trishira.

To begin, find a comfortable position, with your back straight. Breathe yogically. Count from five to one, then from ten to one. Use the Standard Method Exercise to relax the muscles of your physical-material body.

Then assert, *"It's my intent to activate and center myself in my heart chakra."* Continue by asserting, *"It's my intent to become present in my authentic mind."* After you've become present, assert, *"It's my intent to activate my first chakra."* Then assert, *"It's my intent to activate my seventh chakra."* After you've activated your first and seventh chakras, you will perform the Trishira Mudra.

To perform the Trishira Mudra, slide your tongue past your lower teeth until the tip comes to rest at the lowest point. Then put the tips of your corresponding fingers together so that you form a triangle with your hands. Put the soles of your feet together next so that they form another triangle. Continue to hold the mudra while you activate the minor energy centers along the Governor, Ida, and Pingala.

There are twelve minor energy centers along the Governor and twenty minor energy centers along the Ida. Twenty more energy centers are located along the Pingala, in positions that correspond to the energy centers in the Ida. You will have to activate all of these energy centers in order to empower the goddess.

Although this sounds like a big job, it won't be as difficult as you imagine, because you will use your intent to activate the minor energy centers the same way you activated your chakras. The energy centers along the Governor are located in between major vertebrae. The energy centers in the Ida and Pingala are located in corresponding positions along the length to the two meridians (see Figure 22). You will continue the exercise by activating the energy centers along the Governor. Then you will activate the energy centers along the Ida. Finally, you will activate the energy centers along the Pingala.

To activate the energy centers along the Governor, assert, *"It's my intent to activate the energy centers along the Governor meridian that belong to Trishira."* Take a moment to enjoy the shift. Then assert, *"It's my intent to activate the energy centers along the Ida meridian that belong to Trishira."* Finally, assert, *"It's my intent to activate the energy centers along the Pingala meridian that belong to Trishira."* Continue to perform the Trishira Mudra for five more minutes while you enjoy the enhanced flow of energy through the Governor, Ida, and Pingala. After five minutes, release the mudra, count from one to five, and open your eyes. You will feel wide awake, perfectly relaxed, and will experience the benefits that come from empowering the goddess.

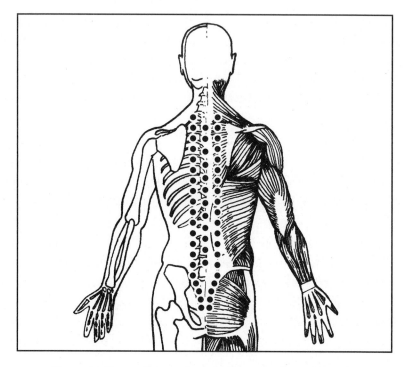

Figure 22: *Energy Centers along the Governor, Ida, and Pingala*

Exercise: The Maithuna Rite

Another way a man and woman can celebrate the goddess is through the Maithuna Rite. In Sanskrit, the word *Maithuna* refers to the intimate embrace that lovers experience when their limbs are intertwined. The goal of the Maithuna Rite is to have partners experience the sexual ecstasy that emerges through the union of Shiva and Shakti. The Maithuna Rite brings partners into an ecstatic state through sexual intercourse by encouraging them to stay centered in their authentic minds while they bring their sexual energy under their conscious control. In practical terms, this means that partners enhance the flow of sexual energy through their energy fields, but keep it from being dissipated by overt sexual stimulation and ejaculation.

In ancient times, the Maithuna Rite was preceded by elaborate preparations that had the release of pent-up sexual energy as their goal. We are told by Georg Feuerstein in *Tantra: The Path of Ecstasy* that after practicing the Maithuna Rite "the practitioners may walk around in absolute bliss, recite poetry, sing, clap their hands, weep with joy, play musical instruments, dance, stagger, and fall down." The author explains that the Maithuna Rite can be accompanied "by the following eight conditions: trembling, (*kampana*), hair-raising thrill (*romanca*), throbbing (*sphurana*), shedding tears of love (*prema-ashru*, written *premashru*), perspiration (*sveda*), laughter (*hasya*), dancing (*lasya*), and spontaneous singing (*gayana*)." [11]

In the Maithuna Rite, partners sit facing each other while they both remain present in their authentic minds. The male partner sits in the lotus position or sits upright with his feet flat on the floor. His female partner sits on his lap, with her legs wrapped around his waist. With her arms, she embraces him around the neck. The man's erect penis is allowed to rest on the opening of the vagina.

This is a static posture that partners assume after they have engaged in spiritual foreplay. Nothing overt or physical is done to arouse the sexual energy any further. If partners remain present in their authentic minds, even without any physical movement or stimulation, the vagina will become fully lubricated and the erect penis will naturally slide into it. After a short time, which can be extended with practice, partners will experience an explosion of sexual energy, which will lead to orgasm and a celebration of the creative power of the goddess.

You can practice the Maithuna Rite directly after you and your partner have engaged in spiritual foreplay or after you've engaged in traditional intercourse. In either case, the explosion of sexual energy that originates by the second chakra will radiate in all directions. As a result, chakras throughout your energy field will become active. You and your partner will share the same sexual ecstasy as the divine couple Shiva/Shakti.

Chapter 13
Your Three Hearts

When the universe was created, the god Vishnu crossed its vast expanse in three easy steps. As cosmic beings, each individual contains the entire cosmos, and can cross its vastness via the three hearts. If you've practiced the Orgasmic Bliss Mudra, then you know that the greatest benefits are concentrated in the region between your solar plexus and throat. This region includes your chest, upper back, and shoulders. What you may not know yet is that this region is central to your experience of transcendent sex and relationships because it's the location of your three hearts.

You may be wondering how you or anyone else could have three hearts. However, as an inter-dimensional being, it's not as strange as it sounds. On the left side of your chest is your first heart—the human heart. If you move horizontally three inches (eight centimeters) to the right, you reach your sternum. Directly in the middle of your sternum is your second heart, your heart chakra. Moving horizontally to the right, another three inches (eight centimeters) you reach your third heart—Atman.

In Sanskrit, *Atman* means "that which cannot be doubled." The Upanishads (a sacred text of yoga) declare that, through Atman, Universal

Consciousness enters your energy field. Through Atman, you experience the yearning for transcendent sex and relationships.

Indeed, it's only because you have three hearts that you can make the transition from traditional sex and relationships to transcendent sex and relationships. However, the transition to transcendent sex and relationships can only take place after you've transcended the limitations of your human heart.

The human heart is limited because it can only reflect energy. The energy it reflects can have either individual or universal qualities. When the human heart reflects energy with individual qualities, the energy can be laced with the same inauthentic desires, emotions, ideas, and attitudes that limit your ability to share pleasure, love, intimacy, and joy.

To move beyond the limitations of the human heart, you must be able to activate and center yourself in your heart chakra, because your heart chakra is a vortex through which sexual energy enters your energy field. Indeed, only by making the transition to your heart chakra can you go beyond the limitations imposed on you by human love and the desires, fears, jealousy, and so on that make it so unreliable and difficult to sustain.

The transition to your heart chakra comes in three phases. In the first phase, you activate your heart chakra and experience the benefits that come from having more sexual energy radiating through it.

In the second phase, you center yourself in your heart chakra. That shifts you into your authentic mind and allows sexual energy to flow through your energy system without disruption. With more sexual energy flowing through your energy system, your personal rights will be secured against the badgering of personas and the intrusion of external projections. Intimacy will become an integral part of your relationship.

In the third phase, you turn your organs of perception inward and emerge from your heart chakra, while you remain centered in it. This will allow you to remain authentic while you experience the world through dual awareness.

Although making the shift from the human heart to the heart chakra will bring benefits, it's only when you make the transition to the third heart—Atman—that intimacy and joy will become permanent and you will experience all the benefits of transcendent sex and relationships.

To make the shift to Atman—the third heart—you must go inward to the place where transcendent love emerges. By doing that, you will become conscious of your a priori union with Universal Consciousness. Once you've become conscious of this a priori union, you will be able to consistently experience and share pleasure, love, intimacy, and joy with your partner.

However, to make the transition from your first heart to your second heart and from your second to your third heart, you will need to know as much as possible about the functions of each heart and how each heart influences your energetic interactions with other people.

The Human Heart

The human heart is often lumped together with the physical heart. However, it has additional functions. The most important is to reflect sexual energy that has emerged from your chakras or from the Kundalini Shakti after it has become active.

When the human heart is functioning healthfully and is not burdened by karmic baggage or external projections, it will reflect sexual energy like a clean mirror reflects light, without any distortion or loss of radiance. However, we rarely see that in the real world. That's because most people carry layers of karmic baggage in their personal field, particularly around their energy centers and their three hearts. They suffer from the intrusion of external projections, which can interfere with the functions of the chakras and the flow of sexual energy through their energy field.

Even when karmic baggage and external projections are not being reflected off the human heart, their presence can block, or at least distort, the sexual energy that's being reflected.

Because the human heart can only reflect energy, it becomes easily blocked or distorted, and that's why human love can't serve as the foundation for transcendent sex and relationships.

In fact, when enough qualified energy is being reflected from the human heart, a person can learn to love almost anything, particularly if he or she obsessively clings to the human heart and the qualified energy being reflected from it. In an amusing passage from *Love and Death*, Woody Allen makes it clear how difficult your relationship can be if it's based exclusively on human love:

> To love is to suffer. To avoid suffering one must not love. But then one suffers from not loving. Therefore to love is to suffer and not to love is to suffer. To suffer is to suffer. To be happy is to love. To be happy is then to suffer. But suffering makes one unhappy. Therefore, to be unhappy one must love, or love to suffer, or suffer from too much happiness.

Although the human heart may burn brightly with reflected sexual energy for some time, the Principle of Rhythm demands that it cannot burn with the same intensity forever. Sooner or later, qualified energy will impair its ability to reflect energy with universal qualities, which means its intensity must sooner or later diminish.

Indeed, under normal circumstances the human heart is almost always burdened by karmic baggage and external projections. The addition of karmic baggage and the intrusion of external energy doesn't necessarily mean that human love is entirely blocked. What it does mean is that human love is usually burdened by layers of karmic baggage and external projections that can make a person judgmental, fanatical, or create the obsessive desire to control or to be controlled.

Desire is a two-edged sword. It compels people in love to seek intimacy with their partner, while at the same time it traps them in the personality issues and personas that emerge from karmic baggage and external projections. Too much dependence on human love, in fact, can lead to the kind of obsessive love that will sooner or later disrupt relationships. By using human love as a stepping-stone to intimacy, however, this trap can be avoided. If you and your partner have fallen into it, you can pull yourselves out by making the transition to the second heart.

The Second Heart

The second heart is the heart chakra. Unlike the human heart, which only reflects energy, the heart chakra serves as a vortex through which sexual energy, which has emerged from Universal Consciousness, can enter your energy field. Because the heart chakra is a vortex and doesn't merely reflect energy, it's much more reliable than the human heart.

With a much more reliable foundation, you will be able to experience more sexual energy. Intimacy will become a stable part of your relationship. A stable relationship with intimacy as its foundation, rather than human love, is essential if partners hope to participate in a long-term intimate relationship with one another.

Your heart chakra also upholds your personal rights. By centering yourself in your heart chakra you can overcome the limitations imposed by your belief system and the personas it supports. Making the transition to your second heart brings additional benefits. It will help you to make the shift from sexual foreplay to spiritual foreplay and from a purely genital orgasm to a multiple and/or full body orgasm.

Indeed, once you've made the transition to your second heart, you will experience more pleasure, love, and intimacy. That will bring you one step closer to experiencing all the benefits of transcendent sex and relationships.

The Third Heart

In order to experience all the benefits of transcendent sex and relationships, including sustained intimacy and joy, you must shift your center of awareness from your second heart to your third heart—Atman.

Atman emerges from the right side of your chest, directly across from the human heart, and to the right of your heart chakra. You can think of it as the doorway through which Universal Consciousness enters your energy field. Although you've always been in union with Universal Consciousness, it's unlikely that you've experienced all the benefits yet. That changes once you've made the transition to the third heart.

By making this transition and recognizing your a priori union with Universal Consciousness, you will become the observer of the movie of your mind. Beliefs and taboos that once restricted your freedom will melt away and intimacy and joy will become permanent qualities of your relationship.

The transition to the third heart is not an easy one. It's not unusual to make the transition into the third heart and then get distracted and pop out of it again. This fitful experience, which can be quite frustrating, will last as long as you believe you're separate from Universal Consciousness and as long as you continue to put your individual needs and desires ahead of transcendent sex and relationships.

You can avoid frustration and make the transition easier for yourself if you accept the objective truth that you're a transcendent being whose Dharma (purpose) is to share pleasure, love, intimacy, and joy with people (particularly with your partner).

Accepting the objective truth may appear difficult from your present perspective, but it will become easier once you've experienced the yearning of your third heart for truth, freedom, or divine love.

The Yearning of the Third Heart

The yearning of your third heart for truth, freedom, or divine love is in reality the yearning to experience union (or intimacy) with Universal Consciousness. Some people experience the yearning of their third heart for one of these three all their lives, others do so when they meet a partner who moves them deeply. Still others experience the yearning only after they've begun the process of transcendence. Indeed, the first hint most people get that Universal Consciousness exists and that they yearn for something more than human love is the yearning of the third heart for truth, freedom, or unconditional love.

Although both human love and intimacy are powerful forces, neither human love nor intimacy is capable of bringing you or anyone else into conscious union with Universal Consciousness. However, if you

intuitively seek more from your relationships than human love and intimacy, human love can motivate you to go deeper, to the place or condition from which Universal Consciousness emerges—your third heart.

Your third heart is the doorway through which Universal Consciousness enters your energy field. By following the yearning of your third
heart inward, you will come into direct contact with Universal Consciousness. However, to go through that doorway—so that you can experience intimacy with Universal Consciousness and by extension experience transcendent sex and relationships—you must recognize that
relationship is not attachment, dependency, or bonding. And you must
be willing to give up the will to power and/or the belief that control
and security are more important to you than transcendence. In fact, unless you've recognized that the experience of transcendence is essentially the ongoing experience of truth, freedom, and unconditional love
and you have the yearning for one of these three, you won't be able to
make the lasting transition to transcendent sex and relationships.

Transcendent sex and relationships are directly related to truth because you can only experience them when you're being true to yourself
and you live with integrity. You can only share the benefits of transcendent sex and relationships with another person when he or she also lives
with integrity.

Transcendent sex and relationships are directly related to freedom
because human beings must be free to express themselves without fear
in order to experience them. Those who are dependent, or who seek to
control or to be controlled, or who must have what they love, cannot
achieve transcendence.

Transcendent sex and relationships are directly related to unconditional love because you must give up all judgment and love uncondi-
tionally, regardless of the consequence, in order to experience the benefits of them both.

That said, it's time to learn more about the yearning of your third
heart for truth, freedom, and unconditional love.

The Yearning for Truth

The yearning for the truth is not the yearning for accurate information. It's the yearning for integrity and personal honesty. Integrity means more than anything else—being yourself—no matter what the personal cost. Being yourself and not what someone else or even your individual mind and ego want you to be is essential if you hope to experience union with Universal Consciousness and share transcendent sex and relationship with your partner.

Indeed, living with integrity means being what you are now, without dressing it up or putting a sugar coating on it. It means letting go of the guilt and shame associated with trying to live up to someone else's expectations or ideals and normally failing. It means doing what is appropriate, even if it means disappointing someone you love.

The Yearning for Freedom

The yearning for freedom is not the same as a desire to be free from external domination or oppression. Nor is it the license to do whatever you want. Freedom in this context is liberty from the domination of karmic baggage and external projections. It's the freedom to be authentic, to be who you are, and to express yourself without being badgered by personas or individual fields of qualified energy.

Freedom of this sort is enduring. It is a state of permanent intimacy, which cannot be taken away by any outside agency. It can only be given away because of ignorance. However, even then the loss of freedom is only a temporary condition because the essential condition of each person is freedom from attachment and of union with Universal Consciousness.

The Yearning for Unconditional Love

The yearning for unconditional love is the innate yearning for union with Universal Consciousness. In fact, on the deepest level of awareness, human beings know that separation is impossible and that union with Universal Consciousness endures from everlasting to everlasting.

Freud called this innate knowledge an infantile belief in immortality. Like many of his generation, he misinterpreted what he observed. The fact is that each human being is an eternal being, not made in God's image, but a vehicle through which Universal Consciousness can manifest pleasure, love, intimacy, and joy on all dimensions of the phenomenal universe.

Because the yearning of the third heart motivates people to consciously re-experience union with Universal Consciousness, the question you're probably asking yourself is whether you have the yearning of the third heart, for truth, freedom, or unconditional love. The exercise that follows should help you to discover whether you have the yearning for one of these three and whether you're ready to make the transition to transcendent sex and relationships.

Exercise: Finding the Yearning of the Third Heart

To find out if you have the yearning for truth, freedom, or unconditional love you must center yourself in your third heart—Atman. Then you must become present in your authentic mind and turn your organs of perception inward, on the level of your third heart. After you've turned your organs of perception inward, you'll assert, *"It's my intent to experience the yearning of my third heart."* If the yearning is there, it will emerge into your conscious awareness. You should be able to discern whether you have the yearning for truth, freedom, or unconditional love.

Before you begin, it's worth noting that the yearning for union with Universal Consciousness will emerge as a yearning for truth whenever your karmic condition demands that you live with greater integrity, in order to overcome personality issues and experience intimacy and joy in your relationships. The yearning for freedom will emerge whenever your karmic condition demands that you break free from attachments in order to experience union with Universal Consciousness. The yearning for unconditional love will emerge whenever your rights have been violated and you must live more authentically.

To begin the exercise, find a comfortable position, with your back straight. Then close your eyes and breath yogically. Continue by counting from five to one, then from ten to one. Use the Standard Method Exercise to relax the muscles of your physical-material body. Then assert, *"It's my intent to become present in my authentic mind."* Continue by asserting, *"It's my intent to center myself in my third heart."* Once you're centered, assert, *"It's my intent to turn my organs of perception inward, on the level of my third heart."* Finally assert, *"It's my intent to experience the yearning of my third heart."*

Many people notice something like bubbles popping off the right side of their chest when they turn their organs of perception inward, on the level of their third heart. They may pop off individually or in clumps. Some of the clumps may be quite large, and your muscles may react by quivering as they pop off. Other people report that the muscles of their chests feel like they were being stretched and flattened one layer at a time. Don't let any of those experiences distract you. If you're patient and remain present, you will experience a unique sensation after a short time that will be the yearning of your third heart.

If you're not sure whether it's the yearning for truth, freedom, or unconditional love, you can check which resonates with you by using the skill you learned in chapter 4. As you know, when something is objectively true, it will resonate. When it resonates, it will enhance the flow of sexual energy through your energy field and keep you present in your authentic mind. When something isn't true, it won't resonate. Instead, it will weaken the flow of sexual energy through your energy field and make it difficult for you to stay present in your authentic mind.

To check whether the yearning of your third heart is for truth, freedom, or unconditional love, remain present and assert three times, *"The yearning of my third heart is for truth."* If the yearning of your third heart is for truth, your sexual energy will flow better and you will stay present without effort. If the yearning is not for truth, the flow of sexual energy through your energy field will weaken slightly, and you will have to remind yourself to stay present.

If the yearning for truth resonated, bring yourself out of the exercise by counting from one to five and then opening your eyes. If the yearning for truth didn't resonate, continue by asserting three times, *"The yearning of my third heart is for freedom."* If the yearning for freedom resonates, bring yourself out of the exercise by counting from one to five and then opening your eyes. If the yearning for freedom didn't resonate, continue by asserting three times, *"The yearning of my third heart is for unconditional love."* If the yearning for unconditional love resonates, bring yourself out of the exercise by counting from one to five and then opening your eyes.

If you don't experience the yearning of your third heart or if it's too weak for you to be sure whether you have the yearning for truth, freedom, or unconditional love, don't dismay. You can enhance the yearning of your third heart by practicing the following exercise.

Exercise: Enhancing the Yearning of the Third Heart

To enhance the yearning of your third heart, you will become present in your authentic mind. Then you will combine your authentic will, desire, and unconditional love. Once you've done that, you will perform the Orgasmic Bliss Mudra. When practiced together, these techniques will quickly enhance the yearning of your third heart.

To begin the exercise, find a comfortable position with your back straight. Then close your eyes and breath yogically. Continue by counting from five to one, and then from ten to one. Use the Standard Method Exercise to relax the muscles of your physical-material body. Then assert, *"It's my intent to become present in my authentic mind."*

Once you're present, you're ready to combine your authentic will, desire, and unconditional love. To do that, assert, *"It's my intent to turn my organs of perception inward and experience my authentic will."* Take a moment to experience your authentic will. Then assert, *"It's my intent to turn my organs of perception inward and experience my authentic desire."* Take another moment to experience your authentic desire. Continue by asserting, *"It's my intent to turn my organs of perception inward and experience unconditional love."* Take another moment to experience unconditional love. Then assert, *"It's my intent to combine my authentic will, desire, and unconditional love."* Take five minutes to experience the shift that takes place once you've combined all three.

You may experience lightness or the sensation that you're floating inside your energy field. Don't be disturbed by either sensation. There is nothing wrong. Feeling lighter indicates that you're centered in universal qualities. The sensation that you're floating indicates that your personal will and desire have temporarily been freed from the influence of karmic baggage and external projections. Take five minutes more to enjoy the effects. Then continue the exercise by performing the Orgasmic Bliss Mudra.

To perform this mudra, place the tip of your tongue on your upper palate. Then bring it straight back until it comes to rest at the point where the hard palate rolls up and becomes soft. Once the tip of your tongue is in that position, put the bottom of your feet together so that the soles are touching. Then bring your hands in front of your solar plexus, with the inside tips of your thumbs together.

Continue by bringing the outside of your index fingers together from the tips to the first joint. Next, bring the outside of your middle fingers together from the first to the second joint. The fourth and fifth fingers should be curled into your palm (see Figure 1). After your tongue, fingers, and feet are in position, close your eyes once again and continue the exercise for ten more minutes.

After ten minutes, release the mudra. Then count from one to five. When you reach the number five, open your eyes. You'll be wide awake, perfectly relaxed, and if you practice the exercise regularly (for as little as five days), you will enhance the yearning of your third heart for truth, freedom, or unconditional love.

Chapter 14

Full-Body, Multiple, and Endless Orgasms

Now that you've learned to celebrate the goddess and have discovered the yearning of your third heart, you're ready to make the transition from a purely genital orgasm to either a full-body, multiple, or endless orgasm.

William Reich recognized the importance of orgasm early in the twentieth century. He declared that people's emotional health and the well-being of their intimate relationships were related to their ability to achieve a complete orgasm. Reich stated that in his work he had never come across a neurotic who had the ability to achieve a complete orgasm because fear made it impossible for him or her to surrender completely.

Reich recognized that a complete orgasm was far more complex than a purely genital ejaculation. In a purely genital ejaculation, sexual energy is actually dissipated. Rather than bringing partners closer together, it has a tendency to push them apart. It might sound counter-intuitive to declare that an orgasm can push partners apart. However, it's possible, because a purely genital orgasm has the tendency to restrict sexual energy to the second chakra and its physical externalization, the genitals. When the sexual energy becomes restricted to the second chakra and the genitals by a purely genital orgasm, it is prevented from radiating freely through the other chakras in your energy field.

If sexual energy doesn't radiate freely through your etheric and physical chakras, less sexual energy will radiate into your physical-material body. It will be difficult for you to feel the sexual excitement that normally accompanies spiritual foreplay and coitus. When sexual energy is prevented from radiating freely through your third and fourth chakras, the tenderness, love, and intimacy you normally feel during and after coitus can be disrupted. When sexual energy is prevented from radiating freely through your fifth chakra, joy and self-expression will be stifled. And when sexual energy is prevented from radiating freely through your sixth and seventh chakras, you will be prevented from making the transition to transcendent sex.

In a healthy orgasm, on the other hand, sexual energy radiating through your second chakra will be transmuted into the complete spectrum of sexual energy needed for a full-body, multiple, or endless orgasm.

Sexual energy will be stepped down to the first chakra and the chakras below personal body space and stepped up to the seventh chakra and the chakras above personal body space. The enhanced flow of sexual energy will radiate through your meridians and pour into the auric fields.

As sexual energy radiates through your etheric and physical chakras into your physical-material body, it will excite your nervous system and your organs of the physical-material body, particularly your sexual organs and skin, which will become flushed and more sensitive.

At the moment of climax, the eleven chakras in personal body space (as well as the chakras above and below personal body space) will explode simultaneously and you will experience all the benefits of transcendent sex. Dr. Jonn Mumford declared, "Orgasm is the only spontaneous, natural experience of a deathless, birthless, timeless, sorrowless dimension."[12]

Orgasm and Relationship

The impact that purely genital orgasms and full-body, multiple, or endless orgasms can have on partners is illustrated by the two anecdotes below.

In the first anecdote, Sam and Marla are at home making love. They're young (in their early twenties) and energetic, having gotten into a routine of making love two or three times a week. They don't engage in spiritual foreplay, and the sexual foreplay they engage in is confined to the same activities each time. They touch each other and kiss for a short time; sometimes they stop and talk. After a while, Marla lies on her back with her legs in the air. Sam kneels in front of her, inserts his penis, and begins to thrust. Marla grinds her hips and moans slightly. Sam thrusts quickly for a minute or two, and after having a genital orgasm, withdraws. They hug and lie together for a few more minutes. Both Sam and Maria feel mildly disappointed, but that's how they normally feel after sex. After a while, Sam rolls over and goes to sleep. Marla stays awake, feeling anxious and mildly depressed.

In the second anecdote, Karen and Jason are in their late forties. They are committed to transcendence and have begun to substitute spiritual foreplay for sexual foreplay. They activate their chakras and become present in their authentic minds before they make love, so that they can share universal qualities with one another. They practice gazing and take plenty of time kissing and touching each other. Then Karen lies on her back and Jason begins to celebrate the goddess. When Jason enters Karen, she is so aroused that she has an orgasm almost immediately. Jason can feel the walls of her vagina contracting. He slows down his thrusting for a few moments until he has stopped completely. Then he withdraws in preparation for the Maithuna Rite. By this time, the enhanced flow of sexual energy has intoxicated them both. It doesn't take long for Jason's erect penis to slide back into Karen's vagina. Jason can feel Karen's breathing change as her body prepares itself for a second orgasm. At the same time, Jason's breathing quickens, and, with an extremely loud moan, he ejaculates.

Afterward, Karen and Jason feel energized and immerse themselves in their mutual afterglow. They're no youngsters. Both are in their late forties. However, age is rarely a factor in the quality of a person's orgasm. Men and women can enjoy full-body orgasms, multiple orgasms, or even endless orgasms, as long as they're sexually active.

In the largest survey of its kind, published in *The New England Journal of Medicine*, researchers found that "older people value sexuality as an important part of life." Indeed, three quarters of the respondents in their forties and fifties reported that they remain sexually active. Even in the highest age group (seventies and eighties), 54 percent of those surveyed who had a partner continued to have sex regularly.

Research has repeatedly confirmed that sex is not exclusively a young person's activity. Whether they're young or old, people value the quality of their sexual lives, which means that the quality of a person's orgasm can have a significant impact on him or her throughout each successive stage of life. The authors of a report in *The Oregonian* recently declared that "when it comes to sexual activity, older people are really just younger people later in life ... There is no reason to believe that they give up the basic human desire for love and intimacy, and the kind of pleasure that comes from intimate relationship."[13]

What We Know About Orgasm

Research since the 1960s has validated what we all intuitively know about the benefits of a healthy orgasm. On the physical side, a healthy orgasm has been shown to reduce stress, lower cholesterol levels, improve circulation, help people lose weight, and even help them to stay younger.

A healthy orgasm promotes the secretion of the hormone DHEA. Dr. Theresa Crenshaw, author of *The Alchemy of Love and Lust*, states, "DHEA may be the most powerful chemical in our personal world. It helps balance the immune system, improves cognition, promotes bone growth, and maintains and repairs tissues, keeping your skin healthy and supple. It may also contribute to cardiovascular health and even function as an antidepressant."

In addition to these benefits, healthy orgasms can enhance your mental health and the health of your relationship by promoting the release of pleasure-inducing endorphins in the brain, which can relieve anxiety and depression, increase vitality, and boost confidence and self-esteem.

Physical Changes During Orgasm

Research has confirmed that men and women both experience complex physical and psychological changes during orgasm. Recent discoveries indicate that a man's orgasm goes through two distinct phases. First, the prostate, seminal vesicles, and vas deferens contract, pouring their contents into the urethra. Sperm mixes with the secretions of the seminal vesicles and the prostate to form the ejaculate. Contractions are the beginning of the ejaculation. This is when men say they feel they're about to come. Masters and Johnson call this point of the phase "ejaculatory inevitability" because once the contractions begin, the process usually happens involuntarily. During the second phase of the ejaculatory process, the fluid is propelled through the urethra by contractions of the pelvic muscles. Although ejaculation occurs in and through the penis, it is in fact a total-body response. According to Dr. Bernie Zilbergeld, "Respiration, blood pressure, and heartbeat increase as a man approaches ejaculation, usually peaking at the moment of 'propulsion.'"

A woman goes through a similar process. When a woman is stimulated through kissing and touching, blood flows into her pelvis, the vagina moistens, and the labia majora and labia minora begin to swell and become duskier and darker in color. As she becomes more aroused, the walls of her vagina start to exude fluid in preparation for intercourse. Lubrication is one of the first signs of sexual arousal in women. Physiologically, lubrication is identical to a male's erection. As soon as the vagina has been lubricated, it begins to elongate, and the uterus moves out of the way to make room for the penis.

From the strictly physiological point of view, a woman's orgasm begins when the muscles of the upper third of the vagina and the uterus begin to contract. However, a lot more is going on as a woman's body prepares itself for orgasm.

1. Muscles tense; heart rate and blood pressure increase.

2. Nipples become erect.

3. The blood-engorged clitoris becomes erect and pulls under the clitoral hood.

4. The labia majora and labia minora enlarge, and lubrication increases.

5. The vagina continues to expand and lengthen, and the breasts engorge slightly.

6. Muscles, including the anal sphincter, continue to tense and then contract, sometimes even spasming as a female experiences orgasm.[14]

Although there has been a great deal of interest in the human orgasm over the last few decades, research into it is not a new phenomenon. More than a thousand years ago, tantric adepts recognized that a healthy orgasm could break down the barriers that separated partners and prevented them from experiencing transcendent sex and relationships. In tantra, three types of orgasm have been identified: genital, full-body, and full-body multiple.

Genital Orgasm

The first type of orgasm is genital orgasm. Kinsey, Masters, and Johnson and other sex researchers, have defined *genital orgasm* as a reflex that occurs when muscle tension and blood flow to the pelvis reach a peak and are dispersed, the pubococcygeal (PC) muscle group that supports the pelvic floor spasms rhythmically at 0.8 second intervals, and the heart rate accelerates rapidly (often as high as 180 beats a minute) and then slows down. For men, orgasm usually includes ejaculation.

From our understanding of the human energy system we know that when a person experiences a purely genital orgasm, he or she will be centered in the individual mind and ego. Although sexual energy will radiate through the second chakra, and additional energy may be reflected off the human heart, the orgasm will not be completely satisfying. That's because the supply of sexual energy will be limited. The limited sexual energy a person experiences (and can share) will be mixed with energy emerging from personas and external projections. Some of this sexual energy will stimulate the etheric and physical chakras once it has been reflected. However, in most cases, there will be a lack of sexual energy available to stimulate additional chakras, fill the auras, or radiate between partners through their energy fields and physical-material bodies.

When the second chakra has not been burdened by an excessive amount of karmic baggage and external projections, more sexual energy will be made available, which means that more sexual energy will be reflected off the human heart. There will be more sexual energy available to fill the auras and radiate between partners.

The more sexual energy the human heart can reflect and the more partners can share, the more satisfying a genital orgasm will be. In some cases, when the second chakra can radiate sexual energy freely and the human heart can reflect it without difficulty, even a genital orgasm can be relatively satisfying. However, there is a wide spectrum of possibilities. The quality of a genital orgasm will always depend on a person's karmic condition and the condition of his or her energy field.

Exercise: The Love Mudra

The exercise that follows is designed to enhance the quality of your genital orgasm. You will begin by becoming present in your authentic mind. Then you will activate your second chakra. Once your second chakra has become active, you will perform the Love Mudra. By performing the Love Mudra, you will enhance the ability of your heart to reflect sexual energy. That will make your genital orgasm more intense and satisfying.

To begin, sit in a comfortable position, with your back straight. Then close your eyes and breathe yogically. Continue by counting from five to one, then from ten to one. Use the Standard Method Exercise to relax the muscles of your physical-material body. Then assert, *"It's my intent to become present in my authentic mind."* Continue by asserting, *"It's my intent to activate my second chakra."* Take a few moments to enjoy the shift.

When you're ready to perform the Love Mudra, open your eyes and keep them slightly unfocused. Then place your left thumb on the acupuncture point on the inside edge of your right thumb, just below the nail. Place the inside tips of your index fingers together. Your middle fingers are curved inward and touching from the first to second joint. The pads of your ring fingers are touching up to the first joint. And your left pinkie is placed over the nail of your right pinkie from the tip to the first joint (see Figure 23).

Hold the mudra with your eyes closed for ten minutes while you stay present in your authentic mind. Then count from one to five. When you reach the number five, release the mudra, and open your eyes. You will feel wide awake, perfectly relaxed, and better than you did before.

To enhance your genital orgasm, practice the exercise for seven days before lovemaking. After practicing the exercise for seven days, your second chakra will become more active, and your human heart will be capable of reflecting more sexual energy. This should make it possible for you to experience a more intense and prolonged genital orgasm.

Full-Body Orgasm

Once you've made the transition to your second heart and have substituted spiritual foreplay for sexual foreplay, you will be able to make the transition to a full-body orgasm. As opposed to a purely genital orgasm, a full-body orgasm will enhance the amount of sexual energy you experience and can share with your partner. It will increase the length of time you can remain sexually intimate.

In a full-body orgasm, sexual energy, emerging from your second chakra, will radiate through your seven traditional chakras. From there it will radiate through your etheric and physical chakras as well as through the meridians that connect them.

Excess sexual energy will continue to radiate through your auras and from your auras into your physical-material body. Sexual energy

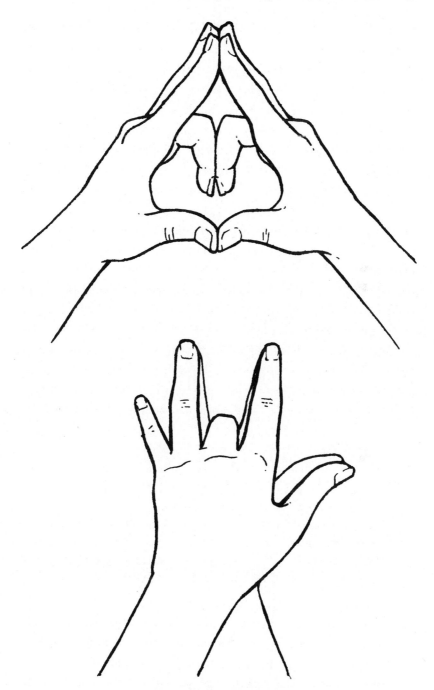

Figure 23: The Love Mudra

flowing into your physical-material body will stimulate your nervous system and enhance your sexual desire. It's at this point, when all chakras in body space have become active and sexual energy has radiated into your physical-material body, that you will experience the explosion of sexual energy that makes a full-body orgasm possible.

In addition to more pleasure and sexual excitement, a full-body orgasm will bring other benefits. Security will increase when your first chakra becomes active. Vitality will increase and gender orientation will become clearer and more balanced when your second chakra becomes active. Your sense of belonging will grow, along with trust and satisfaction, when your third chakra becomes active. Confidence and self-love will increase when your fourth chakra becomes active. Inner joy will increase and self-expression will be enhanced when your fifth chakra becomes active. Personal intent will be strengthened when your sixth chakra becomes active. And a state of transcendence will be realized when your seventh chakra becomes active.

When your etheric chakras become active, you will be able to express and resolve feelings more easily; empathy will increase. When your physical chakras become active, you will become grounded and experience the richness of the physical-material environment without difficulty.

By making the transition to the heart chakra and a full-body orgasm, you will also be able to sense your partner's energetic condition and anticipate what he or she needs and wants. That will make it easier for you to share more pleasure, love, and intimacy with your lover during transcendent sex.

Exercise: Full-Body Orgasm

To experience a full-body orgasm, you must have the will to love what gives you pleasure. That means you must be able to activate your second, fourth, and sixth chakras. Pleasure is associated with the second chakra. By activating your second chakra, you will enhance your experience of pleasure. Personal rights are regulated by your fourth chakra. By activating your fourth chakra, you will gain control over your personal rights, particularly the right to love what gives you pleasure. Personal will is regulated by your sixth chakra. By activating your sixth chakra, you will strengthen your will so that you will love what gives you pleasure, even if there's internal opposition from karmic baggage and/or external opposition from family, friends, and the institutions of your culture. Without the will to love what gives you pleasure, it will be difficult for you to liberate enough sexual energy to have a full-body orgasm.

The following exercise is designed to enhance your will to love what gives you pleasure so that you have enough sexual energy to experience a full-body orgasm. In the exercise, you will activate and center yourself in your heart chakra. Then you will activate your second and sixth chakras. Once your second, fourth, and sixth chakras have become active, you'll become present on those three dimensions and turn your organs of perception inward.

To begin, find a comfortable position, with your back straight. Then close your eyes and breathe yogically. Continue by counting from five to one, then from ten to one. Use the Standard Method Exercise to relax the muscles of your physical-material body. Then assert, *"It's my intent to activate and center myself in my heart chakra."* Continue by asserting, *"It's my intent to activate my second chakra."* Once you've activated your second chakra, assert, *"It's my intent to activate my sixth chakra."* Take a few moments to enjoy the shift. Then assert, *"On the levels of my second, fourth, and sixth chakras it's my intent to become present in my energy field."* Once you've become present, assert, *"It's my intent to turn my organs of perception inward on the levels of my second, fourth, and sixth chakras."*

Take fifteen minutes to enjoy the exercise. After fifteen minutes, count from one to five. When you reach the number five, open your eyes. You will feel wide awake, perfectly relaxed, and better than you did before.

If you practice the exercise for seven days before lovemaking, you will experience more sexual energy radiating through your second, fourth, and sixth chakras. With more sexual energy radiating through those three chakras, you will go beyond the limitations of a genital orgasm and experience the benefits that come from a full-body orgasm.

Exercise: Full-Body Multiple Orgasm

There is a common misconception that only a woman can experience a full-body multiple orgasm. It's time to debunk this myth. The truth is that it's possible for a man to enjoy a full-body multiple orgasm as well. In fact, once a man experiences a full-body orgasm, it's only a short step to a full-body multiple orgasm.

To experience a full-body multiple orgasm, all you must do in addition to what you've done to achieve a full-body orgasm is activate and center yourself in your heart chakra and the corresponding chakra below body space (the fourth chakra below body space). Then you must activate your first and second chakras and the corresponding chakras below body space.

When you can radiate sexual energy freely from your first and second chakra and the corresponding chakras below body space, you will transcend the limitations imposed on your sexual life by your attachment to duality—particularly to good and evil.

By overcoming your attachment to good and evil (at least temporarily), you will find that sexual energy can flow in two directions, up through the eleven chakras in personal body space and down through the chakras below personal body space. This flow of sexual energy in both directions will allow you to feel a full-body multiple orgasm.

This exercise is designed to be practiced along with the exercise to promote a full-body orgasm. If you practice both exercises for seven days before lovemaking, you will experience more sexual energy radiating through your energy field, in both directions. You will find it easier to experience a full-body multiple orgasm.

To begin, find a comfortable position, with your back straight. Then close your eyes and breathe yogically. Continue by counting from five to one, then from ten to one. Use the Standard Method Exercise to relax your physical-material body. Continue by asserting, *"It's my intent to activate my heart chakra and my fourth chakra below body space."* Once both chakras are active, assert, *"It's my intent to center myself in my heart chakra and my fourth chakra below body space."* Take a few moments to enjoy the shift.

Then assert, *"It's my intent to activate my first chakra."* Continue by asserting, *"It's my intent to activate my first chakra below personal body space."* Then assert, *"It's my intent to activate my second chakra."* Continue by asserting, *"It's my intent to activate my second chakra below body space."* Finally, assert, *"It's my intent to turn my organs of perception inward on the levels of my first and second chakra and my first and second chakra below personal body space."* Take about fifteen minutes to enjoy the exercise. After about fifteen minutes, count from one to five. When you reach the number five, open your eyes. You will feel wide awake, perfectly relaxed, and better than you did before.

If you practice both exercises regularly for seven days, you will experience more sexual energy radiating through your energy field in both directions. Once sexual energy can radiate freely through your energy field in both directions, it's just a matter of time before you experience an endless orgasm.

Endless Orgasm

To experience an endless orgasm, sexual energy must radiate freely through your chakras above and below personal body space, and you must be able to shift your center of awareness from your heart chakra to your third heart—Atman.

Once you've met those conditions, you will detach yourself from the "I," as well as from the karmic baggage and personas that compose your individual mind and ego. By detaching yourself from the "I" as well as your individual mind and ego, you will become detached from all internal and external attachments at the same time. At the climatic moment of orgasm, sexual energy will burst forth from your second chakra and second chakra below body space. That sexual energy will activate your chakras above and below body space. With the "I" subdued and nothing strong enough to force you to contract, sexual energy will continue to radiate freely during and after your orgasm. You will experience the joy that comes from an endless orgasm.

Exercise: The Endless Orgasm

In the following exercise, you will prepare your energy field for an end-less orgasm. To do that you will activate your second, fourth, and sixth chakra in and below personal body space. Then you will perform the Orgasmic Bliss Mudra and center yourself in your third heart.

To begin, find a comfortable position, with your back straight. Then close your eyes and breathe yogically. Continue by counting from five to one, and then from ten to one. Use the Standard Method Exercise to relax your physical-material body. Take a few moments to enjoy the shift. Then assert, *"It's my intent to activate my second chakra."* Continue by asserting, *"It's my intent to activate my second chakra below body space."* Then assert, *"It's my intent to activate my fourth chakra."* Next, assert, *"It's my intent to activate my fourth chakra below body space."* Continue by asserting, *"It's my intent to activate my sixth chakra."* Then assert, *"It's my intent to activate my sixth chakra below body space."* Take a few moments to enjoy the enhanced flow of sexual energy through your energy field. To perform the Orgas-mic Bliss Mudra, place the tip of your tongue on your upper palate. Then bring it straight back until it comes to rest at the point where the hard pal-ate rolls up and becomes soft. Once the tip of your tongue is in that posi-tion, place the bottom of your feet together so that the soles are touch-ing. Then open your eyes, bring your hands in front of your solar plexus, and place the inside tips of your thumbs together. Continue by bringing the outsides of your index fingers together from the tips to the first joint. Next, bring the outsides of your middle fingers together from the first to the second joint. The fourth and fifth fingers should be curled into your palms (see Figure 1). Once your tongue, fingers, and feet are in position, close your eyes again. Then assert, *"It's my intent to center myself in my third heart."* Hold the mudra for ten minutes while you stay centered in your third heart. After ten minutes, release the mudra. Then count from one to five, open your eyes, and bring yourself out of the exercise.

You can begin practicing this exercise regularly after you've expe-rienced a full-body multiple orgasm. The effects will be cumulative, which means that once you can center yourself in your third heart and radiate energy freely through your energy field, it's just a matter of time before you experience an endless orgasm.

Beyond Spiritual Foreplay

In tantra, there are a number of positions for coitus. These positions can be used along with the Maithuna Rite to enhance intimacy between partners so that they can experience full-body orgasms, full-body multiple orgasms, and/or endless orgasms.

The following list includes some of the most well-known positions.

Exercise: Putting on the Sock

In this technique, the woman lies on her back. The man sits between her legs and puts his penis at the entrance of her vagina. Using his fingers and hands, he caresses the vagina. Then he removes his hands and replaces it with his penis. The tension created by the man's caresses is satisfied when he finally places his penis in the vagina and begins to thrust vigorously.

Exercise: The Blacksmith's Posture

In this technique, the woman lies down and draws her legs up by spreading them and bending her knees. This position pushes her vagina forward, giving her partner a full view. The male partner mounts her, and teases her by repeatedly inserting and withdrawing his penis. By teasing his partner in this way, the man enhances his erection. He excites his partner and enhances sexual tension so that he and his partner can experience a full-body, full-body multiple, or endless orgasm. After inserting and withdrawing his penis for as long as possible, the man completes coitus by remaining inside his partner until they both climax.

Exercise: The Ostrich's Tail

In the Ostrich's Tail, the woman lies on her back while her male partner kneels at her feet and lifts her legs until only her shoulders and head remain on the ground. Using his hands, the man holds his partner's legs and enters her. The women can either rest her legs on her partner's shoulders or put them around his head. This position leads to deep penetration and will also allow the male partner to control the depth and intensity of his thrusting.

Exercise: The Yawning Position

In this position, the woman lies on her back. She spreads her legs widely with her knees slightly raised. The man holds himself above her on his hands or elbows at first. This allows partners to look into each other's eyes. With her hands free, the woman can caress her own breasts or her partner's head, face, or upper torso. When he is ready, the male partner slides forward, inserts his penis, and remains inside his partner until both climax.

These classic positions described above are designed to enhance sexual tension and pleasure so that partners achieve the most satisfying orgasms possible. However, it's important to recognize that regardless of the position you use for coitus, you and your partner should always keep as much energetic contact as possible. By maintaining energetic contact during spiritual foreplay, coitus, and afterward, you and your partner will be able to share uninterrupted pleasure, love, intimacy, and joy with one another.

You and your partner can practice one or more of the positions described above, as well as the Maithuna Rite, as part of your regular sexual regimen. If there is a complete absence of striving and tension during coitus, you and your partner will experience full-body multiple or endless orgasms. At the moment of climax, searing currents of sexual energy will radiate through your bodies, fusing your genitals together and bringing you both into conscious union with each other and Universal Consciousness.

Exercise: The Afterglow

The tantrics describe the blinding moment of orgasm as going beyond the senses, as if there has been an immediate and profound contact with the truth. There is no voice, no image, no vision—only the experience of transcendent sex and relationships.

It's true that an orgasm can bring partners together and enhance the experience of sexual ecstasy. However, it's also true that the experience of transcendent sex doesn't end with orgasm. Chakras that have become active during spiritual foreplay and coitus will continue to radiate sexual energy even after a full-body, full-body multiple, or endless orgasm. In fact, afterglow, the soft radiation of sexual energy that partners experience after orgasm is an essential part of transcendent sex.

When it comes to post-coital afterglow, partners should continue to maintain as much energetic contact as possible. Partners can ensure that contact is maintained by holding each other closely. Keeping eye contact is especially important, and so is keeping the chakras and energy centers in the hands and feet in close contact.

Because the hands and feet contain important energy centers, partners can use their hands and feet to touch, massage, and stimulate each other, even after orgasm. Rubbing or caressing the back of your partner's neck with your positive right hand if you're right-handed, or left hand if you're left-handed, will stimulate his or her fifth chakra and enhance his or her ability to experience and express authentic emotions, particularly joy.

Caressing your partner's lower back with your positive hand will stimulate his or her second chakra and enhance the flow of sexual energy through his or her pelvis. Stroking your partner along the spine with your positive hand will enhance the flow of sexual energy up the Governor to his or her crown chakra—and beyond.

By activating two special acupressure points on your partner's body, you can produce a powerful energetic experience that will add to their experience of afterglow. The first acupressure point is located in the slight indentation under the coccyx. The second point is located in the back of the head, two inches (five centimeters) behind and under the crown chakra (see Figure 24).

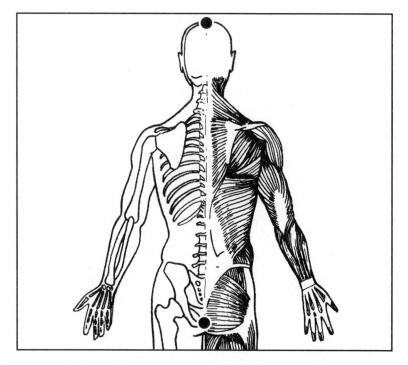

Figure 24: The Acupressure Points to Enhance the Afterglow

To activate these acupressure points, place the middle finger of your positive hand at the point just under the base of your partner's spine and push gently. Then place the middle finger of your feminine hand on the corresponding point, just behind their crown chakra, and push gently. Hold your partner between your two hands and continue to press gently for two or three minutes.

When both points are held simultaneously, sexual energy will radiate freely through your partner's energy field, from the soles of his or her feet to the crown of his or her head, even after the orgasm has ended.[15]

Exercise: The Cradle

Another position that will enhance and even extend your partner's experience of afterglow is the Cradle. In the Cradle, one partner sits upright, with his or her legs crossed. The other partner lies with his or her head in the cradle created by the partner's thighs and crotch. The sitting partner then places his or her hands on the sides of his or her partner's head, with thumbs and forefingers spread apart, to create a cradle for the partner's ears.

The sitting partner must remain present in his or her authentic mind while cradling the partner in his or her hands. On each exhalation, the sitting partner will exhale sexual energy through the mouth, directly at his or her partner's crown chakra. The stream of sexual energy will enhance and prolong the experience of afterglow for the partner being cradled. Partners can perform the cradle for up to ten minutes and then switch positions.

When partners continue to stimulate each other after a full-body, full-body multiple, or endless orgasm while using the techniques described above, the experience of afterglow can be enhanced and prolonged. In some cases afterglow can become so satisfying it will rival the experience of ecstasy experienced during spiritual foreplay and coitus.

Chapter 15

Say Yes to Transcendent Relationships

You already know that there are two types of relationships available to couples. There is a traditional relationship and a transcendent relationship. If partners have the desire to advance beyond the limitations of a traditional relationship, they must make the commitment to be authentic by substituting authentic desires, feelings, and emotions for those that are inauthentic. They must also be able to consistently share pleasure, love, intimacy, and joy with each other. In addition, they must have a clear sense of what differentiates a transcendent relationship from a traditional relationship so that they don't have unreasonable expectations and can recognize a transcendent relationship when they experience it.

In this chapter, you will learn what differentiates a transcendent relationship from a traditional relationship. Then you will learn what you and your partner can do to make the final transition from a traditional to a transcendent relationship.

Traditional Relationship

When viewed from the outside, a traditional and a transcendent relationship look virtually the same. Partners can live together, have children, and so on in both modes of relating. However, the purpose of a traditional relationship is to support the family unit. That will be its highest goal. It will use pleasure, love, and periodic intimacy to achieve that goal. However, it won't take partners any further because the demands of family life will override the motivation to live authentically and to engage in a transcendent relationship.

That's not to say that a traditional relationship can't satisfy partners. In some cases it can, because it can lead to pleasure, love, and intermittent intimacy. However, the final goal of permanent intimacy and joy, which partners share in a transcendent relationship, will remain a distant dream because partners will remain trapped by the mistaken notion that they are individuals, separate from Universal Consciousness and each other.

You're already familiar with a traditional relationship. As an institution, it evolved around the needs of childrearing and the economic realties of a pre-industrial society. I will call it *traditional* because it's the type of relationship that people in Western culture have become accustomed to and have accepted as normal for hundreds of years. Although it evolves and each generation views it from a different perspective, it still dominates in almost all segments of society.

Because traditional relationship values pleasure and human love most, it has limitations and is open to abuse, which means some people in traditional relationships will mistreat and/or neglect their partner.

Although abuse and neglect are not the norm, people in traditional relationships rarely view sustained intimacy and joy as relationship goals. Instead, it's more common for people in traditional relationship to seek security or to become karmically attached to one another. When partners in traditional relationship become karmically attached, their relationship can inhibit personal growth and prevent them from experiencing and sharing sustained intimacy and joy. That's why it's important to recognize that a traditional relationship is about living within limitations.

In contrast, a transcendent relationship is about transcending limitations. That's why a transcendent relationship isn't about attachment, dependency, or bonding. Nor is it something you can have or own. The truth is that transcendent relationship cannot exist in an environment where there is overt or covert oppression or one partner dominates, abuses, or neglects the other. Because permanent intimacy and joy cannot exist in an environment where partners remain trapped by limitations, to achieve a transcendent relationship partners must have the liberty to be themselves and must offer the same liberty to those with whom they share relationships.

Transcendent Relationship

In contrast to a traditional relationship, a transcendent relationship is more difficult to describe. People who choose it rarely talk about it publicly. So, metaphors of divine couples are used to flesh it out and inspire partners to choose it instead of a traditional relationship.

In the Hindu pantheon, Shiva and Shakti are one such couple. In the metaphor, Shiva represents Universal Consciousness and Shakti creative sexual energy. As we know, Shiva and Shakti are in an eternal embrace. According to tantrics, their embrace symbolizes the union of consciousness and energy, which couples share once they've experienced union with Universal Consciousness and with one another.

Although metaphors of divine couples can serve as inspiration, your ability to participate in transcendent relationships will depend on your commitment to transcendence and the choices you make. If you reject the limitations of your belief system; say no to cultural taboos, karmic patterns, and attachments; and choose instead to be authentic and to share pleasure, love, intimacy, and joy, it's only a matter of time before you experience transcendent relationships.

Joy, more than anything else, distinguishes a transcendent relationship from a traditional relationship. Joy will become a permanent part of your relationship when your attention shifts from your heart chakra to your third heart and from the energy centers in the lower part of your body, particularly in the pelvis, to the energy centers in the upper part of your body and above and below personal body space.

The energy centers in your pelvis regulate the expression of vitality, gender, and sexual pleasure. They will stay active in a transcendent relationship. However, the energy centers in the upper part of your body and above and below personal body space will become dominant in a transcendent relationship. These centers regulate self-expression, joy, personal will, and the states associated with transcendent sex and relationships.

In the book *Different Loving: An Exploration of the World of Sexual Dominance and Submission*, we learn that joy is so important that even people who don't consciously embrace transcendent relationships will go to great lengths to experience it in their intimate relationships. People will engage in an astonishing number of sexual and intimate activities with their partners, including all sorts of domination and submission fantasies, as well as bondage scenarios, to achieve a state of joy. Some people use corporal punishment or other forms of intense stimulation as avenues to joy.[16]

When asked how joyful someone would become once they made the transition to transcendent relationships, the renowned spiritual master Ramakrishna said, "When a man attains ecstatic love of God (Universal Consciousness), all the pores of the skin, even the roots of the hair, become like so many sexual organs, and in every pore the aspirant enjoys the happiness of communion with Atman."[17]

Transcendent Relationship and Polarity

You've already learned that to make the transition to transcendent relationships, you must activate your energy centers in the upper part of your body and above and below body space. Also, you must center yourself in your third heart. What you may not know is that you must also change the way you engage in energetic interactions with your partner.

The Principle of Polarity regulates energetic interactions. To facilitate the shift to a transcendent relationship, you must know how the Principle of Polarity influences energetic interactions between partners in both traditional and transcendent relationships.

The Principle of Correspondence is the following list. Everything is dual. Everything has poles, and everything has its pair of opposites; like and unlike are the same. Opposites are identical in nature, but different in degree. Extremes meet. All truths are but half-truths. All paradoxes may be reconciled.

When it comes to the human energy field, there are three types of polarity that influence energetic interactions: back-front polarity, left-right polarity, and up-down polarity.

Back-Front Polarity

From your study of authentic emotions in chapter 6, you already know that the back of your energy field is masculine in relationship to the front, which is feminine. Your back is masculine in relationship to your front because the flow of sexual energy in your back is primarily upward, from the first to the seventh chakra, whereas the flow of energy in the front is primarily downward, from the seventh to the first chakra. Back-front polarity is the same for both men and women. Both men and women are masculine in the back and feminine in the front. This is easy to remember because the back of your body is hard in relationship to your front, which is soft.

When the flow of sexual energy up your back through the main masculine meridian, the Governor, has been disrupted, you will have difficulty asserting yourself and defending your energy field and its boundaries. When you have suffered a disruption in the flow of sexual energy down your front through the main feminine meridian, the Conceptual, you will become overly receptive and reactive to external stimuli.

Left-Right Polarity

Left-right polarity is also the same for both men and women. Men and women who are right-handed are masculine on their right side and feminine on their left side.

Right-handers assert energy through the energy centers in their right palm, right foot, and right eye. They receive energy on their left side, through the energy centers in their left palm, left foot, and left eye.

In contrast, left-handed people are masculine on their left side and assert energy from the energy centers, in their left palm, left foot, and left eye. They're feminine on their right side and receive energy through the energy centers, in their right palm, right foot, and right eye.

People who are blocked on their masculine side will have difficulty asserting themselves; expressing their authentic desires, feelings, and emotions; and manifesting their ideas and creativity. People who are blocked on their feminine side will have difficulty empathizing with other people and being receptive to their authentic desires, feelings, and emotions.

Up-Down Polarity

The third type of polarity is up-down polarity. Although back-front and right-left polarity play their parts in energetic interactions, your relationship to your energy field, your third heart, and up-down polarity will determine whether you can make the transition to a transcendent relationship.

How up-down polarity plays out in a traditional relationship is described below. In a traditional relationship, men are masculine by the second chakra and feminine by the heart chakra. Women are feminine by the second chakra and masculine by the heart chakra. As a function of their polar relationship, men in traditional relationships assert sexual energy from their second chakras, whereas women receive sexual energy through their second chakras. In contrast, women assert energy from the fourth chakra, whereas men receive energy through their fourth chakras (see Figure 25a and 25b).

In practice, a woman's assertiveness (radiating from the heart chakra) will make a man more receptive, empathetic, and gentle. And a man's assertiveness (radiating from the second chakra) will empower a woman and make her more assertive.

The differences in up-down polarity are responsible for the different ways love, intimacy, and commitment are expressed by men and women in a traditional relationship. Women, as a function of the up-down polarity, seek to be embraced by a relationship (especially an intimate relationship) and expect the relationship to affect them deeply. Men, as a function of up-down polarity, have a deep need to retain their individuality and remain detached, even when they're committed to a relationship.

Although men and women use sexual energy differently because of the differences in their up-down polarity, healthy polar interactions in traditional relationship do promote pleasure, love, and periodic intimacy by enhancing the flow of sexual energy between partners.

Figure 25a and 25b shows two figures in traditional relationship, with the organs of their energy systems clearly indicated by arrows showing the movement of sexual energy between them. Although up-down polarity is continually influencing men and women in traditional relationship, it's during sex that the interplay of up-down polarity can be seen most clearly.

When a man in a traditional relationship has been sexually stimulated by a woman, he will react, as a function of up-down polarity, by asserting energy forward from his second chakra. If his female partner is receptive, she will respond, as a function of up-down polarity, by drawing energy from her auric field inward, though her second chakra. The enhanced flow of sexual energy inward will activate the woman's second chakra and enhance its function. Once the chakra has become active, more sexual energy will flow downward through the Conceptual meridian in the front of her body towards her first chakra, at the base of her spine.

When the enhanced flow of sexual energy reaches the center of her first chakra, its polarity will be reversed and it will become masculine because it has entered the back of personal body space, which is masculine in relationship to the front that is feminine. At the same time, the woman's first chakra will become active, and she will feel more secure and comfortable in her body.

By turning once again to Figure 25a and 25b, you can see that the backs of the first six chakras, in personal body space, are immersed in the Governor, the main masculine meridian, whereas the fronts of the chakras are immersed in the Conceptual, the main female meridian.

Sexual energy, which activated the female's first chakra, will continue to move up the back of her energy field, through the Governor meridian. The increased flow of sexual energy will empower her because personal power is largely determined by how much sexual energy can flow up the Governor meridian.

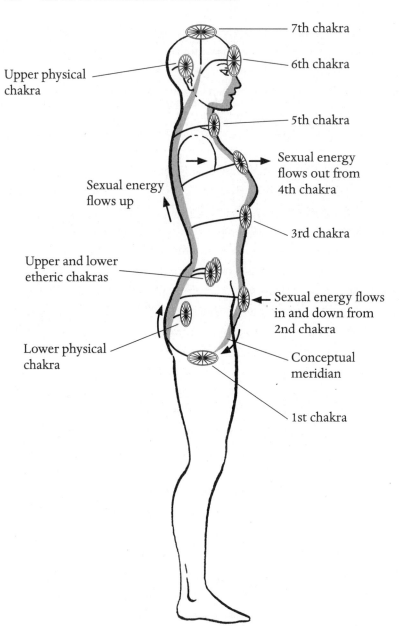

7th chakra

6th chakra

Upper physical
chakra

5th chakra

Sexual energy
flows out from
4th chakra

Sexual energy
flows up

3rd chakra

Upper and lower
etheric chakras

Sexual energy flows
in and down from
2nd chakra

Lower physical
chakra

Conceptual
meridian

1st chakra

Figure 25a: Female Up-Down Polarity

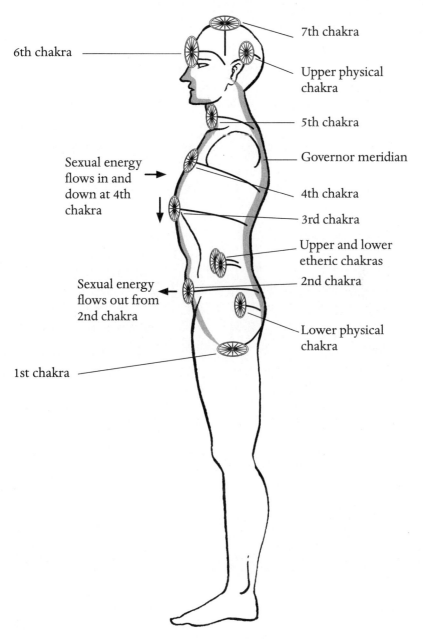

6th chakra

7th chakra

Upper physical chakra

5th chakra

Governor meridian

Sexual energy flows in and down at 4th chakra

4th chakra

3rd chakra

Upper and lower etheric chakras

2nd chakra

Sexual energy flows out from 2nd chakra

Lower physical chakra

1st chakra

Figure 25b: Male Up-Down Polarity

Once the sexual energy reaches her heart chakra (which in a woman is polarized masculine), the chakra will become active. That will enhance the flow of sexual energy through it, which will stimulate her partner's heart chakra and make him more receptive.

Once her partner's heart chakra has become active, more sexual energy will radiate down the Conceptual meridian in the front of his body. If there are no blockages in the form of karmic baggage and external projections, which disrupt the movement of sexual energy, it will reach the front of the second chakra and activate it. That will complete the circuit of energy in a traditional relationship, created by up-down polarity.

It's the differences in up-down polarity that account for the different needs and expressions of love, intimacy, and commitment that men and women bring into a traditional relationship. Evidence of this can be seen in how energetic interactions between men and women in traditional relationship take place. If you bring your attention back to Figure 25a and 25b, you can see that in traditional relationship the front and the back of a woman's energy field, from the first through fourth chakras, are involved in energetic interactions, whereas for a man only the front part of his energy field, from the second through the fourth chakra, is involved. It's not that a woman in a traditional relationship is more committed to love and intimacy than a man. However, the different ways that energy is processed does indicate that men and women bring different needs, expectations, and aspirations to a traditional relationship.

In a traditional relationship, women are empowered and become more self-confident when partners make intimate contact. However, because of up-down polarity, women also seek to be embraced by a traditional relationship. If they're not embraced, many women feel disappointed.

Men are also deeply affected by a traditional relationship. It makes them more empathetic and gentle, and often more receptive to feminine energy. However, even if they're committed to a traditional relationship, men have a deep need to retain their individuality because the back of their energy field remains outside the polar relationship created by up-down polarity.

It should be clear from what you've learned about up-down polarity that energetic interactions in a traditional relationship can enhance pleasure, love, and periodic intimacy. In many relationships, that will be enough to keep partners together and ensure that the family unit stays intact. However, even in the best-case scenario, there will still be a push and pull in energetic interactions based on up-down polarity. That will make it difficult for partners to experience intimacy with Universal Consciousness and permanent intimacy and joy with one another.

In a transcendent relationship, the polar situation is quite different. In fact, in a transcendent relationship, traditional up-down polarity has been factored out of energetic interactions altogether. That's because the traditional needs of partners have been subordinated to a higher purpose—transcendence. Partners have learned to overcome the limitations of up-down polarity by shifting into their third polar field. By giving transcendence a higher priority than the traditional needs of the family, and by shifting into their third polar field, partners will allow sexual energy to flow up the Governor and down their Conceptual meridians without interference.

As soon as sexual energy flows freely, partners will become present in their authentic mind, and their chakras in, above, and below body space will become active.

When all your chakras are active and you and your partner are able to radiate sexual energy without interference, you will transcend the limitations of up-down polarity. At that point, all your energetic interactions will be authentic. The shift into the third heart will become permanent, and you and your partner will experience the benefits of relationship without sacrificing yourselves or compromising your personal integrity.

Exercise: Transcending Up-Down Polarity

You may wonder what I mean by third polar field, because the Principle of Polarity states that everything is dual, everything has poles. Everything has its pair of opposites. However, in the non-physical universe, you are not limited by two polar fields. You can also center yourself in a third polar field, which is neutral. By centering yourself in that field, you can overcome the limitations created by up-down polarity.

In the following exercise, you and your partner will come one step closer to transcendent relationship by activating your second, fourth, and sixth chakras in personal body space and below it. Then you will transcend the limitations of up-down polarity by centering yourselves in your third polar field, on the six dimensions regulated by those chakras. Once you're centered, you will be able to share intimacy simultaneously on those dimensions.

During the exercise, you and your partner will sit six feet apart (two meters), facing each other. Once you're comfortable, close your eyes and breathe yogically. Continue by counting from five to one, then from ten to one. Use the Standard Method Exercise to relax the muscles of your physical-material body. Then you both will assert simultaneously, *"It's my intent to become present in my authentic mind."* Take a few moments to enjoy the shift. Then assert, *"It's my intent to activate my second chakra."* Continue by asserting, *"It's my intent to activate my fourth chakra."* Then assert, *"It's my intent to activate my sixth chakra."* In the same way, activate your second, fourth, and sixth chakras below body space. Once all six chakras are active, assert, *"On the levels of my second, fourth, and sixth chakras in body space and below it, it's my intent to shift into my third polar field."* Then assert, *"It's my intent to turn my organs of perception inward on all those dimensions."*

Take a few moments to enjoy the shift. Then assert, *"It's my intent to radiate sexual energy from my second, fourth, and sixth chakras in body space and below it."*

Once sexual energy begins to radiate, you and your partner will transcend the limits of up-down polarity and begin to experience the benefits of transcendent relationship.

Take fifteen minutes to enjoy the exercise. After fifteen minutes, count from one to five. When you reach the number five, open your eyes. You will feel wide awake, perfectly relaxed, and better than you did before.

You can practice this exercise regularly until you feel comfortable functioning through your third polar field. Then you can take the exercise further by adding additional chakras until you and your partner can function through your third polar fields, in the dimensions regulated by the eleven chakras in personal body space and the first seven chakras above and below body space.

By practicing this exercise as part of your regular regimen, your relationship will reach a new level of intimacy. By transcending the limits of up-down polarity, you and your partner will begin to experience the benefits of a transcendent relationship.

Chapter 16

Make the Commitment to Transcendence Now

In the preceding chapters you've learned how to enhance your level of pleasure, (human) love, intimacy, and joy and to share more of these universal qualities with your partner. However, the final goal, which is participating in a transcendent relationship, will elude your grasp unless you're ready to give up the hidden cultural beliefs that keep you trapped in your individual mind and ego.

In this chapter, we will look at three of these cultural beliefs and at how you can overcome them. The first cultural belief is that you can achieve happiness through relationships. The second cultural belief is that you're an individual being, separate from your partner and Universal Consciousness. The third cultural belief is that transcendence is something that happens to someone else, not you.

We will begin with the belief that you can achieve happiness through relationships. If you examine this belief closely, you will recognize that happiness means different things to different people, so happiness isn't something that can be defined with precision. In fact, happiness is not a specific psychological condition. It's a subjective reaction to external conditions, which will always depend on a person's expectations and their reactions to factors such as health, status, relationships, and even something as innocuous as rhythm.

The following is an example of how subjective happiness can be and how rhythm can influence your intimate relationships. Anna had been a client of mine for two years when the issue of happiness came up. She'd just started seeing a plastic surgeon and she desperately wanted her new relationship to make her happy.

"Rhythm—I'm not sure I understand," Anna said.

"Rhythm is one of the principles that regulate interactions between fields of energy with individual qualities. The Principle of Rhythm states, 'Everything flows out and in. Everything has its tides. All things rise and fall. The pendulum swing manifests in everything. The measure of the swing to the right is the measure of the swing to the left. Rhythm compensates.'"

"It sounds interesting, but how does it apply to happiness?"

"You've heard the saying, 'The greater the saint the greater the sinner?'"

"Of course."

"The proverb expresses the same truth."

"You mean that the further the pendulum swings in the direction of happiness, the further it must swing in the direction of unhappiness?" Anna asked.

"That's right. The only variable is time, how long it will take for the pendulum to swing from one extreme to the other."

"So, you're saying that the problem of happiness is unhappiness?"

"Yes, but that's only part of it, because if a person believes in happiness and unhappiness, he or she may hold on to situations that have made them happy, even after the conditions that made them happy have changed. There is also the issue of hope. People who believe in happiness and unhappiness must also embrace hope, hope that they become happy and hope that they remain happy or don't become unhappy. Unfortunately, when a person embraces hope, he or she must abandon the ever-present now, the only place where pleasure, love, intimacy, and

joy can be experienced. He or she must embrace an uncertain future of hope, where happiness is far from guaranteed.

"Building a life on hope presents serious problems for those who seek transcendent sex and relationships. That's because hope not only push-es a person into the future, it compels him or her to attach to personas, which promise happiness but can't deliver on their promises."

Anna shifted uneasily in her seat, then grumbled, *"Now that I know how miserable I'm gonna be, I feel much better."*

"Anna, there's no reason to be glum. The truth is that in successful relationships the pursuit of happiness has been taken off the agenda."

Anna's eyes widened in surprise.

"That's right, partners in successful relationships intuitively recog-nize the truth about happiness. Instead of trying to achieve the impos-sible, they focus on real issues that can be dealt with systematically."

"Such as?"

"Such as overcoming personality patterns, communicating better, and finding ways to share more pleasure, love, intimacy, and joy with one another. There's something else about partners in successful rela-tionships. They don't have unreasonable expectations. They recognize that their ability to share pleasure, love, intimacy, and joy will depend on the condition of their energy field, not on the qualities that emerge from karmic baggage and personas. When partners have recognized these things, they will use their time wisely to acquire the knowledge and skill they need to bring their energy fields into the appropriate con-dition to participate in transcendent sex and relationships."

The Truth About Individuality

It's not only a belief in happiness that can prevent you from participat-ing in a transcendent relationship. The belief that you're an individual, separate from your partner and Universal Consciousness, can prevent you just as easily.

Both yoga and tantra teach that intimacy is your natural state and that the belief that you're an individual, separate from your partner and Universal Consciousness, stems from ignorance. Unfortunately, your individual mind and ego and your organs of perception appear to contradict this truth. They do that by giving you the impression that you're an individual and that you manifest your individuality through the "I." Of course, this can't be true, for two reasons. First, you're an interdimensional being who exists simultaneously on all physical and non-physical dimensions. Second, on the highest dimension, everything, including you and your partner, are united into one singularity, known as Universal Consciousness.

Fortunately, you can give up the "I" and overcome your sense of individuality by developing detachment from what is unreal, which is the "I," the individual mind and ego, and the field of Maya. Detachment can become a way of life, with the development of discernment.

You will develop detachment once you're committed to living with integrity and you can remain centered in your authentic mind. By living with integrity and remaining centered in your authentic mind, you will become the observer of the movie of your mind. By becoming an observer rather than an actor who is blinded by attachment, you will quickly recognize the true nature of the "I" and the individual mind and ego, and you will recognize their relationship to karmic baggage and external projections. This will mark the beginning of discernment.

Discernment in the strictest sense is the ability to distinguish the difference between what is real and what is only apparently real or illusory. Universal Consciousness is real because it exists outside time-space, in what we call eternity. It's the same in the beginning, the middle, and the end. Your authentic mind is real because it's composed exclusively of energy with universal qualities. It will remain the same as long as the phenomenal universe exists.

On the other hand, the "I," your individual mind and ego, and the field of Maya, which supports them, are only apparently real because they evolve and involve through time-space, and none of them are the same in the beginning, the middle, and the end.

It's by developing discernment that you will recognize personas and external projections, by sensing and/or seeing them, before you become attached to them. That will allow you to stay centered in your authentic mind in all situations. And it will allow you to share more pleasure, love, intimacy, and joy with your partner through transcendent sex and relationships.

It goes without saying that once you've developed detachment and discernment, and once you can experience the benefits of transcendent sex and relationships, you will recognize that you're an eternal being who has always been in union with your partner and Universal Consciousness.

Transcendence Is for Everyone

The final cultural belief we will debunk is that transcendence is something that happens to other people, not to you. In yoga and tantra, the state of transcendence is called Samadhi. Samadhi comes from the Sanskrit root *sam*, which means "with or together." The ancient yogic master Pantanjali declared: "Just as the naturally pure crystal assumes shapes and colors of objects placed near it, so the Yogi's mind, with its totally weakened modifications and attachments, becomes clear and balanced and attains the state devoid of differentiation between knower, (what is) knowable, and knowledge. This culmination of meditation is samadhi."[18]

You've already experienced Samadhi many times. You experienced it when you became present in your authentic mind, when you activated your chakras, experienced orgasmic bliss, and when you centered yourself in your third heart. In fact, Samadhi is a common experience. People experience Samadhi when they recognize the inner truth of something, when they experience sexual ecstasy, and when they participate in an intimate relationship.

This means that you've already experienced Samadhi. You just haven't been able to sustain it and make it permanent. However, your inability to sustain it and make it permanent hasn't been caused solely by the inordinate buildup of karmic baggage in your energy field or the disruption of the synchronistic function of your energy bodies and your energy system. It's your lack of commitment more than anything else that prevents you from making it permanent.

Granted, you may have embraced the belief that transcendence is only for other people lifetimes ago and you've collected additional karmic baggage since then. Nonetheless, the fact remains: you still have free will. Therefore, you can make your commitment to transcendent sex and relationships stronger than any belief, even the belief that transcendence is for other people, not you. It doesn't even matter how long you've been attached to the individual mind and ego. Free will is a fact of life. It can't be lost, stolen, or forfeited.

Indeed, the conflict created by your attachments, including your attachment to the belief in question, can only be resolved by commitment, not by energy work, miracles, or lifestyle changes. Though you may participate in the process of transcendence and may experience many of its benefits, none of that will be sufficient to take you beyond temporary Samadhi (transcendence).

It's choice that brought you to the path of transcendence. However, it's commitment to transcendence with your partner and Universal Consciousness that will make transcendence permanent and enable you to overcome the belief that transcendence is something that happens only to other people, not you.

From Friendship to Union

The relationship you have with your partner and Universal Consciousness, once you've overcome the last obstacles to transcendent sex and relationships, is unique and like no other relationship you experienced before. In the Song of Solomon, this relationship is likened to the relationship between a young woman and her beloved king: "As the lily among the thorns, so is my love," (the committed lover declares). "As the apple tree among the trees of the wood so is my beloved…I sat down under his shadow with great delight, and his fruit was sweet to my taste. He brought me to the banqueting house, and his banner over me was love. Stay with me…comfort me…for I am sick of love."[19]

This poetic expression of transcendent love, intimacy, and joy are echoed throughout devotional, spiritual literature. Ramakrishna describes the experience in this way, "When divine bliss is attained, a person becomes quite intoxicated with it; even without drinking wine, he looks like one fully drunk."[20]

Once you're committed to transcendence, your relationship to your partner and Universal Consciousness will evolve in four predictable stages. In the first stage, you will make the transition from your first heart to your second heart, the heart chakra. Once you've done that, your trust will grow, and you will see your partner and Universal Consciousness as reliable friends. However, friendship will not last long because love and intimacy cannot fully emerge while you're centered in your heart chakra.

In the second stage, the yearning of the third heart will emerge and enhance your yearning for transcendent relationship with your partner and Universal Consciousness. Friendship will evolve into love and intimacy, and the desire for permanent intimacy will replace the simple desire for friendship and more contact. In this stage, the yearning of the third heart will dominate your life and discernment will compel you to be more authentic more of the time.

In the third stage, Universal Consciousness will emerge in its fullness. If you're not fully committed, or your detachment and discernment are not fully developed, the individual mind and ego will retain enough power to disrupt your experience of transcendent relationships. For anyone caught in the middle of the struggle, this can be a torturous period, as the individual mind and ego struggle to retain influence and control. If your commitment to transcendence is strong enough, you will move to the next stage in the process. If your commitment is not strong enough, you will submit once again to the individual mind and ego and identify with the outrage and resentment the individual mind and ego throw up in their defense.

In the fourth stage, the struggle will end. Without the interference of the individual mind and ego, you will remain centered in your third heart permanently, and will recognize that you have an unlimited supply of pleasure, love, intimacy, and joy you can share with your partner through transcendent sex and relationships.

Footnotes

1. Paget, Lou. *Orgasms*. Broadway Books: New York, 2001, p. 25.

2. Saraswati, Swami Satyasangananda. *Sri Vijnana Bhairava Tantra*. Yoga Publications Trust, Munger, Bihar, India, 2003, p. 45.

3. Mumford, Jonn. *Ecstasy Through Tantra*. Llewellyn Publications, Saint Paul, Minnesota, 1975, p. 9.

4. Sivananda, Swami. *Stories from Yoga Vasishtha*. The Divine Life Society, Shivanandanagar, India, 1995, pp. 30–31.

5. http://www.childpastlives.org/titu.htm, originally published in *Reincarnation International Magazine* (vol. 1, No. 2). "The Case of Titu."

6. Paget. *Orgasms*. p. 214.

7. Paget. *Orgasms*. pp. 32–33.

8. Hite, Shere. *The Hite Report on Male Sexuality*. Ballantine Books, New York City, 1981, pp. 508–509.

9. *The Shiva-Purana part 2*, Motilal Banarsidass Publishers, Delhi, India, 1970, chapters 22–28, pp. 554–589.

10. Mumford. *Ecstasy Through Tantra*. p. 15.

11. Feuerstein, George. *Tantra: The Path of Ecstasy*. Shambhala Publications, Boston, 1998, p. 215.

12. Mumford. *Ecstasy Through Tantra*. p. 33.

13. *Oregonian*. Portland, Oregon, August 23, 2007.

14. Paget. *Orgasms*. p. 42.

15. Gach, Michael Reed. *Acupressure For Lovers: Secrets of Touch for Increasing Intimacy*. Bantam Books, New York City, 1997, p. 234.

16. Brame, Gloria G., William D. Brame, and Jon Jacobs. *Different Loving: An Exploration of the World of Sexual Dominance and Submission*, Villard Books, New York City, 1993, p. 76.

17. *Parabola Magazine*. vol XXIII, no 2, 1998, p. 48.

18. *How to Know God: The Yoga Aphorisms of Pantanjali*. trans. by Christopher Isherwood. Mentor Books, New York City, 1969, Part I, vs. 41.

19. *King James Bible*. Song of Solomon, ch. 1 vs. 2–5.

20. *Sayings of Sri Ramakrishna*. Sri Ramakrishna Math, Mylapore, Madras, India, 1993, vs. 939–40.

Glossary

Agape: Unconditional love; sets no conditions and shines like the sun on saint and sinner alike; can't be controlled or limited by inauthentic desires, judgment, or fear. Because Agape emerges directly from Universal Consciousness, we can say that both are essentially the same (God is love). The Sanskrit word for Agape is Ananda.

Ananda: See *Agape.*

Artha: Authentic desire for material comfort or wealth. Provides the energy necessary to create a living environment that supports transcendent sex and relationships.

Atman: The third of the three hearts; a thumb-sized spot on the right side of your chest where universal love emerges into your conscious awareness. Once you become aware of Atman, you will begin to experience the yearning for freedom, truth, and/or universal love. By following the yearning for one of these three inward, you will become aware of your a priori union with Universal Consciousness.

attachment field: External projection; extremely dense and sticky; projected to compel the target to do what the perpetrator wants. Acts like a computer virus; disrupts the target's decision-making process by introducing powerful feelings, emotions, thoughts, and desires into his or her energy field.

auras: Part of your energy system; egg-shaped fields of energy with universal qualities that surround your energy bodies and sheaths on all physical and non-physical dimensions. Protects you from the intrusion of external projections that could disrupt the flow of sexual energy through your energy field, which prevent you from experiencing and sharing pleasure, love, intimacy, and joy.

authentic desires: Desires that come from your authentic mind and enhance the flow of sexual energy, keep you present in your energy field, and support transcendent sex and relationships.

authentic emotions: Anger, fear, pain, and joy; composed of energy with universal qualities; emerge from your energy system—via your chakras—when relationship has been disrupted. Can be resolved by screaming, yelling, crying, or just letting them rise upward to the organs of expression in your face.

authentic mind: A vast interdimensional machine, composed of energy-bodies with different functions and an energy system that nourishes them and provides them with sexual energy. True vehicle of awareness and self-expression; composed exclusively of consciousness and energy with universal qualities. Divided into three essential parts: Paramatman, Jivamatman, and the human energy system.

back-front polarity: A person's back is masculine in relationship to the front because the flow of sexual energy in the back is primarily upward, whereas the flow of energy in the front is primarily downward; both men and women are masculine in the back and feminine in the front. See *polarity.*

blockage: Any field of energy with individual qualities that disrupts the flow of sexual energy through the human energy field and prevents a human being from being present in the authentic mind.

boundaries: Surfaces of the auras; composed of sexual energy in the form of elastic fibers that criss-cross each other in every imaginable direction; will be weakened by interaction with non-physical beings.

chakras: In personal body space there are the traditional seven chakras as well as two etheric chakras and two physical chakras. Sixty-three chakras are stacked above personal body space and seventy chakras are stacked below it.

Sexual energy radiates through all 144 chakras and is continuously being transmuted into the precise frequencies needed to maintain the health of the energy system and the communities of energy bodies, sheaths, and auras that the energy system supports.

Muladhara—first Chakra. Svadhistana—second Chakra. Manipura—third Chakra. Anahata—fourth Chakra. Visuddha—fifth chakra. Ajna—sixth chakra. Sahasrara—seventh chakra.

Chao Yang / Chao Yin: The (two) Chiao Yang meridians rise from a central point in the soles of the feet and pass through the outer sides of the ankles and legs, where they connect with additional meridians at the base of the penis / vagina. Along with the two Chiao Yin meridians they form minor energy centers in the feet.

Chiao Yin: The Chiao Yin meridians rise from a central point in the soles of the feet and pass through the insides of the ankles and legs, where they connect with additional meridians at the base of the penis / vagina. They are called negative leg channels because they are yin in relation to the Chiao Yang meridians.

Ching Shing Li: cosmic energy (chi).

commitments: Strengthens your auric boundaries and liberates your sexual energy; will make you less reactive to external projections and make it easier for you to stay centered in your authentic mind.

Conceptual: Main feminine meridian in the front of personal body space.

controlling waves: External projections; waves of subtle (non-physical) energy with individual qualities. Normally projected by someone who seeks to control and/or change an aspect of another person's personality.

cords: External projection; more dense than controlling waves. Manifestations of dependency, need, and/or desire that can border on obsession; manifest the perpetrator's desire or need to hold on to or have contact with his or her target.

Dharma: Authentic desire; "that which holds together" (in essence that which prevents worldly relationships from dissolving into chaos). Dharma has two applications: shared Dharma, which is the duty that everyone has to seek transcendence, and individual Dharma, which is the specific path each person must follow in order to achieve transcendence.

DHEA: hormone released during orgasm. Helps to balance the immune system, improves cognition, promotes bone growth, and maintains and repairs tissues, keeping your skin healthy and supple; it may also contribute to cardiovascular health and even function as an antidepressant.

dual awareness: The ability to maintain your awareness of the external environment while you are centered in Paramatman and Jivamatman.

energy bodies: Subtle bodies in the field of Jivamatman and Paramatman; interpenetrate your physical-material body and are the same size and shape; composed entirely of energy with universal qualities. Allow you to be present in your energy field and experience the activities of the physical and non-physical universe via your awareness and your organs of perception.

energy system: Supports Paramatman and Jivamatman. Composed of chakras, meridians (auras), and the minor energy centers. See Paramatman; Jivamatman.

energy with individual qualities: Energy that evolves and involves through time-space. It emerges from the field of Maya; attachment to it disrupts the flow of sexual energy through a human's energy field and prevents him or her from being present.

energy with universal qualities: Energy that never fundamentally changes. It goes by many names: shakti, prana, chi, and so forth. It is the energy that flows through your chakras and meridians. It emerges into conscious awareness as pleasure, love, intimacy, and joy, as well as truth, freedom, and bliss.

Eros: Sexual love.

ever-present now: The eternal present; the space in time where humans are not driven into the past or future; the space you inhabit when you are present in your authentic mind.

external projections: Energetic projections with individual qualities, which one person can project at another. Once you've become attached to an external projection, it will be integrated into your individual mind and ego and become part of the karmic baggage that you carry in your energy field. See: *controlling waves*; *cords*; *attachment field*.

field of Maya: see *Maya*.

Filio: Brotherly love.

Governor: Main masculine meridian in the back of the human energy system.

Ida: One of the main meridians in the body, the Ida originates on the left side of the first chakra and works its way up the left side of the Governor meridian, passing through the left nostril. It combines with the Pingala and Governor to become one giant meridian when the Kundalini Shakti has risen to the crown chakra and beyond.

inauthentic desires: Emerges from karmic baggage and external projections; restricts the flow of sexual energy.

inauthentic emotions: Composed of energy with individual qualities; cannot be expressed and resolved via your energy system and your organs of expression. Keeps you attached to the karmic baggage and/or the external projections that support them.

individual mind and ego: Composed of karma; not structural parts of the human energy field or functional parts of the authentic mind, but composed of an evolving community of individual energy fields that have only individual qualities. Filters or even distorts a person's perception of people, places, and things; can weaken a person's commitment to him- or herself. Can't express or share love. Part of the field of Maya. Activities: worrying, judging, and comparing yourself to others (actually all activities that emerge from inauthentic desires), as well as any activities that block the flow of sexual energy through your energy field and prevent you from remaining present.

Jivamatman: Part of the authentic mind; *Jiva* (Sanskrit) means "embodied soul." Differentiated into spirit, intellect, soul, and body; composed exclusively of energy with universal qualities (energy bodies, sheaths, and auras whose structure vary according to their function). Through Jivamatman, Universal Consciousness can express universal love that has been differentiated into pleasure, (human) love, intimacy, and joy.

Kama: Authentic desire, which denotes pleasure as well as the desire for pleasure. Kama enhances the energy necessary to experience pleasure, love, intimacy, and joy.

karma: Sanskrit word; comes from the root *kri*—"to act," and it signifies an activity or action. In the West, karma has been defined as "the cumulative effect of action," which is commonly expressed as "You reap what you sow."

karmic baggage: Main obstacle to the experience of transcendent sex and relationships. Dense energy with individual qualities in your energy field, it creates pressure and muscle ache when you're stressed; produces anxiety, self-doubt, and confusion when it's consciously or unconsciously activated.

Kundalini Shakti: Greatest repository of sexual energy in your energy field; emerged from Shakti, via the tattvas, along with you and everything else in the phenomenal universe. Comes in two forms: as structural Kundalini, and as the serpent energy.

left-right polarity: Men and women who are right handed are masculine on their right side and feminine on their left side. Right-handers assert energy through the energy centers in their right palm, right foot, and right eye, and they receive energy on their left side through the energy centers in their left palm, left foot, and left eye. Left-handers are masculine on their left side and assert energy from the energy centers in their left palm, left foot, and left eye. They're feminine on their right side and receive energy through the energy centers in their right palms, right foot, and right eyes. See *polarity.*

Maithuna Rite: The intimate embrace that lovers experience when their limbs are intertwined; a form of tantric coitus. The goal of the Maithuna Rite is to have partners experience the sexual ecstasy that emerges through the union of Shiva and Shakti.

Maya: The appearance of reality; a field of energy with individual qualities that exists alongside authentic fields of energy on all physical and non-physical dimensions.

meridians: Part of your energy system; streams of energy that transfer sexual energy from the chakras to the energetic vehicles in Paramatman and the energy bodies, sheaths, and auras in Jivamatman. The flow of energy with universal qualities through the meridians enables a human to remain present in the authentic mind, to form an authentic identity, and to participate in transcendent sex and relationships.

minor energy centers: Part of your energy system; located throughout your body. Four principle centers are located in the extremities—one in each hand and one in each foot. Others are scattered throughout your energy field. Two principle functions: facilitate the movement of sexual energy through the energy field, and balance the pressure within it.

Moksha: Authentic desire; the true state of every human being. Denotes transcendence, which is spiritual freedom and liberation from karmic attachment and external projections. Motivates people to engage in activities that lead to transcendent sex and relationships.

mudra: Symbolic gesture that can be made with the hands and fingers or in combination with the tongue and feet. Each mudra has a specific effect on the human energy field and the energy flowing through it.

Mulabandha: The Root Lock; exercise designed to temporarily release blockages that have forced the muscles by your first chakra to contract.

non-physical beings: Composed of the three elements necessary for life: consciousness, energy, and subtle matter—as well as awareness and a limited degree of feeling and sensation. Feeds on your sexual energy if they get the chance. The primary activities that introduce non-physical beings into your energy field are channeling and/or the invocation of gods and angels, elementals, spirit guides, deceased human beings, ascended masters, nature spirits, and/or power animals (for guidance, comfort, and/or sustenance).

orgasmic bliss: An enduring condition deep within your energy field, created through the union of consciousness (Shiva) and sexual energy (Shakti). The merging of consciousness and sexual energy provides a safe haven, deep within you, where you already experience oneness and where nothing can interfere with your experience of transcendent sex and relationships. A state that combines the anticipation and increased sexual excitement; experienced during the moments before a full-body orgasm, with the satisfaction and release that takes place during and after it.

Paramatman: Part of your authentic mind; *Para* (Sanskrit) refers to the supreme or universal. In conjunction with the word *Atman*, it refers to that which is transcendent; transcendent or universal mind; one unified field or body, composed of consciousness and energy with universal qualities. Contains everything necessary to be present.

past-life lover: A lover from a past life to whom you are still attached via a cord, control wave, or attachment field.

personas: Fields of karmic baggage that share same or similar resonance; building blocks of your personality issues. Can be used as tools for transcendence.

Pingala: In the tantric system of yoga we are told that the Pingala serves as one of the ruling meridians. The Pingala works its way up the right side of the Governor and passes through the right nostril. Both the Ida and Pingala join the Governor again in forming one giant stream of energy when the Kundalini Shakti has risen to the crown chakra and beyond.

polarity: The degree to which your energy field is polarized masculine or feminine. See *back-front polarity; left-right polarity; up-down polarity.*

Prana: Sexual energy; energy without qualities; universal energy.

Principle of Desire: "Desire is a function of mind." Desire manifests in all fields of activity. Desires that are stronger and more active will dominate weaker, less-active desires in all energetic interactions that take place in both the physical and non-physical universe.

Principle of Correspondence: "As above so below; as below so above."

Principle of Polarity: "Everything is dual." Everything has poles; everything has its pair of opposites; like and unlike are the same; opposites are identical in nature but different in degree; extremes meet; all truths are but half truths; all paradoxes may be reconciled.

Principle of Field Dominance: "All fields of energy interact." Fields with a higher vibration will have a greater impact and/or effect than fields with a lower vibration. In all field interactions, fields with a higher vibration dominate and/or displace fields with a lower vibration.

Principle of Gender: "Gender is in everything." Everything has its masculine and feminine principles; gender manifests on all planes.

Principle of Rhythm: "Everything flows in and out." Everything has its tides. All things rise and fall: the pendulum swing manifests in everything. The measure of the swing to the right is the measure of the swing to the left. Rhythm compensates.

qualified energy: Energy with individual qualities.

ohm: Universal vibration; the creative vibration of Shakti that permeates the physical and non-physical universe.

resonance: The vibration or mean frequency that emerges from, and is the signature of a field of energy or living being. Every living being and/or field of, energy with individual or universal qualities has its own resonance.

restrictive belief system: Restricts the flow of sexual energy through your energy system. Karmic baggage can manifest its qualities through a restrictive belief system that enhances self-limiting and/or self-destructive tendencies. In extreme cases a restrictive belief system can even create obsessions, which can cause anti-self and anti-social behavior.

Samadhi: Culmination of meditation; orgasmic bliss experienced when you're centered in your third heart—Atman.

self-love: To enhance self-love, Jivamatman must receive more love from Paramatman. It's through Paramatman that universal love in the form of sexual energy enters your energy field. If you center yourself in your authentic mind, you can enhance the amount of sexual energy Paramatman receives from Universal Consciousness. Then you can enhance your self-love by transferring the excess of sexual energy from Paramatman to Jivamatman.

sexual energy: Energy with only universal qualities; experienced whenever you experience or share pleasure, love, intimacy, and joy with your partner.

sheaths: Interpenetrates your physical-material body like the energy bodies; composed of energy with universal qualities. Allows you to interact directly with your external environment and other sentient beings; gives you the flexibility to express yourself and to participate in transcendent sex and relationships.

Shekina: According to Jewish mystics, the Indwelling of Universal Consciousness.

Shiva/Shakti: Shiva and Shakti are revered as both the divine couple and as the archtypes for consciousness (Shiva) and energy (Shakti).

spiritual foreplay: Enables people to make the energetic shifts necessary to experience the full spectrum of pleasure, love, intimacy, and joy possible; the ultimate goal of spiritual foreplay is the experience of transcendent sex and relationships.

tantra/tantrics: Tantra is an ancient school of Indian thought that views energy with universal qualities and consciousness as essentially the same. Shiva, who represents consciousness, and Shakti, who represents energy, were depicted in tantric iconography in eternal embrace, which means that they are considered fundamentally the same. Tantrics sought to enhance the amount of sexual energy they had and could share by participating in the activities of the world, rather than adopting the aesthetic idea of yoga, which was to give up worldly activity for an exclusive life of contemplation and meditation.

tattva: Steps in evolution. From the Sanskrit root *tat*, which means "that," and *tvam*, which means "thou" or "you." Thus *tattva* means "thou are that"—signifying the ancient truth that you are always in union with Universal Consciousness and that you can experience the benefits of union (which include pleasure, love, intimacy, and joy) by remaining present in your authentic mind. According to yoga and tantra, evolution in the physical and non-physical universe has gone through thirty-six steps already.

three hearts: As an inter-dimensional being you have three hearts: the human heart, your heart chakra, and Atman. It is from Atman that Universal Consciousness emerges into your conscious awareness.

transcendence: The state of union or intimacy with Universal Consciousness, your self, and your partner. In the transcendent state you can experience and share the universal qualities of pleasure, love, intimacy, and joy without disruption.

transcendent relationship: A relationship in which you can share pleasure, love, intimacy, and joy freely with a partner without blockages, karma, or anything else getting in the way.

Tree of Authentic Desire: The four branches of authentic desire (Artha, Kama, Dharma, and Moksha). These four branches of authentic desire enhance the flow of sexual energy, keep you present in your energy field, support transcendent sex and relationships, and are the natural functions of earthly life. See *Artha; Kama; Dharma; Moksha.*

Trishira: The Ida, the Pingala, and the Governor meridians are known as Trishira. In Sanskrit, *tri* means "three" and *shira* means "that which carries." The energy that radiates through Trishira has its origin at the base of the spine—in the coiled serpent energy. Many of the practices of yoga and tantra are aimed at enhancing and balancing these three meridians of energy.

Universal Consciousness: Singularity that people are yearning to reunite with through relationship, particularly transcendent relationships and sex. Root cause or creator of everything; foundation of your authentic mind as well as everything else in the physical and non-physical universe, including time, space, energy, and consciousness; has no individual qualities.

universal qualities: Universal qualities include pleasure, love, intimacy, and joy, as well as truth, freedom, and bliss. Universal qualities do not create attachment; they support transcendent sex and relationships. Sexual energy is a form of energy that has only universal qualities.

up-down polarity: Men are masculine by the second chakra and feminine by the heart chakra; women are feminine by the second chakra and masculine by the heart chakra; men in traditional relationship assert sexual energy from their second chakra, whereas women receive sexual energy by their second chakra; in contrast, women assert energy from the fourth chakra, whereas men receive energy by their fourth chakra. See *polarity.*

Veda/Vedic: Refers to the books that are sacred to both yoga and tantra. The Bhagavad Gita and the Upanishads are two of the best known Vedic texts.

vehicle: An energetic vehicle. Energy bodies are energetic vehicles, as are sheaths and auric fields.

Yang Yu/Yin Yu: The (two) Yang Yu meridians are the masculine arm channels located in both arms. They link the shoulders with the centers in the palms, after passing through the middle fingers. Along with the Yin Yu, they form the minor energy centers in the palms. The Yin Yu are feminine arm channels, which link the centers in the palms with the chest. They travel along the insides of each arm.

The energy centers in the palms play a significant role in healing and in regulating pressure in the human energy system and are considered energy centers in their own right. They are often referred to as minor energy centers or minor chakras.

Yin/Yang: Yin represents femininity, body, soul, earth, moon, water, night, cold, darkness, contraction. Yang is masculine, mental, spirit, heaven, sun, day, fire, heat, sunlight, expansion.

yearning: The yearning for either truth, freedom, or divine (unconditional) love comes from your third heart, Atman, and is the yearning to experience union (or intimacy) with Universal Consciousness.

yoga: Union; an ancient scientific method developed in India to achieve transcendence.

yogic breath: A breathing technique used in yoga; by breathing yogically you will restore your breathing to its natural state and enhance the level of Prana (sexual energy) that radiates through your energy field.

yoni: Sanskrit; female genitals.

Index

Afterglow, 233, 256, 269–271

Agape, 48, 297

Ajna chakra, 139

Anahata chakra, 138

Ananda, 48, 297

Anger, 35, 77, 112–114, 117, 120–121, 137, 160, 221

Artha, 26–28, 72, 297

Aryan, 212–213

Atman, 49, 241–243, 245, 249, 265, 276, 297

Attachment field, 13, 31, 33, 67–68, 75, 109, 111–112, 119, 159–160, 180–186, 188, 194, 214, 216–219, 230, 264, 290, 297

Auras, 7, 39, 50–53, 80, 83, 100–101, 127, 134, 151, 158–159, 163–169, 176, 188, 259–260, 297

Authentic desires, 22, 24–29, 31, 33, 35–36, 38, 45, 50, 72, 76–77, 95–96, 99, 130–132, 138, 150, 180, 199, 214, 273, 278, 297

Authentic emotions, 29, 33, 50, 72, 76–77, 93–94, 96, 99, 110–120, 124–126, 130–132, 138–139, 142, 145, 150, 163, 180, 197, 199, 269, 273, 277–278, 297

Authentic mind, 15, 22, 24–29, 35–36, 44–46, 48–50, 53, 55, 61–62, 68, 74–76, 81, 93–96, 98–101, 103–106, 111, 114–116, 120–124, 130–133, 138–139, 142, 145–146, 150–153, 159, 167, 175–177, 182–185, 190, 192, 197, 199, 203–204, 208, 210, 214–215, 218–219, 224–225, 236, 242, 249–251, 259–

260, 271, 283–284, 290–291,
293, 298

Awareness, 7, 10, 12, 14, 17, 22,
25–26, 43, 45, 49–50, 55, 57–59,
61–62, 68–69, 72, 78, 95–99,
101–102, 140, 145, 150, 163, 189,
225–227, 242, 245, 248–249, 265

Back-front polarity, 277–278, 298
Belief systems, 91, 133, 140
Bhagavad Gita, 4, 67
Blame game, 11, 188
Blockage, 147, 184, 219–220, 298
Body part, 16, 60–63, 66, 198
Boundaries, 7, 51, 137, 157–158,
188–190, 277, 299

Chakras, 7, 38–41, 51–53, 59–60,
76–78, 80, 106, 111–112, 114,
117–127, 134, 136, 140–143,
145–147, 149–153, 156,
164–173, 188–189, 194, 198,
204–206, 215–218, 221–224,
226–227, 231, 233–237, 239,
243, 254–255, 259–260, 262–
265, 269, 278–285, 291, 299
Chanting, 40–41, 121–122, 233
Chao Yang, 144, 204. 299
Chao Yin, 204, 299
Chemistry, 2, 19, 65, 130, 160
Ching Shing Li, 193, 299
Commitments, 189–190, 299
Conceptual, 113–114, 135, 137–
139, 194, 215–216, 218, 224,
277, 279–280, 282–283, 299

Controlling waves, 31–32, 180–
181, 185–186, 216–219, 299–300
Cords, 31–32, 180–181, 185–186,
216–219, 300

Detachment, 290–291, 293
Dharma, 26–28, 72, 246, 300
DHEA, 256, 300
Discernment, 139, 290–291, 293
Dual Awareness, 43, 55, 57–59, 78,
98–99, 225–227, 242, 300
dualistic, 55, 70, 214

Ego, 9, 23, 25–26, 28–29, 36, 44–
46, 51, 54–55, 68, 71, 76, 78, 89,
94, 96, 107, 109, 111, 120, 130,
132, 138–140, 150, 157, 166,
177, 192, 203, 214, 225, 230,
248, 258, 265, 287, 290, 292–293
Energy bodies, 12–13, 25, 49–53,
75–76, 83, 98, 100, 134, 142,
155–159, 161, 163–164, 166–
168, 176, 180–181, 194–196,
200–201, 203, 225–226, 258–
259, 268, 291, 300
Energy field, 1–17, 19, 22–36, 38–
40, 44–46, 49–55, 58, 61, 66–76,
78–79, 83–85, 88–89, 93–106,
108–112, 117–120, 124–126,
133–136, 142–143, 147, 150,
155–161, 163–164, 166–169,
176–178, 180–190, 192–196,
203–204, 207, 214–221, 224,
230–231, 233, 235–236, 239,
242–245, 247, 250, 252–254,

258–259, 263–267, 269–270, 276–279, 281–284, 289–291

Energy system, 12–13, 25, 39, 44, 49, 51, 53–54, 69, 76, 78, 80, 88, 111–112, 115, 120, 127, 133–135, 137, 142, 151, 176, 204, 216, 236, 242, 258, 279, 291, 298–301, 306, 309

Energy with individual qualities, 1–2, 8, 19, 22–24, 26–28, 30–32, 35, 44–45, 49–51, 53–54, 67–68, 70, 77–78, 88, 95–98, 100–101, 103, 105, 108–109, 111–112, 114–115, 135–136, 176–178, 180, 189, 214–216, 218–220, 224, 229, 242, 288–289, 300–301

Energy with universal qualities, 1–2, 4–9, 11–13, 19, 24–27, 35, 38–39, 44, 49–51, 53, 70, 93, 108–112, 114–115, 131, 135–136, 142, 158, 176–178, 214–215, 224–226, 229–231, 243–245, 254, 289–290, 301

Eros, 4, 48, 59–60, 132, 301

Etheric chakras, 51, 53, 127, 134–135, 140–142, 156, 163–169, 194, 203–204, 254, 259–260, 262, 280–281

Evolution, 4–5, 49, 108

External projections, 22–25, 27, 29–31, 33–36, 44–45, 51, 53, 78, 111, 114–115, 119, 125–126, 131–132, 136–137, 158–161, 163–164, 167–169, 178, 188,

190, 194, 196, 216–217, 230, 242–244, 248, 252, 259, 282, 290

Fear, 7, 24, 33, 40, 48, 69, 77, 89, 91, 94, 112, 114, 117, 122, 138, 195, 247, 253

feminine, 84, 106, 110, 113–114, 118–119, 124, 143, 145, 180, 192–194, 204, 215, 230–231, 233, 270, 277–279, 282

Field of Maya, 45–46, 157, 176–177, 289–290, 301

Filio, 48, 301

Fragmentation, 159–161

Gender, 9, 110, 117, 119, 137, 145, 149, 151, 191–197, 200–201, 203, 207, 227, 262, 275

Gender orientation, 149, 191–197, 200–201, 203, 207, 227, 262

Goddess, 2, 5, 93, 95, 110–111, 142, 212–214, 229–231, 233–239, 253, 255

Governor, 114, 119, 136–140, 155, 194, 215–218, 223–224, 235–238, 269, 277, 279, 281, 283, 301

Hermetic Principle, 71

Hope, 186–187, 245, 248, 288–289

Ida, 223–224, 235–238, 301

Inauthentic desires, 22–24, 26–29, 34–36, 38, 41, 45–46, 48, 54, 69, 72, 96–98, 130, 132, 196–198, 242, 301

Inauthentic emotions, 45, 72, 96–98, 110–111, 114–118, 120, 124–126, 130, 132, 197–198, 242, 301

Individual mind, 2, 23, 25–29, 36, 44–46, 48–49, 51, 54–55, 68, 71, 76, 78, 89, 93–94, 96, 98–101, 104–105, 107–109, 111, 114–116, 120, 130, 132, 138–140, 150, 157, 166, 176–177, 189–190, 192, 203, 214, 219, 225, 230, 242, 248, 258, 265, 287, 289–290, 292–293, 302

Integrity, 9–10, 75, 110, 138, 145, 157–158, 247–249, 283, 290

Interdimensional being, 108, 177, 181, 290

Internal dialogue, 89, 91, 96

Jivamatman, 44, 49–51, 53, 55–59, 83, 302

Kama, 26–28, 72, 195–196, 302

Karma, 1–2, 34, 67–68, 78, 88, 230, 302

Karmic baggage, 2, 22–25, 29, 32–36, 44, 47, 51, 53–54, 66–69, 71–76, 78, 83–84, 87–89, 91, 93, 95–96, 98, 100, 102–103, 111–112, 114–115, 119, 137, 161, 163–164, 167–169, 180–182, 188–190, 194, 216–217, 219–220, 243–244, 248, 252, 259, 263, 265, 282, 289–292, 302

Kundalini Shakti, 137, 214–217, 220–221, 224, 236, 243, 301, 303, 305

Left-right polarity, 277, 303

Maithuna rite, 238–239, 255, 267–268, 303

Manipura chakra, 138

masculine, 106, 110, 112, 118–119, 143, 145, 192–194, 204, 215, 277–279, 282, 298, 301, 303, 305, 308–309

Maya, 46, 157, 177, 290, 303

Meeting, 25, 130–131

Meridians, 7, 39, 51, 53, 80, 134, 151, 204, 215–216, 223–224, 235–237, 254, 260, 283, 303

Minor energy centers, 7, 39, 51, 53, 80, 134–135, 143–144, 188–189, 204–205, 236–237, 303

Moksha, 26–28, 72, 304

Mudra, 17–18, 36–38, 40, 59, 80–83, 89–92, 161–162, 167–169, 201–202, 231–234, 236–237, 241, 251–252, 259–261, 266, 304

Mulabandha, 217, 222, 304

Muladhara chakra, 136–137, 223

Non-physical universe, 24, 31,35, 46, 49–50, 67, 71, 142, 215, 284

Ohm, 40, 60, 233–235

Oneness, 1, 6, 10, 12

Organs of perception, 25, 28, 30,
    49–50, 56–58, 68, 74, 77–78,
    96, 98, 100, 105, 108, 110,
    125–126, 142, 151–153, 163,
    165, 168–169, 172–174, 176,
    183, 205–206, 216, 218, 221,
    225–227, 242, 249–251, 263,
    265, 284, 290
Orgasm, 2, 10, 196, 211–212, 239,
    245, 253–260, 262–267, 269–271
Orgasmic bliss, 3, 5, 10–11, 14,
    17–19, 27, 72, 133, 150, 159,
    234–235, 241, 251–252, 266,
    291, 304

Pain, 77, 112, 114, 117, 123, 139,
    147, 149, 175, 177
Paramatman, 44, 49–51, 53, 55–
    59, 83, 304
Past-life lover, 175, 178–182, 184–
    185, 188
Patriarchy, 9
Patriarchal cultures, 8–9, 70,
    116–117
Personality issue, 11–12, 31, 67, 96
Personas, 88–89, 91, 93, 95–102,
    109, 115, 119, 125–126, 132,
    139, 159, 178, 194, 196, 209,
    216, 230, 242, 244–245, 248,
    259, 265, 289–290, 305
Phenomenal universe, 46, 69, 71,
    118, 193, 215, 249, 290
Physical chakras, 51, 53, 127,
    134–135, 140–142, 145–146,
    151, 156, 163–169, 188, 194,

203–206, 215, 226, 239, 243,
    253–254, 259–260, 262, 280–281
Physical material body, 169, 174,
    184
Physical universe, 4–6, 12, 24, 30,
    44, 46, 49–50, 67, 69, 71, 108,
    141–142, 204, 212, 215, 290
Pingala, 223–224, 235–238, 305
Polarity, 2, 46, 68, 117–119, 151,
    195, 215, 276–285, 305
Positive affirmations, 88, 93
Positive intent, 93–94
Prakriti, 4
Prana, 78–79, 305
Principles, 3, 192, 288
Principle of desire, 22, 24–25, 67–
    68, 177–178, 193–194, 244, 305
Principle of correspondence, 71,
    117–118, 276, 305
Principle of polarity, 68, 117–118,
    276, 284, 305
Principle of field dominace, 177–
    178, 305
Principle of gender, 117, 192–194,
    305
Principle of rhythm, 244, 288, 305
Purusha, 4

Qualified energy, 31, 33, 35, 45–
    46, 51, 54, 67–68, 89, 100–101,
    105, 180–181, 197, 216, 220,
    230, 236, 244, 248

Reintegration (of subtle bodies),
    167

Relating, 130–131, 273

Resonance, 29, 73–75, 88, 96, 121–122, 164, 306

Restrictive belief systems, 87–88, 91, 140, 306

Sahasrara chakra, 140, 223

Samadhi, 291–292, 306

Self-Love, 41, 43–44, 48, 54–56, 58–61, 217, 262, 306

Serpent energy, 215–222, 224, 229, 236

Sexual energy, 2, 4–14, 23, 26–28, 30–34, 36, 38–40, 46, 49, 51, 53–55, 58, 60–63, 66, 68–70, 72–80, 83–84, 87–89, 93, 95, 100–101, 103–106, 110–114, 116–126, 130–134, 136–139, 142–143, 146–147, 149–151, 156, 158–160, 163–164, 176, 181, 184–185, 187–190, 192–201, 203–215, 217–218, 222, 224–227, 231, 235–236, 238–239, 242–245, 250, 253–255, 258–260, 262–266, 268–271, 275–284, 291, 306

Shakti, 2–6, 10, 12–13, 126, 137, 145, 196, 212–217, 220–221, 224, 229–230, 234–236, 238–239, 243, 275

Sheaths, 50–51, 53, 83, 98, 100, 134, 142, 155–159, 163–169, 176, 306

Shekina. 155, 307

Shiva, 2–4, 10, 195–196, 212–213, 234, 238–239, 275, 307

Singularity, 4, 55, 108, 290

Soulmate, 179

Spiritual foreplay, 2, 207–210, 212–216, 224, 226, 229, 231, 235, 239, 245, 254–255, 260, 267–269, 271, 307

Standard method, 15, 17, 38, 56–58, 62, 74, 77, 81, 98–99, 105, 121–126, 145–146, 151–152, 165, 167–168, 172–174, 183–184, 197, 205, 218–219, 221, 225–227, 236, 250–251, 259, 263–264, 266, 284

Subtle bodies, 155–159, 161, 163

Svadisthana chakra, 137

Tantra, 4, 10, 26, 43, 46, 54, 71, 136, 176–177, 224, 229, 231, 236, 238, 258, 267, 289, 291, 307

Tantrics, 7, 14, 269, 275, 307

Tattva, 4, 48–49, 307

Three hearts, 241–243, 307

Traditional relationship, 35, 60, 73, 119, 130–131, 133, 136, 147, 226–227, 273–276, 278–279, 282–283

Traditional sexual foreplay, 208, 210, 213

Transcendence, 2, 4–6, 8–10, 13–14, 17, 23, 27–28, 41, 72, 83, 88, 95, 100, 103–105, 131, 133, 151, 164, 190, 195, 203, 225,

246–247, 255, 262, 275, 283, 287, 291–293, 308

Transcendent relationship, 1–2, 4, 6–7, 9, 12–13, 26–27, 34–35, 43, 65, 67, 72–73, 75, 94–95, 107–109, 116–117, 130–131, 133–134, 136, 139, 145, 156, 158, 178, 187, 203, 227, 242–243, 245, 247–248, 254, 273–276, 278, 283–285, 287, 289, 291–293, 308

Trishira, 235–237, 308

Trust, 7–9, 60, 74–76, 91, 93, 110, 117, 132–133, 138, 145, 149, 160, 201, 209–210, 227, 262, 293

Unconditional Love, 5, 9, 48, 108, 246–252

Union, 3–4, 10, 27, 49–50, 109, 150, 229, 238, 243, 245–246, 248–249, 268, 275, 291–292

Universal Consciousness, 1, 4–5, 9, 12–13, 25–28, 39, 44, 46, 48–50, 54–56, 71, 76, 85, 104, 108–110, 134, 136, 150, 155, 158–159, 177, 194, 214–215, 229–230, 241, 243–249, 268, 274–276, 283, 287, 289–293, 308

Universal qualities, 1–2, 4–7, 9, 12–13, 19, 25–28, 36, 39, 44, 46, 49–51, 54, 71, 93, 108–112, 115, 132, 136, 142, 158, 176–178, 203–204, 212–215, 224–227,

229–231, 234–235, 241–242, 244–246, 252, 255, 287, 290, 308

Upanishads, 4, 241

Up-down polarity, 277–285, 308–309

Veda / vedic / vedic texts, 4, 26, 67, 309

Vehicle, 4, 7, 12, 14, 25, 44, 68, 133, 160, 167, 249, 309

Visuddha chakra, 139

World of intellect, 46, 76

World of soul, 46, 76–77

World of spirit, 46, 70, 76

Yang, 2–4, 144, 192–193, 204, 309

Yang Yu, 144, 204, 309

Yin, 2–4, 144, 192–193, 204, 309

Yin Yu, 144, 204, 309

Yearning, 1, 49–50, 108, 179, 182, 184, 195, 242, 246–253, 293, 309

Yearning for freedom, 49, 108, 246–252

Yearning for truth, 49, 108, 246–252

Yearning for unconditional love, 108, 246–252

Yoga, 4, 26, 46, 71, 78, 136, 175–177, 224, 230, 236, 241, 289, 291, 309

Yogic breath, 78–81, 309

Yoni, 231–235, 309

To Write to the Author

If you wish to contact the author or would like more information about this book, please write to the author in care of Llewellyn Worldwide Ltd. and we will forward your request. Both the author and publisher appreciate hearing from you and learning of your enjoyment of this book and how it has helped you. Llewellyn Worldwide Ltd. cannot guarantee that every letter written to the author can be answered, but all will be forwarded. Please write to:

Keith Sherwood
℅ Llewellyn Worldwide
2143 Wooddale Drive
Woodbury, MN 55125-2989

Please enclose a self-addressed stamped envelope for reply,
or $1.00 to cover costs. If outside the U.S.A., enclose
an international postal reply coupon.

Many of Llewellyn's authors have websites with additional information and resources. For more information, please visit our website at http://www.llewellyn.com.